D0016497

Happily Ever After

WITHDRAWN

Happily Ever After

The Romance Story in Popular Culture

CATHERINE M. ROACH

INDIANA UNIVERSITY PRESS

Bloomington & Indianapolis

This book is a publication of

Indiana University Press
Office of Scholarly Publishing
Herman B Wells Library 350
1320 East 10th Street
Bloomington, Indiana 47405 USA

iupress.indiana.edu

"i carry your heart with me(i carry it in". Copyright 1952, © 1980, 1991
by the Trustees for the E. E. Cummings Trust,
from COMPLETE POEMS: 1904–1962 by E. E. Cummings,
edited by George J. Firmage.
Used by permission of Liveright Publishing Corporation.

© 2016 by Catherine M. Roach
All rights reserved

No part of this book may be reproduced or utilized in any form or by any means,
electronic or mechanical, including photocopying and recording,
or by any information storage and retrieval system, without permission in writing
from the publisher. The Association of American University Presses' Resolution
on Permissions constitutes the only exception to this prohibition.

The paper used in this publication meets the minimum requirements
of the American National Standard for Information Sciences—
Permanence of Paper for Printed Library Materials, ANSI Z39.48–1992.

Manufactured in the United States of America

Library of Congress Cataloging-in-Publication Data

Names: Roach, Catherine M., author.
Title: Happily ever after : the romance story in popular culture / Catherine M. Roach.
Description: Bloomington : Indiana University Press, 2016. | Includes
bibliographical references and index.
Identifiers: LCCN 2015033975 | ISBN 9780253020444 (cloth :
alk. paper) | ISBN 9780253020529 (e-book)
Subjects: LCSH: Love stories, American—History and criticism. | Love stories,
English—History and criticism. | Women in literature. | Love in literature.
| Popular literature—United States. | Popular literature—Great Britain.
Classification: LCC PS374.L6 R58 2016 | DDC 813/.08509—dc23
LC record available at http://LCCN.loc.gov/2015033975

1 2 3 4 5   21 20 19 18 17 16

To Theo

Such is my lover and such my friend

i carry your heart with me(i carry it in
E. E. CUMMINGS

i carry your heart with me(i carry it in
my heart)i am never without it(anywhere
i go you go,my dear;and whatever is done
by only me is your doing,my darling)

i fear

no fate(for you are my fate,my sweet)i want
no world(for beautiful you are my world,my true)
and it's you are whatever a moon has always meant
and whatever a sun will always sing is you

here is the deepest secret nobody knows
(here is the root of the root and the bud of the bud
and the sky of the sky of a tree called life;which grows
higher than soul can hope or mind can hide)
and this is the wonder that's keeping the stars apart

i carry your heart(i carry it in my heart)

Contents

Acknowledgments

I've been working on this book since 2007 and spent the last year finishing it during a sabbatical in England. Accordingly, I have a lot of people and institutions to thank for their help.

To start with, I'd like to thank everyone in the UK who ever called me "luv." May I say that I love being called luv? As George Bernard Shaw is reputed to have quipped, "England and America are two countries separated by a common language." In the romance fiction world, perhaps the best proof is furnished by the example of the spunky heroine. A gal full of spunk means something startlingly different in our two lands. Thanks to new colleagues overseas for that lesson learned. Thanks also to our Roundhay neighbor who offered me a Pimm's Cup, the Cornish bartender who pulled me a real cider, and our Yorkshire butcher who kept us well fed on local lamb. I have never passed a happier year.

I gratefully acknowledge the generous support that made this book possible from the Romance Writers of America (Academic Research Grant, 2009–10) and the Research Grant Committee of the University of Alabama (2012–14), as well as ongoing research support from the College of Arts and Sciences Dean's Office and my home program of New College at the University of Alabama. I am especially grateful to the Fulbright Program of the US Department of State and to their British partners in the US–UK Fulbright Commission for granting me the Fulbright–University of Leeds Distinguished Chair (2013–14). My year in residence at Leeds's Centre for Interdisciplinary Gender Studies in the School of Sociology and Social Policy allowed me to complete the research and finish the book manuscript. Thanks as well to the Greece Fulbright Commission and Aristotle University of Thessaloniki for a Fulbright Intercountry Lecturing Award that year.

Many of the book's arguments took shape in thirteen different talks that I gave over the past five years. I owe a debt of gratitude to the innumerable audience members and fellow conference-goers whose questions and conversation contributed to my thinking on this project. I mention in particular the conferences of the International Association for the Study of Popular Romance, the Popular Culture Association, the UK Romantic Novelists' Association (RNA), and the Romance Writers of America (RWA).

I am equally grateful to a long list of colleagues who contributed in varied and crucial ways to this project: Sally Hines and Ruth Holliday, my brilliant hosts at the Centre for Interdisciplinary Gender Studies (with special thanks to Ruth for letting me use the "sex in your eyes" line); Julia Cherry, Barbara Brickman, Michael Steinberg, Ted Trost, Natalie Adams, Jim Hall, Jennifer Purvis, Tom Fox, Lane Busby McLelland, Fred Whiting, Jeremy Butler, Deborah Weiss, and Carmen Mayer, among a slew of wonderful colleagues in Tuscaloosa, for conversation and valuable suggestions on the project; Eric Murphy Selinger, Sarah Frantz, Bill Gleason, An Goris, Pam Regis, and Betty Kaklamanidou for their leadership in the field of popular romance studies and their individual support; Pia Fenton, Sue Moorcroft, Linda Hooper, and Jo Beverley of the British RNA and my fellow writers in the Yorkshire Flying Ducks chapter, who all generously welcomed me to the UK and enlightened me about romantic fiction there; and many others whose aid, encouragement, or insight benefited the project, such as Mary Bly/Eloisa James, Madeline Hunter, Kate Dresser, Courtney Miller-Callihan, Jonathan Rowe, Samantha Holland, Mark Priestley, Dave Bauer, and Naomi Goldenberg. My thanks to you all.

I'd like to express my gratitude as well to anonymous peer reviewers at the *Journal of Popular Romance Studies* and at *Mosaic,* where earlier versions of portions of this book appeared, for their careful readings that helped me to see my text more clearly, and especially to the two reviewers commissioned by Indiana University Press, whose astute feedback helped to sharpen and improve this book.

My undergraduate students in the New College seminar "Gender, Sexuality, and Popular Culture" read drafts of this book material and provided useful critiques; I thank especially Chris Chirino and Tiffany Brown. For several years now, the seminar students and I have read and discussed popular romance together; we've created romance fiction cut-up projects, experimented with online collaborative romance writing, and run a romance lending library. I thank all these students, and many others who have come through my office, for their help in thinking through this book project and for providing me with endless examples of the romance narrative in popular culture.

I thank my family in Ottawa, Canada, and in Tuscaloosa for encouragement and support: my parents for always believing in me, my sons for reading romance fiction out loud in goofy voices, and my husband to whom I dedicate this book.

Finally, as this book's research is rooted partly in ethnographic and participant observation work conducted at annual conferences of the Romance Writers of America and other sites of popular romance authorship and readership, including a year spent as a participating member of the UK Romantic Novelists' Association, I thank the many readers and writers who talked with me about this project. To everyone who answered my question, "What do you think about romance?"—thank you for your stories.

Earlier versions of this book material appear in:

- Catherine M. Roach. "Getting a Good Man to Love: Popular Romance Fiction and the Problem of Patriarchy." *Journal of Popular Romance Studies* 1.1 (August 2010), http://jprstudies.org/2010/08/getting-a-good-man-to-love-popular-romance-fiction-and-the-problem-of-patriarchy-by-catherine-roach/.

- Catherine LaRoche [Catherine M. Roach]. *Master of Love.* New York: Pocket Star–Simon and Schuster, 2012. *The Society of Love,* Book 1.

- Catherine M. Roach. "'Going Native': Aca-Fandom and Deep Participant Observation in Popular Romance Studies." *Mosaic: A Journal for the Interdisciplinary Study of Literature,* special issue, *Romance.* 47.2 (June 2014): 33–49.

- Catherine M. Roach. "Love as the Practice of Bondage: Popular Romance Narrative and the Conundrum of Erotic Love." In *Romance Fiction and American Culture: Love as the Practice of Freedom?* edited by William A. Gleason and Eric Murphy Selinger. Farnham, UK: Ashgate Publishing, 2016.

Happily
Ever
After

Prologue

Journey into Romancelandia

You've all heard the story, in its thousand and one variations. You know what I'm talking about.

The bar. The drinks. The hook-up or the pick-up. The sweaty sex.

Advertising's favorite emotional well.

The internet dating.

The rom-com date movie.

The Disney princess movies soaked up by three year olds.

The lyrics of almost every pop tune ever written.

The diamond ring.

The trashy romance novel. The bodice-ripper.

Fifty Shades of a billion dollars. Mommy porn. Women snaking around the bookstore in a line five hundred long, waiting to get their copies signed. Mimosas circulate: "I read it through lunch breaks and I'm giggling."[1]

You've heard the stories from your friends. They call you up, needing to talk. They've met Mr. or Ms. Right, and now hope's gone wild and hormones are running high. Or they need to vent and a shoulder to cry on: Mr. or Ms. Right has turned out wrong, yet again.

You've probably been in love yourself. Or thought you were, you poor sod. Maybe you were just in lust, struck stupid by desire or lit up to your brilliant, beautiful best: sex in your eyes, glowing like a rainbow.

Maybe you are still in love now. Maybe it did all work out.

Maybe you don't believe in love. It's sappy, sentimental drivel. A cultural construct in the service of capitalism and patriarchy. A trap.

Maybe you don't care about sex. Too busy, too tired, too smart for that messy shit.

But still, no matter where you fall—you know what I'm talking about, don't you?

I'm talking about the romance story: Find your one true love and live happily ever after.

We might as well capitalize the whole damn thing, it's got such iconic status as the meta-story of what life is supposed to be all about: FIND YOUR ONE TRUE LOVE and LIVE HAPPILY EVER AFTER!!!

That's what we're going to think about and try to understand. How does this narrative function? Why, how, and to what effect does this story have such a hold on us?

Gear up. We're going into Romancelandia.[2]

1

Find Your One True Love

Book Lovers and the Romance Story

The romance narrative is a central storyline of human culture. Pushing the thesis further: The story of romance is the guiding text offered by contemporary American culture and the culture of the modern West on the subject of how women and men (should) relate. Find your one true love—Your One and Only—and live happily ever after. To the ancient and perennial question of how to define and live the good life, how to achieve happiness and fulfillment, American pop culture's resounding answer is through the narrative of romance, sex, and love. According to Stephanie Coontz's history of marriage, a "gigantic marital revolution had occurred in Western Europe and North America during the Enlightenment." Prior to the late eighteenth century, notions of marriage tended to be pragmatically based on economic and political considerations of money, resources, power, and alliances. The sentimental and passionate love-based marriage stood in radical contrast to this older sense. Through the nineteenth and twentieth centuries, the romantic love match came to dominate as the ideal for marriage in Western culture. This romance narrative is now arguably the most powerful one at work in American culture. The core story about finding true love and happiness has come to have great resonance and pervasive influence, both in people's lived experience and in the representations of love in the wider culture. Since its ascendance in the nineteenth century, romance may well be the prime cultural narrative of the modern Western world.[1]

By calling the romance story a cultural narrative, I mean a guiding story that provides coherence and meaning in people's lives. The truth value of this story lies in the extent to which it is held to be true by people who shape their lives around that story, whether consciously or unconsciously. In this sense, there is a mythic or religious nature to the romance narrative. It functions as a foundational or idealized story about the meaning and purpose of life—even when it fails to deliver on its promised happy ending and leads instead to heartbreak and tragedy. According to this story, despite the risks, love is what gives value and depth to life. Our purpose is to bond with a well-suited mate worthy of our love and to love and be loved by this mate within a circle of family and friends. Here, life is a high-stakes quest for the Holy Grail of One True Love. This search is driven by yearning and desire for the paradise of this romantic happily-ever-after. We chase romance, we structure our lives around it, we fashion much of our art and culture from it. The romance story is not only a narrative but becomes also, more disturbingly, an imperative. The happily-in-love, pair-bonded (generally, although increasingly not exclusively, heterosexual) couple is made into a near mandatory norm by the media and popular culture, as this romance story is endlessly taught and replayed in a multiplicity of cultural sites: Disney princess movies, the wedding industry, fairytales, Hollywood movies, pop music lyrics, advertising, the diamond jewelry industry, and more.

One of the most interesting cultural sites where romance is taught, retold, and—a crucial point—experimented with in new forms is in the literal "romance story" of mass-market genre fiction. There are obviously significant differences among the cultural sites listed above, as there are differences among the subgenres and storylines in romance publishing. Nonetheless, the basic plot of the romance narrative—find somebody to love, work through problems, be happy—holds true as a common storyline across all these categories and across all of the books, despite the variation. As such, likening these various cultural forms allows us to look at the phenomenon of the romance narrative as a whole. Moreover, when we focus in on genre romance fiction, we find a particularly rich cultural site to study the workings of the broader romance narrative.

Romance fiction is America's bestselling genre. According to industry research compiled by the professional trade organization Romance Writers of America (RWA), romance novels constitute the largest segment of fiction publishing and of the consumer book market. Romance fiction had a readership of almost 75 million Americans in 2008, including 29 *percent of all Americans over the age of thirteen.*[2] That's about the age when I got hooked on the books. As a girl, I'd been an avid reader (British pony stories, Nancy Drew, the Chronicles of Narnia). By the time I hit my teens, I added the classics and my mother's romance collection. Among romance's various subgenres, I read single-title historical romance, as those big medieval and nineteenth-century romances—*misunderstood privateers! hot-blooded Highland lairds! rakish English dukes!*—best provided for me that rush of fantasy pleasure and the escapist feeling of otherness that I sought in my reading experience. The romance novels were a treat, a reward to be savored. When I finished my school exams or handed in a research essay, I allowed myself to read one novel. I chose my book with care, buying it or trading with a girlfriend or snagging one of my mom's from the giant stack teetering beside her bed. I looked for poignant stories with strong heroines who overcame long odds to win happiness and a man. I wanted the book to make me cry and then to sigh as I closed the back cover. I chose a day when my schedule was clear. I'd get up for breakfast but go back to bed to read. It took me about eight hours to finish the book cover to cover, an entire day lying in bed immersed in the story from lovers' first meeting to happily ever after. If anybody tried to enter my room, I'd yell at them. Sometimes, I'd put a sign on my door, "Reading—do not interrupt!" I didn't want to come out of the story or have anything loosen the book's emotional grip on me.

This massively popular genre now racks up over a billion dollars in annual US publisher revenue. It accounts for half of all mass-market paperbacks sold. The vast majority of these books are bought by women; the gender breakdown ranges from 84 to 91 percent women buyers, with men accounting for 9 to 16 percent of sales. Globally, 200 million novels by Harlequin/Mills & Boon (publishers of romances in series formats) are sold every year, and romances are translated into over ninety languages worldwide. These stories have ancient literary roots. Although the current form of woman-oriented genre romance fiction dates from the appearance of 1970s bestsellers such as Kathleen Woodiwiss's *The Flame and the Flower* (whose bold and bodacious narrative thrilled me as a teenager), we can trace a much longer lineage for such stories. A lot depends on definition. If by *romance novel* one means an Anglo-authored, love-based courtship plot resolving to a happy marriage, then the literary ancestry traces back through highlights such as the Harlequin/Mills & Boon publishing empire, the Regency-set novels of Georgette Heyer, and the nineteenth-century masterworks of Jane Austen to Samuel Richardson's 1740 bestseller *Pamela*. If one adopts a broader definition that encompasses stories about the trials and tribulations of romantic love and erotic desire, then the earlier and wider context can include the seventeenth- and eighteenth-century British amatory fiction of bestselling writers Aphra Behn and Eliza Haywood, Shakespearean comedy, the poetry of the medieval troubadours, the earliest extant European novel *Callirhoe* (named after its beautiful heroine) by the Greek first-century CE author Chariton of Aphrodisias, and the unapologetically erotic love poetry of the biblical Song of Songs.

What fascinates me is how, even with the possibility of new and more open twenty-first-century norms for gender equality and sexual experimentation, the romance narrative continues to thrive. The power of the story does not die. In fact, romance sales show new dominance in the market. The number of titles released increased from 5,184 in 2003 to 10,497 in 2007. With the meteoric rise of self-publishing and e-books soon after that date, the number of new titles published yearly further exploded and became harder to pin down. In print format only, 9,513 romance books came out in 2013. E-books added thousands more to that count as, according to book data sources Bowker and BookStats, romance has emerged as the most popular category in self-published books, and e-books now account for 49 percent of the romance market.[3]

These romance titles spread across a variety of subgenres both traditional and new. Contemporary-set romances remain popular, as well as romantic suspense and the historical romances that I grew up reading. A setting in nineteenth-century England continues to predominate for the historicals, with Scottish settings that allow for covers of bare-chested and muscled Highland lairds also popular. (Sometimes the giant sword clasped upright in the hero's hand is not just a sword.) But the genre has developed in many ways over the thirty-five years I've been following it. New romance subgenres have popped up such as gay and lesbian, urban fantasy, science fiction, erotic, paranormal (I read a shape-shifter ménage story about three wolf-humans the other day), and inspirational romance (stories with a religious context, typically conservative Christian, and what some cheekily call a ménage à trois with God, although theoretically an inspirational romance could be Buddhist or Zoroastrian).

In academia, the study of romance is also thriving. Scholars have been writing a lot about love recently, in its broadest strokes, with a new field of "love studies" emerging. Examples include philosopher Simon May's *Love: A History* (2011), sociologist Eva Illouz's *Why Love Hurts* (2012), and professor of English Susan Ostrov Weisser's *The Glass Slipper: Women and Love Stories* (2013), to name just a few. Within the last decade the field of popular romance studies has vigorously taken off. In 2004, Romance Writers of America launched its annual Academic Grant competition to fund research on the romance genre. In 2009, the field gained a crucial scholarly apparatus with the establishment of the International Association for the Study of Popular Romance and the *Journal of Popular Romance Studies*. Thanks to a grant from the foundation of top-selling author Nora Roberts, in 2011 Maryland's McDaniel College created the Nora Roberts Center for American Romance in support of library collection, teaching, and scholarship in the field. The US Library of Congress and its Center for the Book hosted a 2015 public outreach conference on "Romance Fiction in the Digital Age" at which award-winning filmmaker Laurie Kahn previewed her new documentary about the global romance community, *Love between the Covers*. Academics, generally working from the discipline of English literature, have produced field-defining monographs and anthologies: Pamela Regis's 2003 *A Natural History of the Romance Novel,* Lisa Fletcher's 2008 *Historical Romance Fiction,* Sarah S. G. Frantz and Eric Murphy Selinger's 2012 *New Approaches to Popular Ro-*

mance Fiction (which includes a useful history of the development of the field), and Jayashree Kamble's 2014 *Making Meaning in Popular Romance Fiction,* among others.

Amid this interest in thinking about love and romance, I aim to engage the question a little differently. My goal is to broaden both the angle of study and the audience reached by writing a different style of book: wide-ranging instead of based in one academic discipline; written not only for a scholarly audience but for a general readership who wants to think about the role of the romance story in society; not an outsider study but a personal interpretation of the romance offered by a reader and a new author of the genre. Accordingly, I work from an interdisciplinary humanities background of cultural studies, religious studies, gender studies, sex-positive feminism, and more. I bend and blend the genre of academic writing with the genre of popular fiction, as I write analytically about the romance story while at the same time learning how to write romance fiction in a self-reflexive experiment that allows these two genres of writing to inform each other. I intend by this project to bridge boundaries between academics and the general public who read romance novels in such happy numbers. My lessons in fiction-writing carry over into the style of this book, which I am writing as accessibly as possible for a broad audience. I use a first-person voice throughout, include a lot of stories, and deliberately minimize the traditional academic apparatus of notes, analysis of theory, and discussion of prior scholarly literature. With the books sexier and more diverse than ever, with more empowered and kick-ass heroines, an accessible bridge from academia to the public seems crucial so that scholars can contribute to the important public conversation that the genre prompts.

In this book, then, I seek to understand my fascination with romance novels by understanding how the romance narrative functions and how it is currently changing. The book's big-picture context is romance as a cultural story about the key role that erotic partner love plays in granting happiness, wholeness, and healing. Romance is a powerful and perennial theme in cultural representations both high- and middlebrow. It is a force that structures people's lives and shapes their relationships. While keeping in mind this backdrop, I give shape and focus to my inquiry by centering it on the literal romance story of popular genre fiction. I place romance fiction in the broader cultural context of the romance narrative in order to ask questions about meaning, fantasy, fear, and desire in how stories of love play out in pop culture. Unlike some lines of previous academic inquiry into romance fiction, my goal has little to do with either critique or defense of the genre, nor do I aim for close literary reading of individual authors or texts. Like Tania Modleski did in her *Loving with a Vengeance: Mass-Produced Fantasies for Women*, I seek to read romance fiction "symptomatically," not intending by this metaphor for the genre to be taken as illness or pathology but simply as an incredibly rich cultural site that yields much insight into changing norms for gender roles, sexuality, partnership, and romance.[4] Romance novels, in short, let us think about how we think about love.

I deliberately write as if my audience knows and reads romance novels. I realize—indeed, I hope—that my assumption is not always true. I hope that some of you who are now reading this book don't know much at all about these novels or, even better, that you have a passive prejudice or an active disdain for the genre. Maybe you've flipped through a paperback romance at some point. Maybe you once found a Harlequin in your grandmother's basement and read it down there in the dark. Maybe you—along with about a billion other people—saw a copy of *Fifty Shades of Grey* in the summer of 2012 and read the juicy bits. But you wouldn't call yourself a *romance reader*. Nevertheless, for the purposes of this book, I am making you—all of you, anyone now reading these pages—into honorary romance readers.

I make this move because I want to swing discussion about popular romance in a different direction. Janice A. Radway's seminal 1984 study of the genre in *Reading the Romance* is powerful in all sorts of ways and important in that her methodology of reader-response criticism aimed to take romance readers and their interpretation of texts seriously (in her case, the community of romance-reading ladies from the pseudonymous town of Smithton). Nevertheless, the book and its author approached the genre as an outsider. Although Radway brings her academic readers into the circle of romance fans, these readers of her text are kept separate and held at bay outside that romance community by the scholarly conventions of objectivity and distance. I am up to something different: I'm taking us in. All the way, and all of us—whether, like me, you've read romance since puberty as a lifelong fan or whether you swear to God you've never picked up one of those books in your life and never will.

I do this to make a point: You—we—already *are* astute and well-informed readers of the romance story. You know the story inside out. Even if you don't read actual romance novels as I do, you sop up this storyline through your daily doses of pop culture and have done so since you were a child. Whenever I tell people that I'm looking at the narrative "Find your one true love and live happily ever after," everyone nods their head in familiarity. *Everyone.* It's the soup we swim in. So when I say *we* in this text, I refer to this community of romance story insiders of which I am making you, dear reader, an honorary member for the duration of your time with my book. *We* here also refers to the creators and consumers of contemporary popular culture in the United States, with its diaspora of near global reach and its Anglosphere pop culture siblings in Canada, the United Kingdom, Ireland, Australia, New Zealand, and wherever else the romance story plays out in similar if not identical ways.[5]

With the project thus defined, I launched my study by talking to everyone I could about the romance story: students, family, friends, and colleagues both academic and romance-writerly. I startled acquaintances with my eager question: "Do you read romance novels?" ("Yes," answered one fellow carpool mom cautiously, "if I'm allowed to say that.") I set up a romance lending library in my office. My younger son decorated a poster in magic markers that we hung outside my door for borrowers to write down comments about the novels they've checked out. The poster filled up as all sorts of people stopped by: lots of students, a professor from another department, a book-buyer, a custodial staffer who smiled at me and said, "You be the one with the books" (she became my most frequent borrower). I incorporated a unit on romance fiction into my annual "Gender, Sexuality, and Popular Culture" undergraduate seminar. In this class, students choose romances from a big box that I carry to class and write reader responses about the books. I workshopped chapters from my research with the students. We did cut-up exercises with the novels to create alternative storylines and published our results in a campus magazine. We wrote a collaborative online branching romance story with scenes ranging from romantic suspense and comedy to the spiciest of erotica. I engaged in four years of participatory ethnographic research within communities of romance authors and readers in the United States, based around Romance Writers of America.[6] I wrote, and eventually published, two romance novels myself. In the project's last year, a Fulbright sabbatical grant sent me to the Centre for Interdisciplinary Gender Studies at the University of Leeds in the UK. There, I joined the Romantic Novelists' Association (RNA) and attended monthly chapter meetings in a Yorkshire pub with a wonderful group of writers, including a charming ninety-year-old man nominated for an RNA Romantic Novel of the Year award for his twenty-first romance novel, all of which he writes under a female pseudonym.

Through this research and building on previous academic interpretations of romance, I developed the approach to the romance story unpacked in this book's chapters. My core argument is that romance novels are popular because they do deep and complicated work for the (mostly) women who read them. There is a reparative aspect to this work, to try to make up for the costs to a woman's psyche of living in a culture that is still a man's world. There is a transgressive and empowering nature to this work, often one of raucous fun and sassy sisterhood, a refusal to be limited or lessened by narrow gender roles and toxic ambivalences about women's sexuality. And there is a mythic or religious nature to this work, a testament of faith in the redeeming power of love as of ultimate concern in human life.

For another way to put all this, let me quote this doozy of a Biblical verse: "Your desire shall be for your husband and he shall rule over you" (Genesis 3:16). Let's say you are a heterosexual woman. You want a man. Why, God knows. But you want one anyway. All right, you sort of know why you want him, despite the fact that men can be, well, "men": domineering or worse, emotionally closed-off, unfaithful, or just plain slobs. You want him because you want a boyfriend, a sexual partner, a helpmeet, a father to your children, a breadwinner, or someone to change the light bulbs and take out the garbage. You want him because he—or a series of he's; it doesn't have to be a one-and-only "one true love"—can be supportive, open, devoted, and sexy. You want him because you love him. What's wrong with that?

But God knows why, indeed. According to Genesis, God knows *exactly* why you want that man, since making women desire men is part of God's plan of punishment. Intriguingly, the tale of Adam and Eve functions as a foundational story both for the origin of erotic romance and for the origin of patriarchy. In the account, God as matchmaker notes that "It is not good for the man to be alone." So God creates Eve as a partner for Adam, to Adam's delight: "This one, at last, is bone of my bones and flesh of my flesh," says Adam when God presents the newly made Eve to him. Here is the origin of marriage, as the narrator explains: "That is why a man leaves his father and mother and clings to his wife, and the two of them become one body" (Genesis 2:18, 23–24). Oddly enough, after the fall, when Adam and Eve eat the forbidden fruit, God metes out female heterosexual desire as a *punishment* for Eve and all her daughters. The context here is childbirth and motherhood: "In pain you shall bring forth children," God curses Eve as the penalty for her disobedience. Yet despite this pain, "Your desire will be for your husband," God further ordains, ensuring that Eve will still *want* to cling to Adam. Female heterosexual desire ensures that women will have children, despite the difficult labor of birth. But the curse is not over, and God now invents patriarchy. This final retribution entails more pain for Eve and the race of women. God says to Eve that her husband "shall rule over you" or, in another translation, "shall be your master" (3:16).

What a perfect trap: to be made to want someone who will subordinate you. It is a vision of male-female relations that continues to speak truth in the twenty-first century. As a woman, is there any way to get out of this trap? You could resist desire and relationship, but that's tricky to do and maybe not so much fun. So you deal with it: desire, vulnerability, compromise, the costs of relationship, and so on. And you tell yourself that surely the progress of women's rights and feminism in the twenty-first century means that no one is really ruling over anyone else as master anymore, right? But still, it's a lot to figure out and try to work through. And dealing with it takes a damn lot of energy: men, maybe some kids, a job, keeping the home together, grooming for the beauty game that is part of all this fuss. Even sex is complicated and tiring. Post-*Tootsie* and second-wave feminism, now you're even responsible for your own orgasm; you've got to work for that too, on top of everything else.

So you're buffeted by mixed messages about being sexy but not tawdry, independent but in the perfect relationship: today's Superwoman, somehow having and doing it all. You're worn down. You want some time to yourself and you want to talk with other women who understand. You want to relax and play. Here's one possibility: You could read romance stories. One way to loosen this Gordian knot of female heterosexual desire is to turn it into the magic potion of a love that softens and sweetens the complications of desire into the guarantee of a happy ending. In this reading, as others have argued before me in different ways (e.g., Janice Radway in *Reading the Romance,* Tania Modleski in *Loving with a Vengeance,* and Ann Barr Snitow in "Mass Market Romance: Pornography for Women Is Different"), romance stories are a creative respite for women, an imaginative play space to roll around in the fields of fantasy with sister readers of the genre, all the while affirming the reality of love as a force that can work good in the world. And the fantasy is this: a good man, devoted to you, with whom even the orgasm takes care of itself.

It comes up later, but a few words about my usage of *patriarchy* are in order here. *Patriarchy* can be an overused term, a too-easy shorthand or form of jargon that treats as monolithic very different cultural and socioeconomic realities. To say that I—as a Western, educated, professional white woman—live under a patriarchal culture certainly means something very different than to say the same of a girl of color in the developing world who is denied the right to education or who faces genital mutilation. Allan G. Johnson's *The Gender Knot* is helpful here in his definition of patriarchy as a cultural system that "promotes male privilege by being male dominated, male identified, and male centered" and as one that valorizes violence and control.[7] High rates of sexual assault, sexual harassment, and violence against girls and women form a central part of such culture, as do high rates of violence against men. I share in Johnson's analysis that contemporary American culture remains marked by such patterns, although these patterns have clearly lessened through the nineteenth and twentieth centuries thanks to successive waves of social justice movements such as civil rights, gay and lesbian rights, the women's movement, and feminism.

While a key point of Johnson's radical feminist analysis concerns the deep cultural root (Latin *radix,* thus "radical") of male privilege, an equally important implication pertains to the value system of this cultural arrangement. As opposed to a system that values cooperation and the sharing of power with others, patriarchy as a cultural system (along with its partner system capitalism) values competition and the wielding of power over others: the tough guy stance, in other words. It is a system that encourages and rewards hierarchical leadership, domination, and control—over one's body and emotions, over others, over technology, over nature. As a means to gain and enforce such power, violence is often expected, tolerated, and even glamorized (think of every Hollywood big-budget guns-and-explosion movie you've ever seen). The extent to which men suffer from shaming, emotional straightjacketing, and brutality in this competition for power—as men with more power push those with less into lower-caste positions further down the hierarchy—demonstrates how men, as well as women, suffer in a patriarchal system. Women can move up the hierarchy and win power—again, think Buffy the Vampire Slayer and Wonder Woman–type heroines, both real-life and fictional—but the name of this game remains patriarchy, with the ultimate prize a form of control that is gendered as masculine.

In this sense, the modern capitalist Western world is a culture still very much marked by patriarchy with its values of male-inflected power, domination, and control and with leadership positions dominated by men. It's still a man's world out there. The dangers this game of patriarchy poses to women include greater physical vulnerability to both general and sexual assault and the attendant lifelong low-level anxiety about dark alleys and deserted streets, about acquaintances or family intimates who could become abusers; disadvantages that endure in the workplace such as lower pay rates, employment discrimination, glass ceilings, and pressures of the "second shift"; issues around reproduction such as unwanted pregnancy, access to affordable birth control and abortion, the burdens of childcare, absentee fathers; greater media and cultural pressures to be young, slim, attractive, sexy, and coupled as part of misogynist double standards: in sum, the pressure of living in a culture that is always, at least potentially, in certain ways against her.

All this is a background although central concern of the romance story: How to win at this game that is stacked against women? As earlier romance critic Ann Snitow said about Harlequins, the books have "their own dream-like truth: our culture produces a pathological experience of sex difference." So, given this dream-truth, how to enjoy playing the game? The answer of the romance story to this conundrum of living as a woman in a man's world, or, more specifically, as a heterosexual woman whose desire is for men, is to offer a fantasy safe space that addresses these anxieties and has them all work out. This imaginative space provides resources for thinking through the conundrum and for feeling its contours differently.[8]

In taking on this project, I experimented with writing voices. Chapters 2, 4, 6, and 8 are the more traditional academic sections. In alternation, chapters 3, 5, and 7 are more fully narrative in style, with passages of my romance writing and with stories based on my time spent among romance communities of readers and authors. There is some deliberate repetition of material between these two sets of chapters. You can choose to read one set over the other and still get the gist of my argument, or you can read both sets in order to see how these different styles of writing interrelate.

More specifically, chapter 2 lays out my method for how an academic interested in popular romance fiction might study this bestselling genre. It sets out a practice for negotiating the "aca-fan" tension in the growing field of popular romance studies based on methods of observant participation and performative ethnography.

Chapter 3 turns to full-fledged narrative mode with a fictionalized scenario presenting scenes of my romance fiction and an imagined boisterous dialogue between Catherine Roach, romance studies academic, and Catherine LaRoche, her fiction-writing alter ego. Here, I aim for play—albeit of a serious kind—to make a point about the experimental potential of ludic research. I introduce arguments that I work out in more academic detail in later chapters about the pleasure and danger of seduction, the romance narrative as imperative, whether the genre passes feminist tests, and how to interpret the alpha hero.

In chapter 4, I explore the notion that romance fiction functions as a form of woman-centered, feminist pornography. I've come to believe that the guarantee of women's sexual pleasure is one of the aspects of romance fiction of most challenge to the culture. Furthermore, the mainstream growth of erotic romance (in a rainbow of sex-positive, informed-consent shades well beyond *Fifty Shades of Grey*'s publishing impact) signals important changes in cultural attitudes toward women's and queer sexuality and perhaps, finally, a loosening of double standards and restrictive norms around allowable sexual expression.

Chapter 5 recounts vignettes from my four years of fieldwork at Romance Writers of America conferences, in an analysis of this romance fiction community as a powerful and creative female space of freedom, fantasy, play, and professional accomplishment—and as one that challenged and opened me up to a rollicking new sense of academic self.

In chapter 6, I work to untangle the nature of erotic love as one of the most dangerous things we do to ourselves. Romance—as a life practice among lovers and as a literary-cultural narrative—is a complicated conundrum of freedom and bondage. This conundrum entails love as a practice of avoiding what I term bad bondage while accepting—even delighting in—good bondage. I analyze BDSM (a portmanteau acronym for bondage and discipline, dominance and submission, and sadism and masochism) erotica and the fascinating figure of the "pussy whipped man" in order to unpack notions of masculinity and the more egalitarian models featured in romance fiction, whereby love allows a good man to emerge from behind the patriarchal mask of the alpha hero.

Chapter 7 narrates an account of my writing journey as I follow the aspirational path of a historical romance novelist. This path has a steep learning curve littered with far more rejections than I'd hoped for, but it offers as well the opportunity to master professional writing skills—the discipline of the daily word count, the mystery of the query letter—that I find profoundly engaging.

Chapter 8 arrives finally at consideration of the romance story's happily-ever-after ending, wherein love conquers all and heals all wounds. I introduce concepts of erotic faith and reparation fantasy to make two interrelated arguments about what is at stake in the ending of the romance story, namely that romance functions as a religious belief system offering guidance on the end goal of how to live a worthy life and as a reparation fantasy about the end of patriarchy itself. Gay and slash (same-sex fanfiction) romances in particular help to make this argument.

The epilogue presents lessons learned from this project of romancing the academic—turning me into a romance writer and turning the romance story into an object of academic analysis.

At this point, you might be wondering who this woman is who invites you along on this tour through the territory of the romance genre that insiders playfully name Romancelandia. What sort of a guide will she be? What does she bring to the table, in terms of her own personal investment in these love stories? To help situate this project, let me tell you a little more about the background that brings me to the study.

As I mentioned, I grew up reading romance novels, a white, middle-class girl in suburban Canada in the 1970s and 1980s. My adolescent Christmas stocking often held an historical romance novel delivered by Santa Claus. I used to call the books—with amused affection—"trashy novels." My friends and I and my mother and some of my mother's friends all bought, read, traded, and discussed our trashy novels. To parse this descriptor now, looking back, I see in it two things. On the one hand, we called the books *trashy* in a fondly intended labeling of the genre as lowbrow. Romances weren't the "good" or "high" literature that I had to read for school. On the other hand, naming the books trashy betrayed a somewhat titillated adolescent sense that I was getting away with something naughty. I wouldn't have been allowed to read *Playboy* or watch porn videos in the house. Although the romance stories were in some cases equally sexually explicit, and thus in that sense trashy or smutty, the books were acceptable because they were *romances,* with the legitimizing factor of the committed happily-ever-after ending, and *novels,* thus better than reading nothing at all. Eventually, I went away to graduate school, became a cultural studies and gender studies professor, and published feminist research into gendered fantasy spaces in popular culture. And still, throughout it all, I read romance novels. At night, when the kids were finally asleep and the day's work was more or less done, I would read romances, usually books set in nineteenth-century Britain. I found them relaxing and enjoyable, a quiet me-time and escapist pleasure. Throw in a glass of wine and maybe some chocolate, and I was a contented woman.

But why? What is this pleasure? What is the appeal of this romance story that has such a hold on me and millions of other readers, most of them women? I wrote this book in order to get answers. I wrote to interrogate my own lifelong fascination with the genre. I wrote the novels that went along with this academic study—*Master of Love!* *Knight of Love!*—in order to dig deeper, in a more fully engaged way, into the meaning of the romance narrative as well as for the sheer craft pleasure of learning a new and emotionally intense form of writing.

Here is another bit of biography that seems relevant. I live some version of the romance story myself: less Disney and fairytale than the narrative's pure ending promises, but happy nonetheless with my darling Theo. We met in the angst-ridden corridors of academia, so long ago now. Twenty-five years ago? We were both starting Ph.D.s in the same department, assigned to the same residence hall. By the time we graduated, we had lived together for years, celebrated our marriage at the university's Faculty Club, conceived our first child, and accepted jobs at the University of Alabama. In Tuscaloosa, we built a life together, renovated an old house, raised two children, and gathered a warm circle of friends.

So to what extent does my status as a heterosexual professional woman and mother in a longstanding marriage shape my analysis of the romance narrative? What if I'd had my heart broken in a messy divorce? What if I were lesbian and the state had refused me the right to marry my beloved? What if I were asexual and annoyed by sex and romance as a boring waste of time? What if I'd spent the last thirty years happily romping through a series of torrid affairs of the most varied description but saw settling down and monogamy as synonymous with impossible compromise, loss of freedom, and the end of real love? Were any of this so—were any of a million other things different about my life history—I am sure this book would be different, as I expect is true of most books and their authors. But it's impossible to say how.

I don't believe in love at first sight. I'm leery of young love. I certainly don't believe in giving up career ambition or educational goals for love, especially for women. I advise my college students to focus on school and self-development; choices about long-term relationships and family can often wait. And partnering up remains just that: a choice. Not everyone has to fall in love, marry, or have children. There are obviously other ways to live a happy and fulfilling life. But I do believe in romantic love. I love passionately a good man, and I know down to my bones that he loves me back. Our love has helped us to build a home, careers, a family, and a community of friends.

There is another level, then, to my attempt to write an insider account of the romance narrative. I have gone inside the community of romance authors to become one of them. But I am also one of *them*: that sappy and self-satisfied tribe of the happily partnered. Thus, I write as a woman in love. It's an interesting phrase: *in love.* I am in it. Within the embrace of love. Pierced by Cupid's arrow. Drugged by love's wine. Does this insider status as a lover mean that I know *more* or *less* about the function of the romance story? I believe myself to experience in some authentic manner the power of romantic love as a force for good—for joy and strength and creativity—in the joining of two lives. But maybe I am just caught in a deep delusion, bound by a lifetime of romance-novel chains to a Plato's cave of flickering Prince Charming shadows. Am I naive or blind to the more negative side of the romance narrative, because I live out a measure of its happily-ever-after?

You, dear reader, will have to form your own judgment.

*   *   *

One final delimitation of this project aids its launch. I've been bandying about the clichéd tagline "Find your one true love and live happily ever after," but what does that line really mean? What exactly *is* this romance story? In my reading, there are nine essential elements to the romance narrative, nine key components to the core story about romance. I discuss these elements throughout the book but begin by outlining them here.

Pamela Regis provides a fruitful and oft-cited breakdown of the romance novel into eight essential elements in her 2003 text *A Natural History of the Romance Novel.* The eight elements that Regis identifies as central to the genre story of a successful courtship between hero and heroine

are (1) society defined, (2) the meeting, (3) the barrier, (4) the attraction,
(5) the declaration, (6) the point of ritual death, (7) the recognition, and
(8) the betrothal. In my own take on the romance narrative, I present a
different list of essential elements, nine this time, intended not to replace
Regis's list but to replicate it from a different angle.

Regis works within the discipline of English literature, and her elements pertain largely to the structural components of the romance plotline taken sequentially from the beginning of the story to the end (although authors creatively play with mixing up the standard sequence as
well). I work instead from an interdisciplinary gender and cultural studies perspective, and my elements pertain to a different category of description. Instead of chronological narrative, I am interested in the deep
structure of the romance story. I seek not to define the plot points of the
novel but to identify the core claims about romantic love made by the
broad romance narrative and then exemplified in cultural products such
as romance novels (as well as romantic comedy movies, pop lyrics, advertising, etc.). Taken together, my nine essential elements describe the deep
storyline or foundational premises that tellers spin out through a million
and one variations into the tales of romance that we read and watch and
hear in pop culture. This type of breakdown of the romance story allows
for examination of its central messages and reveals the work that the story does for its audience in offering pleasure and support but also posing
potential pitfalls or traps in the messages that the story feeds to readers.
Furthermore, listing the essential elements in this way provides explanation for romance's overwhelmingly female authorship and readership,
as in my analysis the story addresses itself to typical female experiences,
interests, and anxieties.

The story of love, as a noun, reduces down in its essence to a verb. In
its most condensed form the story is a command, a verbal imperative:
"Love!" Connect, outside yourself, in a positive and fruitful way. The culture, of course, offers us multiple narratives about who and how to love:
love your nation (be patriotic), love your school (show school spirit, be
a loyal alum), love your god (be pious), love your parents (practice fil-
ial devotion, be a good son or good daughter), love your children (be a
devoted parent), love your friends (be sociable), love your pets (be an

animal-lover), love your job (find your calling), love your co-workers (be collegial), love your town (be civic-minded), love yourself (have self-es-teem). But according to the core cultural story told about love, all of this loving is incomplete without the icing on the cake: You need to find a spe-cial "Somebody to Love," as Jefferson Airplane (1967), Queen (1976), and Justin Bieber (2010) all agree. A *lover,* tellingly, does not mean a generic person whom one loves and who loves one back—such as a parent, child, or friend. We reserve the term *lover* for a romantic partner, that Special Somebody, our One True Love. As we will see, this view of love is not without its problems, but such is considered the pinnacle of love or, we may say, the essence and very heart of love.

In the romance story, the imperative "Love!" can be fleshed out into nine key elements that are always present, even if only implied. These essential elements of the romantic love story are: (1) IT IS HARD TO BE ALONE, especially (2) as a WOMAN IN A MAN'S WORLD, but (3) romance helps as a RELIGION OF LOVE, even though it involves (4) HARD WORK and (5) RISK, because it leads to (6) HEALING, (7) GREAT SEX, and (8) HAPPINESS, and it (9) LEVELS THE PLAYING FIELD for women. Let me lay out each point in more detail.

1. *It is hard to be alone.* Humans are social animals. Most people need and want love, of some kind. We are deeply relational be-ings. As babies, we need love—close, affectionate, physical at-tachment—as much as we need food or shelter. Without some form of loving caregiver, babies fail to thrive as healthy children. While there are models for the solitary life and the hermit, most adults continue to seek connection through family, friends, and community. Positive and loving relationships, in a variety of forms, are a sign of health; they are the glue that holds a life to-gether and the sweetener that makes life good.

2. *It is a man's world.* In this world wherein we seek connection, the stakes are higher for women. Compared to men, women often have less power, less money, fewer choices, and suffer from greater vulnerability and double standards. Women are often socialized into looking after men (and children and elders) and have their

needs and interests overlooked by men. "Men," of course, is not a monolithic category in which all men are the same (nor, obviously, is "women"). A hierarchy of value grants more power to able-bodied heterosexual men who conform to standard norms of straight masculinity (thus is the romance hero "manly"—tall, muscled, and ruggedly handsome). This hierarchy shames and devalues non-conforming men, as it also limits women; it justifies violence as a means of exerting mastery, control, and power over others both male and female. Using the terms of feminist theory, we can describe and analyze this situation as gender inequality, sexism, homophobia, misogyny, and patriarchy. In terms of the romance story arc, this situation adds to the initial unhappiness of the heroine. Women suffer at the story's beginning, in various fashions small to grand, from living in this man's world wherein the balance of power is stacked against them and where they have not yet found love to rebalance the equation. The woman's conflicts may include shaming or lack of knowledge about her sexuality, anxiety about weight or appearance, the threat of rape, the memory of past trauma caused by a man, an overbearing or inattentive boyfriend, full-blown domestic or sexual abuse, low self-esteem, family pressures to get married, workplace discrimination, financial vulnerability due to an inability to earn or control an income, or solo caregiver responsibilities (often for a child). Embodiment and sexuality entail further challenges and vulnerabilities for women due to disparities in the enjoyment of sex, unintended pregnancy, miscarriage, difficulties of childbearing and birth, and abandonment with children. Often, despite a heroine's best efforts, she is unable to fully resolve her problems without the aid of a powerful male. The romance story opens and begins to play out in this corrupt world that could also be described as the real world.

3. *Romance is a religion of love.* The romance story offers this answer to these problems: romantic partner love. The romance story believes in the redemptive or resurrection power of love. Romance entails faith in love as a positive force for the good in people's

lives. In this sense, love functions as religion, as a source of ultimate concern (to use an influential definition by theologian Paul
Tillich). Romance approaches the role of the divine as the locus
of ultimate significance. This religious function of the romance
narrative partly explains the success of Christian or inspirational
romance publishing, with its subgenres such as Amish, African
American, or evangelical Protestant romance. Stories of the
Christian God and romance intertwine easily because both entail
belief in the divine power of love. Romance is a storyline that
stakes its claim on the belief that the world is a good place and
that despite all of life's injustice and suffering, both love and love
stories make the world a better place. We see here that the genre
is life affirming. The romance narrative is not cynical or pessimis-
tic; its tone is not that of irony. It believes that love brings out the
best in people. In a jaded world, such an optimistic stance is easy
to mock as sentimental sappiness. But the stance is hard, if not
impossible, to deny. Love, of course, *does* make the world a better
place. The genre is quite rightly unapologetic for this faith in love.
The romance story becomes problematic, however, if and when it
privileges romance over other forms of love as the best and highest love.

4. *Romance requires hard work.* In the plotline of a romance story,
   conflicts between the main characters must be resolved and ob-
   stacles—both internal and external—must be overcome, often
   through great difficulty and deep struggle. Writers talk here of
   torturing their characters, of making them earn their happy ending. In love, giving up individuality for coupledom requires a
   willingness to make changes in one's life for the sake of another
   and generally involves sacrifice. Even more so, to fall in love is
   to take off the social masks that we wear and to bare our self to
   another, sharing insecurities and anxieties, hopes and dreams,
   willing to see the other and to be seen. Such openness makes you
   vulnerable. Opening body, soul, home, finances, heart to another
   is hard work. It requires trust, self-love, and a willingness to take
   on risk.

5. *Romance involves risk.* Love doesn't always work out. In fact, it may fail spectacularly. The story of romance novels, which are technically romantic comedies in that they end happily, can all too easily turn into the failure of love in romantic tragedies such as the iconic *Romeo and Juliet*. This knowledge haunts romance stories as a shadow text, often present within the story as the path avoided: The book opens with a bad boyfriend whom the reader knows is on his way out. A previous generation's failed romance is redeemed through the current characters. Or secondary characters are left hanging with an unresolved love story until a future book in the series. Readers feel this risk in the main story itself, which in "real life" would be unlikely to work out but which within the fantasy space of the romance always, miraculously, does: The heroine sleeps with the hero while he's still the emotionally closed-off cowboy or the philandering rake, but instead of the obvious scenario wherein he leaves her heartbroken, her act of giving herself to him opens his heart, such that he reforms his wandering ways and declares himself to be forever hers. Women get hurt in romance. Men do, too, of course, but as I argued in point no. 2, the romance story is particularly an exploration of women's vulnerability in this regard. Romance storytelling is the safe, imaginative space to explore the meaning and shape of this landscape of risk.

6. *Romance facilitates healing.* Love heals all wounds. Love conquers all. While these are clichés that stretch beyond realism into a mythic ideal, love in all of its forms does grant strength to endure many of life's hardships. Because love pulls us out of and beyond a narrow egoism into genuine care for another, it can lead to maturity, generosity, strength of character, and a type of spiritual fulfillment in finding a purpose in life greater than oneself. When someone loves you, well and truly, that love affirms your worth and value as an individual. Such love can give you greater confidence, heal past hurts, and grant resilience. It can be easier to take on life's challenges with a good partner at your side.

7. *Romance leads to great sex, especially for women.* The romance
   story is sex-positive. Although life and romance are horrifically
   replete with endless examples of how people misuse the power
   of sexuality to hurt and control others—generally, although not
   exclusively, how men use sex to hurt women—true love romance
   heals the scars of past sexual abuse. Lovers bloom in sexual joy.
   Whether the intimacy is cozy or spicy, sex shared lovingly with a
   partner adds joy to life and depth to a relationship. The romance
   teaches that sexuality is meant to be a good thing, an important
   and positive part of being human. Sexuality is not shameful,
   dirty, or sordid but natural, healthy, and empowering. It is a key
   part of what bonds two lovers into one, through the trust and
   vulnerability entailed in real intimacy. Women in romance novels
   are always sexually satisfied, even if such satisfaction is only implied by the quality of the lovers' relationship and the story's happy ending. For readers, the romance genre can connect women to
   their sexuality in positive ways. The equation works in both directions: In the romance story love leads to great sex, and sex is only
   great if experienced with the beloved. In this sense, love solves
   the problem of sexual desire, with its Dionysian gusts of unpre-
   dictable and disruptive energy, by focusing that desire solely on
   the beloved. By the ending of the romance story, love guarantees
   the constancy of the lovers. "I only have eyes for you" is the lover's
   refrain (and a perennially favorite jazz standard).

8. *Romance makes you happy.* One of life's delights is a special someone to love who loves you back. The supportive love of a good
   partner—what the romance story calls "true love"—is a sweetness to be treasured. When that sweetness is seasoned with the
   spiciness of shared erotic desire, the feast is delightful indeed.
   But despite the romance story's tagline about "living happily ever
   after," the happiness that romantic love leads to is not a simple
   or facile one. It is a mature happiness, rooted in the poignant
   knowledge of the inevitable loss of the beloved in death and open
   to the ongoing challenges inherent in any relationship. There can,
   however, be an over-the-top aspect to this element. The excess of

the lovers' commitment can strike some who are not fans as ridiculous lovey-dovey campiness. Hence the eye-rolling the genre
can provoke. But the story must complete its narrative arc. Begun
in the suffering and unhappiness of the real world, the romance
story must end in the healing and happiness of the mythic world.
This is not to say that neither love nor happiness are real but that
the romance story narrates their reality in a mythic way, pushing it into a more perfect fantasy space. Sometimes you can feel
this shift from realism to the mythic happening. The hero turns
around and walks back instead of leaving. Someone comes back
to life after a near-death experience. (These moments make my
eyebrows go up at the same time they make my heart beat faster.)
The more problematic and dangerous version of this essential
element is the implication that a person *must* be in a romantic
relationship in order to be truly happy. Here, the romance story
becomes oppressive if it mandates coupledom for everyone. The
story can place immense pressure on people to find a True Love
soulmate and can make them feel like failures if they don't find it.
Happiness, I repeat, does not require romantic love.

9. *Romance levels the playing field for women.* Here is the real happy
   ending for women. In a romance story, the woman always wins.
   By the end, the heroine is happy, safe, financially secure, well
   loved, sexually satisfied, and set up for a fulfilling life (as is the
   hero). A warm circle of friends supports her; bad guys have been
   brought to justice; families are reconciled. The main characters
   go from conflict to harmony and from disequilibrium of power to
   equality. Unlike in real life and much of literary fiction, women
   always gain power in these stories. Women never lose in the love
   relationship. The romance story is a woman-centered fantasy
   about how to make this man's world work for her. The payoff for
   the reader is the pleasure of this reparation fantasy. The problem,
   however, is if the fantasy obscures the extent to which there are
   options other than romance whereby women can thrive and become empowered. Romance may level the playing field and rebalance the odds that are stacked against women, but the romance

story does not necessarily change the name of the game. The reparation fantasy doesn't fundamentally challenge man's world, or, if it does, the challenge is too subtle and not pointed enough for the tastes and politics of some. But the story and the imaginative play space it makes possible are obviously very appealing for many readers and for many women—myself included—living as we all are in a still-patriarchal world, even when women have significantly more power than before and a (tiring) mandate to have and do it all.

And there you have it.

The romance story.

An analysis of the human condition. A prescription for happiness. A blueprint for how to live the good life. An illusion. A recipe for disaster. An addiction. A universal truth. Esteem enlivened by desire. The bonding of two into one. The brainwashing of individuals by power structures with something to gain.

You decide.

Me, I think it's some of all of the above.

And more.

In the rest of this book, let me tell you how.

2

Going Native

When the Academic Is (Also) the Fan

Here's a moment. I am in Tuscaloosa, Alabama's one really good sea-food restaurant—fish trucked in daily from the Gulf of Mexico—having lunch with Eloisa James/Mary Bly. She's the guest of the University of Alabama; we invited her down in her capacity as Dr. Mary Bly, Shakespeare and Renaissance scholar at Fordham University, but also in her capacity as Eloisa James, *New York Times*–bestselling author of historical romance novels. She delivered a campus-wide talk in the English department, visited my gender studies seminar, and spoke with my students about romance fiction. *Mary* is a respected academic with scholarly publications and degrees from Harvard, Oxford, and Yale. *Eloisa* is a high-level, successful romance writer. I am there in that moment eating lunch as a fan of Eloisa James, asking when her next book is coming out. I am there as an academic who works in popular romance studies, talking with Mary over shrimp salad about American cultural ambivalences around women's sexuality. And I am also there as a beginner writer—what's called a *wannabe*—eager for and honored by Eloisa's volunteered advice on my own historical romance manuscript. She reads and critiques my first chapter over key lime pie: "Core idea intriguing, but opening scene no good—not enough tension! Raise the stakes! Make the heroine suffer more! And the hero, his eyes could be sky blue." All great advice, except I keep his eyes brown, "chocolate brown," influenced I suspect by an early boyfriend.

Here's another moment. I'm at a university conference on the romance genre where I've presented a paper on an earlier version of this book's material. The floor opens to discussion, and one woman raises her hand. "I was very offended by your paper," she announces. The speaker says that she has a background in academia and is also a romance author with multiple published novels: an authentic, credentialed insider, in other words, to the romance community of authors and fans. Academic conferences are supposed to generate debate, but disagreement doesn't often get expressed in quite such emotionally charged terms. This woman, however, seems to be a straight-talker deeply engaged by these issues. Her concern, she explains, has to do with my attempt to function simultaneously as a romance novelist and a romance studies professor. "I want to read a novel written by someone who has poured her heart into it," she says, "not a book written to make money." She adds that a romance novel "should be a book of the heart. You're doing it as a cold-blooded experiment."

I seek to assuage her concern by recounting my own insider credentials. I describe how I've read romance novels since I was a young teenager, how my mother is a fan of the genre and that our home was always full of romances. I consider myself a fan, although I think about romance novels analytically—critically but sympathetically—as do many readers. The historical romance manuscript I am writing *is* the book of my heart, I tell her, starting to wax rhapsodic and adopting her language. My romance-writer self is not a fake self, nor is my romance-academic self a "beard" donned to provide legitimating cover for this aspiring novelist within me. Both of my personas are authentic and fully intertwined, both *are* the "voices of my heart." But she remains unconvinced. "What I heard is that you needed an excuse to write a romance," she says, shaking her head. "I don't know how I feel about a researcher studying us and being a romance writer. You are treading on sacred ground for me."

The point of these stories? Multiple identities are in play for those involved: literally for Mary/Eloisa, with her two names and the two identities she, like many romance novelists, long kept separate. I, too, have a multiplicity of identities, of positionality, in play: fan, academic, and beginner writer. There are tensions—productive, yet also complicated—in these separate but overlapping communities of the academics who study popular romance and the fans and authors who read and write it. Who gets to speak for the romance narrative? Who gets to tell and retell its story and to study its broader cultural reach? Using what methods and to what ends should this analysis proceed? What anxieties does the romance story address and does its study provoke? Boundary disputes can occur between the outsiders looking into this territory of Romancelandia and the insiders who inhabit it and identify as its natives. These different communities may guard the boundaries of Romancelandia out of concerns over how the genre is portrayed: whether romance fiction gets due respect or is unfairly criticized or dismissed. As we will see, these concerns have to do with questions of cultural capital, literary quality, sexual content, women's empowerment or disempowerment within the genre, and more.

My interlocutor at the conference functioned as a type of border patroller for this territory. Her concern was that I, as an outsider, had overstepped or overreached. In my attempt to understand the function of the romance narrative in popular culture, I had determined early on not only to study these romance stories from the outside as an academic researcher but also to enter within the romance fiction community by seeking to write novels myself. It is precisely this boundary-crossing move into participatory research—admittedly a bit of an unusual one—that disturbed the woman. My experimental method highlights and in some cases triggers these tensions among the communities interested in romance fiction; the method complicates but also enriches the study material. I was grateful for the woman's honesty, as it helped me to see how a "real" insider could read my participatory research as disrespect, infiltration, inauthenticity—even as blasphemy. What she called my "treading on sacred ground" blurred boundaries between inside and outside. Was I an interloper forcing my way under false pretenses into the territory of Romancelandia in order to take advantage of the genre or set it up for betrayal? Insiders don't want academic outsiders criticizing their genre based on false or incomplete understandings about romance novels—understandably so. And they certainly don't want an undercover spy in their midst, listening in on their conversations, partaking in community activities under false pretenses, and then reporting to the outside world about "silly novels by lady novelists," to use George Eliot's nineteenth-century phrase. So is it the insider-expert (the author of romance novels and the avid reader of the genre) or the outsider-expert (the academic or cultural commentator) who has status as the more authoritative reader of the romance, as they all—we all—engage, albeit differently, in sussing out the mystery of this thing called love?

The more I've pursued work in popular romance studies, the more I've come to see these tensions and multiplicities of identity as of key relevance for issues of methodology in the field. If the past few years have been a time of development and professionalization for this field, as I noted in the last chapter, then there is a need for serious attention to methodological questions of how we carry out the critical practice of popular romance studies. To undertake the project of this book—to understand how the romance narrative functions in popular culture, how it dominates the publishing industry as the bestselling fiction genre, and how it is now changing in conjunction with evolving norms for gender and sexuality in the culture—my own practice of the field of romance studies led me to dive into the romance community itself for answers. But, first, I needed an understanding of the terrain, of its bumps and points of tension; I needed a plan for how to proceed. This chapter lays out such a roadmap.

My claims here are twofold. First, we can think through the significance of the multiplicity of identities by drawing on the concept of *aca-fandom* to analyze the status of academic attention to popular romance. Figuring out how to negotiate the tension in play between the academic and the fan is central for the exploration I propose into the world of popular romance—and, more generally, for any academic study of pop culture. Second, this analysis can then yield purposefully theorized methodological pathways to help carry out this task. Based on my own fieldwork and the work of ethnographic theorists, I discuss three terms as part of such a methodology: *the aca-fan-author, observant participation,* and *performative ethnography.*

COMING OUT AS AN ACA-FAN . . .

Mapping out the territory and tension of aca-fandom requires situating this category within the broader romance community. If we think about the community interested in genre fiction romance as a large whole, we can divide it into four sub-communities: (1) fans, (2) romance writers, (3) industry professionals, and (4) academics; or those who consume the genre of romance stories as readers, produce it as authors, sell it as editors/agents/publishing professionals, and study it as academics. These people all read romance novels but do so in different ways. Interactions among these different sub-communities of reading practice and identity position are complex and not infrequently fraught with tensions of various sorts having to do with maintaining and/or bridging the boundaries among the sub-communities.

The category of romance fans, in more academic and perhaps fruitful terms, can be referred to as ludic readers, that is, people who read for play and pleasure. Within the romance community, the term *reader* seems preferred over *fan* to describe one who enjoys reading these novels for pleasure. In *Lost in a Book* (1990), psychologist Victor Nell coins the term *ludic reading*—from the Latin *ludus*, or play—to highlight the engagement and trancelike absorption that can result from reading. This pleasure derives in part from novels' intense components of emotion and fantasy, such that readers' imaginative engagement with the story shapes who they understand themselves to be.[1] Media studies scholar Henry Jenkins develops another helpful concept in his 1992 book *Textual Poachers* with an analysis of how fans function as rogue readers who "poach" from their chosen media genre or texts in order to engage critically and creatively in lively fandoms of participatory culture. From this perspective, fandom is not only intensely private, as the reading experience can be, but also powerfully communitarian.

In the romance community, participants range from casual and occasional readers of romance fiction, to voracious connoisseurs of the genre, to professional reviewers and bloggers. Community participation may take the form of trading books and recommendations among friends, reading and posting on any of the numerous fan-based romance review websites (e.g., *Dear Author, All about Romance, Smart Bitches Trashy Books, RT Book Reviews, The Romance Reviews, Romance in Color, Romance Junkies*, etc.), or attending playful reader-oriented events like the annual *Romantic Times* Booklovers Convention. Whether fans' engagement is private or participatory, fandoms are often highly creative and productive.[2] Engagement within any fandom earns fans capital within the economy of their fandom in the form of renown, respect, friendship, and membership in lively fan worlds—such as romance fiction's Romancelandia. Participation creates a sense of identity that is unique to the individual but also one that is shared in collective activities and fan talk. Engagement results as well in prolific textual productivity. In the participatory culture of romance, fans write *a lot:* online comments, book reviews, blog posts, fanfiction, and even book manuscripts, since romance writers almost invariably start out as ludic readers of the genre who eventually try their hand at writing with the hope of becoming published authors themselves.

Like such aspirational writers who start out as fans, a number of academics in popular romance studies are ludic readers who began to think critically about the genre and to share such reflections in academic venues. Thus arises the category of the aca-fan. In my lunch with Mary/Eloisa, I was an aca-fan; it was an aca-fan moment. Here's another such instance:

 INTERNATIONAL ASSOCIATION FOR THE STUDY OF POPULAR ROMANCE

The clever joint logo for the International Association for the Study of Popular Romance (IASPR) and the *Journal of Popular Romance Studies* (JPRS) is a dialogue bubble enclosing those organizations' initials, placed within a red heart. This graphic could be read, "IASPR & JPRS talk about and study the romance genre," where the heart represents this genre. Or it could be read, "IASPR & JPRS love the romance genre," where the heart represents love. It's an interesting ambiguity. Academics analyze the romance genre but may love, hate, or be indifferent to it as ludic readers. Fans love the genre (even when some novels and authors drive them crazy) but may or may not analyze it in a manner described as academic. What happens, then, in those moments when the fan is also an academic or when the academic is also a fan?

The terms *aca-fandom* and *aca-fan* (sometimes with a hyphen or slash sign between the compounds, sometimes not) gained currency in the early 1990s to describe the overlap of academia and fan cultures. *Aca-fan* refers particularly to those academics who self-identify as pop culture fans—that is, academics who aren't shy to admit publicly and write professionally about how they love *Madmen, True Blood, Lord of the Rings, Game of Thrones, Star Trek,* or *Star Wars,* or how they are members of any other fan culture based around a media text or genre of film, television, or fiction—such as popular romance fiction. Aca-fans take these fan cultures seriously as objects of scholarly analysis and carry out such study from a perspective both inside that world, as fans themselves, and outside it, as academics. They take inspiration from, but also take further, earlier audience ethnographies in cultural studies and literature—such as Janice Radway's influential work on romance fans in *Reading the Romance—* that validated fan communities as objects of study without themselves being fannish or insider accounts. The aca-fan concept was popularized by such leading texts as Henry Jenkins's *Textual Poachers* and Matt Hills's *Fan Cultures* (2002). Jenkins's own ongoing, influential blog is entitled *Confessions of an Aca-Fan.*

It is true, of course, that all academics, at some level, are fans of their area of study—be it nineteenth-century British fiction or coastal wetlands or early Chinese history or rural sociology. Otherwise, why devote one's life and career to such? Although the term *fan* isn't generally applied to scholars, such lack of usage may speak simply to high-culture bias and elitist discrimination.[3] Academics generally study what intrigues them—we study what we love—explained often by some personal motivation or familial history of association. The aca-fan, however, seeks to meld to a greater degree public work and private hobby, professional persona and personal pleasure, high culture and popular culture. Aca-fans, in other words, come out of the closet. To the question, "What do you read for fun or do for leisure?" they answer, delightedly, "The same as for work!" This delight has a political purpose as well. Aca-fans believe academics shouldn't talk only to other academics; they seek to move analysis out of the ivory tower, away from jargon, and into a wider participatory culture of public engagement. As Jenkins writes on the

"About Me" page of his blog, "The goal of my work has been to bridge the gap between these two worlds. I take it as a personal challenge to find a way to break cultural theory out of the academic bookstore ghetto and open up a larger space to talk about the media that matters to us from a consumer's point of view."[4]

Aca-fandom is thus a realm of intersection and hybridity. The aca-fan is the hybrid offspring of two species of parent. The typographic hyphen or slash represents the union of academic and fan but also their ongoing tension in a complex new mode that holds together two distinct forms of engagement with a text. In romance aca-fandom there is both conjuncture and disjuncture between academics' investment as fans reading the genre for pleasure and their investment as scholars analyzing it for insight. Or, to put the matter differently, at stake is the attempt to conjoin two very different pleasures of the text. On the one hand is the pleasure of reading for escapist fun: for the vicarious emotional appeal of gripping characters and a strong story. On the other hand is the pleasure of reading for evaluative study: for the intellectual payoff of probing a text as a telling artifact of a particular cultural place and time. Aca-fans try to join both brands of pleasure. Further at stake is the very purpose of the reading activity itself. Aca-fans read for the reward of these variously conceived pleasures of the text at the same time that they are invested in the more political goal of reading to break down the ivory tower and to open up academic analysis to public engagement. Aca-fans operate here both from a pleasure position, relishing their ludic frolic through their media field of choice, and from a missionary position, preaching to colleagues both within and without the academy an ecumenical gospel of union between university and mall, between academic journal and online review site.

None of this is to say that fans can't also be whip-smart and influential analysts of their chosen media texts—or that academics always are. Such is Jenkins's point about readers' creation of participatory culture, wherein they appropriate and use texts with intentional skill and creative verve to serve their own needs and interests. The resulting fandoms can be influential. In the media realm of television, for example, the "quality television" debate argues that fans play an important role in advocating

for high standards in their particular realm of interest and thus in moti-
vating producers to maintain quality and break new ground. Similarly,
Matt Hills coined the term *fan scholar* to describe non-academics whose
primary identity is as fans and who produce high-level analysis of a work
or genre.[5]

In the fandom of popular romance fiction, prime exemplars of such
fan scholars are the writing partners Sarah Wendell and Candy Tan, the
eponymous "Smart Bitches" of the wickedly funny, unapologetically
fan-based, and critically astute *Beyond Heaving Bosoms: The Smart Bitches'
Guide to Romance Novels* (2009). Wendell continues analysis of the romance genre in her ongoing web-based review blog *Smart Bitches Trashy
Books*. Other sophisticated romance genre fan scholars with online sites
include romance author Olivia Waite, who offers a blog series on intersec-
tional feminism in romance; a political science professor at Washington
University in St. Louis who writes as Vacuous Minx; *Wonk-o-Mance*, a
group blog and review site with a genre-expanding manifesto to celebrate
"the whole messy spectrum of human behavior, packaged up for consumption in romance novel form"; Jackie Horne's *Romance Novels for Feminists*
with its tagline, "For readers who like a little equality with their love"; and
the chair of a college English department who writes the romance-heavy
blog *Something More*.[6]

On the back cover of *Bosoms*, bestselling romance novelist Jennifer
Crusie offers this telling blurb: "I love the Smart Bitches. They look at
romance with clear but loving eyes." Precisely therein—in this metaphor
of eyes that are clear *but* loving—lies the tension of the aca-fan. This tension is productive but also complicated and fraught with risk. A fan reads
romance with loving and passionate eyes—but as even the besotted dupe
finds out eventually, love can be blind. The lover does not see the beloved's flaws; loving eyes see past these shortcomings. However, put more
cynically (or more realistically), love doesn't *allow* us to see these flaws;
love blinds and so dupes us. Accordingly, a fan whose eyes are loving may
not see with full clarity. A fan may be defensive about the beloved, lack
objectivity in its evaluation, be unwilling to weigh its weaknesses or be
resistant to wider critiques of the genre (although the fan scholars cited
above provide proof of the willingness to post challenging and skepti-

cal evaluations of the romance genre and its books). An academic who is too fannish may fall prey to these risks. A disinterested academic, on the other hand, reads romance with clear eyes—but as anyone who has ever sought a soulmate knows, we open our deepest selves only to those we trust to love us, only to those whose eyes burn with a passion most interested indeed. A reader who is too academic may be left unmoved by the storylines and characters, miss the beating heart of the genre, lack a sensibility for its poignancy or emotional draw, just "not get it" in terms of why or how the genre is so popular, and may thus treat the genre with a certain distrust or disdain. Sometimes, this "not getting it" is a matter of access. The academic may be shut out of certain spaces and conversations open only to insiders, who may for their part distrust academics or feel inhibited around them.

The question, then, is how to preserve the rigorous analytic evaluation of the academic and yet meld it with the fan's engagement, the lover's delight, the insight made possible by a deep passion for a genre. It is, of course, no new argument—indeed, it is a banal argument—to warn that excess enthusiasm can compromise critical clarity of insight or, alternately, that academic analysis can destroy the passionate feel for a text. But to be enthusiast *and* critic at the same time, practitioner *and* analyst—to argue and embody that one can be deeply and equally of both camps—perhaps gets us somewhere more interesting, with implications for research methodology and especially for fandom research. One example similar to my project is the participatory autoethnography of film scholar-fan Tom Phillips, who argues that "embracing an 'overly confessional' approach to my academic writing is integral to the fidelity of my research." This "confessional" mode can add to an academic's authority, certainly in order to establish access and trust with research subjects in a fan community, but also within the changing academic contours of popular culture studies itself. Jenkins and colleagues' "Manifesto for a New Cultural Studies" *requires* that pop culture scholarship embrace "new epistemologies and new modes of expression that preserve rather than ignore this 'immediacy'" of pop culture texts involving intensity of emotion, identification with characters and storylines, and imbrication into our daily lives. They reject in their manifesto "the distant authority of traditional academic writing" and are suspicious "of attempts to write about popular culture from a distance."[7]

How, then, to produce academic scholarship from within the process of seeing into the beloved's heart—where the beloved here is the genre of popular romance fiction? How to contribute to a deeper public understanding of the genre without losing the creative, participatory play of the fan that keeps the enterprise pleasurably fun? How to be political without lapsing into a tired old missionary position? I approach this as a methodological question: How do we negotiate these tensions of the aca-fan in order to carry out a critical yet deeply engaged practice of popular romance studies?

. . . AND CROSSING THE BRIDGE INTO ROMANCELANDIA

And so is born my answer: In my research, I proceed as a multi-positioned *aca-fan-author* through a practice of *observant participation* in order to produce a *performative ethnography*. Together, these three terms constitute my alternative approach to the traditional fieldwork method of participant observation, as I apply it to the academic study of genre romance.

Soon after beginning romance research, when I moved from casual ludic reader to engaged aca-fan, I came to see that upcoming generations of novelists sprang from the participatory fan culture of romance. Since highly engaged readers often became aspirational or wannabe authors, I needed to become precisely that in order to complete my arc of engagement in the romance community. Only by becoming the romance writer, by embodying that form of creative production, would I be able to participate fully in all subgroups of the romance community (leaving aside the publishing industry professionals of agents and editors, which my triple positioning admittedly lacked the ambition and range to reach). I intended for my aca-fandom to become creative by intertwining my academic writing *about* the romance genre with fiction writing *within* that genre: I resolved to become the romance *aca-fan-author*. I coined this triple hybrid term to capture the multiplicity of identity I started out describing in my lunch with Mary/Eloisa, wherein I was simultaneously the academic outsider, studying the genre; the fan consumer, reading it; and the insider practitioner, writing it. I thus set out to write a romance manuscript, following all the norms for mainstream historical romance fiction. To inspire and capture this project I gave myself a pseudonym—"Catherine LaRoche"—more exotic and romantic than "Roach."

By sinking deep into the romance narrative as a fiction writer, I found myself able to inhabit the inside of that storyline and trace out its pathways in a fictional, emotionally driven writing experiment that reflexively informed and enriched my nonfiction, analytically driven writing. I believe there is methodological value to this approach, but I'm not arguing that an academic *must* be an aca-fan-author in order to study the genre. It's an experiment I have undertaken because of my interest in the romance narrative and for the challenge and pleasure of a new writing craft. I'm vastly engaged by this writing and by the creation of a romance writer persona to go along with my academic persona: Catherine LaRoche favors décolletage over tweed and packs long velvet gowns for conferences instead of standard business suits. She allows me to write purple prose along with solemn academic jargon, steamy sex scenes along with dry analysis. But if, partly, I'm doing this writing for fun, equally, I'm arguing that the fun matters: It stands as testament to the option of a different mode of academic research. I'm the aca-fan-author for the pleasure of the writing it yields and for the witness it provides to the fruitful possibilities of an alternative form of engaged and participatory academic research.

I have carried out this work-play through my second adopted term of research methodology, *observant participation*. This qualitative fieldwork method departs from the more standard practice of *participant observation* followed in cultural anthropology and sociology wherein an outside researcher seeks to observe insider participants of a cultural group, joining in enough to gain access but in an important sense remaining an objective outsider. According to norms of the field, the researcher should participate within the culture to the extent necessary to observe participants freely and to produce thick cultural descriptions analyzing these observations. Success may even require the researcher to in some sense become a member of the culture under observation—although herein starts to arise the danger of that problematic term *going native*. Researchers must not go too far, lest they cross a line after which objectivity is lost, the tale can no longer be told, and a point of no return occurs when re-acculturation and going back home become difficult. Think of Kurtz, feared lost in more senses than one, up the Congo in Joseph Conrad's *Heart of Darkness*. Or as aca-fan researchers Jen Gunnels and M. Flourish Klink put it, in reference to this "very white, very Western stigma," the fear is that by "going native" and "experiencing the subject on the subject's terms, all else will be eschewed and our cultural clothing rent as we become intellectual savages running naked through the streets beneath the Ivory Tower."[8]

Debates and experiments are perennial within fieldwork as to how far into the realm of active participation or intensive enculturation a researcher may safely venture. Anthropology has, in fact, a long history of researchers deliberately "going native" in various ways in their fieldwork and written ethnographies for self-conscious, experimental reasons of method and theory.[9] The tension of "where to draw the line" is by no means new. The necessary self-reflexivity of participant observation has always raised questions about the resulting status of the researcher and of how to maintain methodological rigor—indeed, what such rigor might mean—in the complicated situation wherein the researcher is participating as an observer of participants. In this sense, there is a long-recognized paradox at the heart of anthropological fieldwork: One must participate fully to understand, but not participate *too* fully, lest one never come back out to tell the tale one entered the community to understand. Since the 1970s and especially in the last ten to twenty years, a growing minority trend of ethnographers has critiqued the norms of distance, objectivity, and neutrality entailed in the insider/outsider divide, or what anthropologists differentiate as the *emic* (the perspective of a person already within the social group) and the *etic* (the perspective of an observer outside the social group). Such a divide places the academic in what anthropologist Luke Lassiter terms "an authoritative (and inherently exploitative) relationship with the exotic, distant, normalized Other." Increasingly, ethnographers have evolved field methods and writing styles to blur that divide in order to address questions of ethics, access, and validity.[10]

These self-reflexive and experimental practices have the effect of flip-ping participant observation on its head into a method of observant par-ticipation, wherein the researchers participate more deeply and more fully as insiders to the culture and then reflexively observe themselves as participants, as well as their own process of observation, along with the native cultural participants. Researchers move from reactive to proactive participation and then theorize the role of this move in the ethnographic encounter. Michaela Pfadenhauer, for example, states of her approach, "observant participation means that we go into the social 'field' we are examining as intensively as possible and try to become as similar as pos-sible—up to their linguistic and habitual customs—to the people we are examining." Such a practice of observant participation in ethnography is quite similar to the stance of the aca-fan in the embrace, and even privi-leging, of the insider perspective. We see this claim in "Manifesto for a New Cultural Studies" when Jenkins and his co-authors write that "the best cultural critics speak as 'insiders' as well as 'outsiders'."[11]

By stressing this relationship between insider and outsider, or be-tween self and other, and by observing oneself as much as the other, this approach addresses another problem with the metaphor of going native, namely the power dichotomy of the metaphor's colonial taint. To go na-tive can carry overtones of condescension, as it implies and risks reaf-firming a problematic power structure of imperial self versus colonial other. Although the term carries this history of alienation from the very people with whom one seeks to work and bond, I am nonetheless drawn to its expressive potential. I use the term partly because it suggests, as Jenkins points out, that "by definition, academics cannot be fans."[12] I seek to use the term with playful and ironic self-awareness, in campy, cheeky protest against this very bias: Yes, I am Kurtz, gone native up the river, in velvet and spangles. This research felt to me like a movement and departure, with the creation of a new critical practice and new self in relation to that practice. I *was* going somewhere new and into some new researcher-self. I was coming out of the closet as a romance fan and an academic who wanted to write popular fiction. I was crossing over into new territory, into Romancelandia. That land where romance writ-ers and readers live and play is where I, too, wanted to be. My research project became to map the contours of Romancelandia by becoming its native daughter.

This approach of observant participation, or that of the aca-fan, poses challenges for a researcher. If academics too far abandon the outsider etic perspective of neutral and objective analysis, if they too far adopt the insider emic perspective of emotional and subjective investment in the culture, they can become too fully the fan. They can lose authority and credibility, and their account can lose hermeneutical power to interpret that culture outside its sphere. This concern is not an idle one and does not merely accede to reductive notions of the fan as the obsessed and self-deluded dupe to ideological hegemonies—in the case of the romance fan, to notions of the bonbon-eating, brainwashed housewife mindlessly consuming patriarchal bondage narratives of One True Love. Academics cannot, *must* not, no matter how devotedly fannish their tastes may be, or how deep they seek to travel into insider territory of the participant, abandon the fundamental mode of critical inquiry and skepticism so central to the academic task. As digital media scholar Ian Bogost puts it in a much commented-upon blog post entitled "Against Aca-Fandom,"

> The media scholar ought to resist aca-fandom, even as he or she embraces it. The fact that something feels pleasurable or enjoyable or good (or bad) need not be rejected, of course, but it ought to issue an itch, a discomfort. As media scholars, we ought to have self-doubt about the quality and benefit of the work we study. We ought to perform that hesitance often and in public, in order to weave a more complex web around media.... Embracing aca-fandom is a bad idea. Not because it's immoral or crude, but because it's too great a temptation.[13]

This caution is important. I am a lifelong ludic reader of the romance genre, ever since I first snuck peeks at the intriguing bosom-covered paperbacks that my mother kept in her room. I read romance for relaxation, reward, amusement, and as a form of play, but I'm aware, in Bogost's terms, that it elicits for me an "itchiness" as well. I don't easily say that I *love* the genre (although I sort of do). The style of aca-fan engagement I seek is characterized by skepticism, generosity, generativity, fascination—but not by *love*. I seek hermeneutics, not apologetics. I want to be expansive, not defensive. My claim, then, isn't that popular romance studies should privilege insider accounts based on observant participation nor that such accounts provide better or deeper readings of the genre. For the current critical practice of popular romance studies to thrive, it needs a broad variety of accounts: insider, outsider, and insider-outsider. But perhaps the aca-fan approach of deep observant participation, by aiming to dissolve as much as possible the emic/etic divide, produces an elusive and distinctive quality of information: a fully insider account of experience in the romance community, contextualized and interpreted for an outside community through a wider analytical lens.

In my field research, I strived for such a deep insider approach of observant participation in three ways: by observing members of the romance community through interviews and field participation in conference gatherings and online forums; in a self-reflexive observation of myself as I engaged in this fullest form of participation; and through my aca-fan-author practice in "observing" or adhering to the prescribed behavioral norms of this community of practice, like an observant Jew or Catholic practices the norms of their faith community. My aim through such deep participation was to go native within the community while bringing my tweed-jacketed academic self along for the ride, not as a stand-in for colonial oppressor but as a critical engagée trying to think hard about what is at stake in this addictive genre. I became a native of Romancelandia, writing "from the heart" (as the disgruntled woman at my talk said), from my dual but not dueling hearts, simultaneously crafting academic and fiction writing about falling in love.

Another challenge has been this: How to write up the results of such fieldwork? Turned on its head, this challenge represented an opportunity for a different type of writing and scholarship to emerge. And so the question of how to present the data leads to the third and final term of my research methodology: *performative ethnography*. Ethnography is the product field researchers write up; it refers, literally, to storytelling about a particular cultural group. The problem, of course, is what to include in that story and how to tell it. Those researchers following broadly postmodern field methods of observant participation often seek to produce a different type of ethnographic write-up—more experimental, narrative-based, first-person, self-reflexive, and up-front about the role of the researcher in the ethnographic encounter. My adaption of this method in popular romance studies has led me to write performative ethnography, defined as the use of expressive form or artistic performance (most often theater but also visual art, fiction, dance, poetry, music, multimedia, etc.), often encompassing value-laden and emotionally charged work, in the production of an ethnography.[14] I am going deep in this field, becoming a full participant, not in order to defend or advocate for the genre but in order to *perform* it. The result of my research is my performance of, and as, a romance writer.

I align myself here with researchers such as anthropologist Neil L. Whitehead, sociologist Loïc Wacquant, and art historian Lianne McTavish: ethnographers who respectively formed a Goth/Industrial band, trained as a boxing prize-fighter, and competed in a female body-building event as they simultaneously researched the communities in which they immersed themselves as full observant participants. The activity of the community under study becomes the performative vehicle for the research. The professor performs as "Detonator" of Blood Jewel, as "Busy Louie" in the ring at the Golden Gloves, as "Feminist Figure Girl"—or as romance writer Catherine LaRoche. Through such performative engagement, one becomes the research one conducts. One links cultural performance to cultural analysis.[15] These experiments transgress orthodox norms of academic writing and, in my case, transgress as well a certain form of feminist and highbrow politics that views romance writing as a no-no (politics that have led some women academics who publish romance to remain closeted, hiding their romance identity from their academic peers).[16]

While there are clearly risks to this auto-ethnographic and performative mode—solipsistic self-regard, self-deluded confessional biography, fannish lack of skepticism—there is also, at the very least, an honesty in admitting to the role of personal desire and fantasy in the research choices of the academic. As Whitehead notes further, "In order to understand desire, we must become desiring subjects ourselves"; such desire can get us far, can be, indeed, "the vehicle for participation in other cultural worlds." We all study what we do for a reason. The performative auto-ethnographer makes that personal reason public in a purposefully structured engagement of self and other. Researchers working with these alternative field practices argue that resulting ethnographies should be meaningful to the community under study and should recirculate back into the community in some significant way. Barbara Tedlock writes about public ethnography as an engagement with the general public wherein researchers produce novels, plays, op-ed pieces, and more that serve as "mimetic parallels through which the subjective is made present and available to its performers and witnesses."[17]

The form of performative ethnography in which I engage is an attempt to address this issue by writing up what I have learned from the romance community in a manner of interest to it that permits me to participate fully within that community. My fiction writing becomes *mimesis,* my mimicry or imitation (sincere, engaged, respectful) of this community's work and my expressive presentation of self performed within it. Much of this ethnography emerges, then, in a different voice and style than traditional academic writing, in a deliberate experimental attempt to produce and embody, in fiction performance, generative writing for and about the popular romance community.

LUDIC RESEARCH

What I've sought to offer in this chapter are methodological lessons learned for the critical practice of popular romance studies and a proposal for one way to conduct such scholarship. What I'm after is an engaged and practical but not reductive interpretation, a rich interweaving of insider and outsider perspectives. I believe it is possible in such work to listen closely to a wide variety of voices—including my own such voice, as I make explicit my desires for romance reading and writing—and to gather these voices, without succumbing to false sentiment or misplaced belief in the transparency of people's accounts of their experience, in order to make sense of how power and expectation shape our most intimate inner lives.

Finally, a revelation. What's emerged as a conclusion for me in this work is how much I *like* it. So here's a fourth methodological term, tossed in as lagniappe: I'm a *ludic researcher,* one who engages in research as play, for pleasure. When I started out this project, I was unsure where it was going—where it was taking me, what it was making of me. I sometimes felt guilty about my giddy enjoyment—surely my work should not be this rip-roaring when others have to scrub out the tanks of river barges to earn a living. Eventually, however, I worked through my confusion. I shed the guilt. I embraced the project. I decided that enchantment can be a legitimate part of research.

Other researchers who engage in versions of this methodology echo such sentiments. Wacquant, for example, as a sociologist working in urban ethnography, spent three years in a Chicago gym in fieldwork for his academic study of boxing. For the book, he explicitly took up a method of observant participation and talks about the importance of "moral and sensual conversion to the cosmos under investigation" and the "intoxication of immersion" that results. A ludic researcher indeed, he includes a long footnote of material from his field notebook:

> Today I had such a ball being in the gym, talking and laughing with DeeDee and Curtis sitting in the back room and just *living* and *breathing* there. . . . I feel so much pleasure simply *participating* that *observation* becomes secondary. . . . I find the idea of migrating to Harvard . . . and participating in the *tutti frutti* of academe totally devoid of meaning and downright depressing, so dreary and dead compared to the pure and vivacious carnal joy that this goddamn gym provides me. . . . I'm already way beyond seduction![18]

This "carnal joy," I submit, is serious and important stuff. It has wider implications for the status of academic research, traditionally steeped in norms of objectivity and distance, staid and sober. The style of research for which I'm aiming suggests there are other ways to live a life of inquiry and to share its fruits with interested communities both inside and outside that sphere of inquiry. I am heartened by the growing body of similar methodological approaches: by the Goth music anthropologists, figure-girl competition art historians, and gloved-up boxing sociologists out there. As a pair of aca-fan scholars ask, "How can the critical study of any text succeed without the passionate and knowledgeable participation of the scholar?" Or as Feminist Figure Girl puts it, "Look Hot While You

Fight the Patriarchy."[19] This playful pleasure, this frisky humor, this carnal joy—this *ludus*—of our research is seriously seductive stuff indeed.

So, yes, I am seduced by the women of the romance community, by their embrace of a writing life of love and desire and fantasy, by their siren call to dress up my fanny and schmooze a chocolate-fountain midnight dessert buffet on the RWA conference final night. Champagne in hand, I am Kurtz in my sparkly velvet, lacking only a boa (mental note: buy one next year), gone native, up the river, out of any closet—who needs a closet when such interesting questions are at stake out here?!—over the bridge into Romancelandia, exactly where I want to be.

I am the academic, thinking endlessly about dynamics of fantasy, desire, shame, power, reparation, and imagination.

I am the fan, excited by all the free books they're throwing my way.

I am the newbie writer, shy, unsure, dreaming of publication.

3

Notes from the Imagination

Reading Romance Writing

Wherein Catherine Roach and Catherine LaRoche,
in Feisty Dialogue, Comment upon LaRoche's Fiction

As Monty Python says, "And now for something completely different." In this chapter, I eschew the theoretical. In its place, a confession: While I truly believe in the value of bringing fan and scholarly communities together, a big part of why I'm doing this work is because it's a whole bucket of fun. And I want you, gentle reader, to have fun along with me. Without drowning you in jargon and theory, I want to engage you in performative ethnography and in debates about that omnipresent romance narrative directing us to hot and steamy love. Accordingly, there's a deliberately goofy aspect to what I'm up to, an academic-lite approach that involves poking fun at myself, at certain conventions of sober analysis, and at insider/outsider boundaries that can make conversation—serious conversation—difficult across the divide between academics and the general public.

So here's the setup. We're in Starbucks at the Ferg, which is the University of Alabama's student services building more formally known as the Ferguson Center. A recent survey of the undergraduates has revealed that a stunning 45 percent of them had not read a book cover to cover in the past year. The Creative Campus initiative responded with a controversial campaign entitled "Seducing the Reader," featuring giant posters hanging around campus emblazoned with taglines such as "Are You a Book Virgin?" and "Lose Your Innocence between the Covers This Term!" In a further dodgy effort at engaging students in the lost art of book reading—and in an ill-conceived attempt at copy-cat programming spurred by the success of *Fifty Shades*—Creative Campus has invited Catherine LaRoche to give a reading from her recently released Victorian romance e-book *Master of Love*. Catherine LaRoche is a member of Romance Writers of America; she has a two-book publication contract with the Simon and Schuster e-book imprint Pocket Star. In an initiative by the College of Arts and Sciences designed to highlight faculty publications, the dean's office has displayed cover art of all the faculty members' books in buildings around campus. Outside the office door of Catherine Roach, professor in the university's interdisciplinary program of New College, hangs a beautifully framed giant blow-up of LaRoche's cover for *Master of Love*.

Some of this, I swear, is actually true.

Picture this, then: For the reading, Catherine LaRoche sports a Chanel suit in bright red (this is, after all, the home of the Crimson Tide). Aiming to be practical yet stylish, she wears medium heels and a few pieces of good jewelry, subtle makeup, and crimson lipstick. Compared to Catherine Roach, she is the prettier one. LaRoche doesn't like to be too flashy but certainly doesn't want to look like an *academic*. Everybody knows they have no fun. Unless they're continental Europeans, they can't risk dressing fashionably for fear that colleagues will conclude they are having an affair or are intellectual lightweights lacking dedication to the life of the mind. LaRoche, in contrast, enjoys her clothes. At Romance Writers of America conferences, she gets to wear long velvet sequined gowns to the award ceremonies. Roach, nerdy romance studies academic, never gets to dress like that at her conferences.

Now, dear reader, if this tomfoolery taxes your patience, stick to the academic chapters. But if such an experiment in alternative academic discourse and multiplicity of interpretation intrigues you, I urge you to forge on.

I crook my finger at you.
I cast you a wink and a saucy smile.
Take my hand, and let us forge on together.

*   *   *

Here she is: Catherine LaRoche, striding to the microphone in that red Chanel suit. She provides a short introduction before beginning her reading. The passage comes from *Master of Love*. The scene, she explains with a smile, is one of seduction, set in the library of the Viscount Rexton's London mansion after an 1847 dinner party. All the guests have left—save one. The point of view character is the book's heroine, an impoverished but genteel book dealer whom our hero, Lord Dominick Rexton, has commissioned to organize his library. (Our text now switches to a font named Rockwell, which I intend to be taken in the most salacious sense.)

Truly, she couldn't disagree with Lord Rexton's logic; she *did* need to be kissed, and by him. There seemed a quality of magic to the moment, a suspension of normal reality. When again would she, the Honorable—the prim and oh so respectable—Miss Callista Higginbotham ever find herself in the arms of London's most handsome and notorious lover?

For years, she'd had no illusions a life of passion and romance would ever form any part of her fate. And yet here, now, was passion—kindling an inner fire with an intensity that shocked. If he was offering love-making, she'd not back down now. To say no would be like saying no to breathing, to tilting one's face to the sun, to one's heart beating. Here was the fire of life, and living.

Heavens, *he* needed to kiss her? *She* needed to kiss, to know what it was to be desired, to be treated tenderly and with fierce passion as a woman, and not only as a sister, a household manager, a friend, a female book dealer tottering on the edge of ridicule and financial collapse.

As Dominick's mouth nibbled at the corners of hers, she knew she would freely give all he asked, greedily

take all he offered, and deal with the damn consequences tomorrow. Tonight she wanted to be—*for once in her
life!*—impulsive and improper and wayward and loved.
Some back part of her mind, where rationality sat banished but not silenced, warned her there lay the rub. This
wasn't about love, but about bedding down; she would
forget that distinction at her peril.

"Shhh." The sound whispered from her, meant for her
wiser self. She *knew* she'd never have him all. But she
could have some, for now. Surely that was enough?

It would have to be, because it was more than she could
turn down. She felt a fluttering within her breast, an opening up and release of a new self beginning to stretch wings.

"Callista?" There was inquiry in his voice, but seduction in his mouth. He used his tongue to trace a wet path
along the edge of her lower lip and lick into the corners
of her mouth. "Mmm, delicious . . . cream and honey and
wine."

He rubbed his smooth-shaven cheek against her own.
"Rose petals and velvet," he murmured into her ear.

And then he dipped his head to inhale deeply along the
column of her throat. "And your scent is that of the ocean
at night and the deep forest and some indescribable essence of Callista."

He leaned his forehead into hers, his voice thickened
with passion. "Let me make love to you, beauty. I'll see no
harm comes to you, I promise."

She wasn't entirely certain what this promise was in regards to—her reputation? the pain of her virginity? the
possibility of breeding?—but discussion seemed beside
the point. She had needs of her own, and, at the moment,
they involved having his mouth on hers, doing those delightful little tricks with his tongue.

She realized with a start he'd already seduced her long
ago, perhaps from that afternoon when he'd gifted her
with Pliny's *Historia* and confessed abashedly he liked to
read it himself, all the while standing there like Adonis
incarnate.

For answer, she looped her arms around his neck and pulled him close. He was still on his knees in front of the low crimson leather chair, and he set his hands on her own knees to spread her full skirts and push into the vee of her body. It felt horribly wanton to open her legs like that and yet thrilling at the same time.

With a low growl, he set one hand against the shoulder blades of her back and another on her bottom and slid her into full contact with his form. The breath fled her body, and she heard herself moan.

His hard chest crushed her breasts, his hand kneaded her buttocks, and that other hard piece of him began to rock rhythmically into the juncture of her thighs. (What *were* those secret parts of them called? She knew the names in Italian slang and ancient Sanskrit, but had no terms to use in English.) Her stomach clenched, and heat seared her. Their position seemed to align them perfectly for a joining, the details of which were still murky but rapidly becoming clarified.

"Your hair. I need it down, now." He began to pull pins from her coiffure and toss them aside. "Do you know how much I think about this fiery hair of yours, how often I've imagined you with it down, caressing your naked body as you tease me to come to you?"

Good Lord, she thought, stunned by his words. *That was her, in his fantasy!?* He thought about her that way? Could she be that erotic image he painted?

He needed two hands to get out all the pins and loosen the complicated twists and ringlets and ribbons Marie had woven for the evening. But his other hand didn't seem to want to leave her bottom, where it kept her tightly tucked against his insistent rubbing.

Not wanting him to stop that intoxicating pleasure herself, she reached up her arms to dismantle her coiffure. The movement caused her breasts to arch toward his face, and she watched with some amusement as his gaze dropped into her cleavage and his breath caught. He was like a boy opening too many presents at once and abandoning the favorite of a moment ago for a new excitement.

He brushed a thumb pad across the tops of her breasts pushed up by her corset. The full brilliance of Marie's dressmaking skills became clear to her. This low-shouldered gown became more enticing the more one was seduced in it, so to speak. It gave a lover something to play with. The stiff horizontal bands of fabric pleated around the bodice shielded her bosom from the gaze of onlookers. But a lover, holding her close and gazing down, was treated to a lovely shadowy area that begged to be explored.

Dominick was quick to comply. He undid the upper hooks at the back of her gown and loosened with practiced skill the top set of corset laces. Her ruffled silk sleeves slid down to trap her arms while freeing her breasts to spill out over the edge of her corset. Looking down, she was amazed at the picture she presented: hair tumbling around her shoulders—all right, maybe it *was* a rather vivid red—emerald silk binding her arms, the creamy tops of her breasts bared to the dark golden head bent over them, a puckered pink nipple disappearing into his mouth. . . . *Could this be her?*

The shot of sensation as he tugged at her breast with tongue and lips brought her out of her reverie. She hadn't known her body could *feel* like this! Hot and tingling pleasure spiraled from the nipple in his mouth down to the base of her spine and gathered there to feed the growing fire. Her bosom and womb seemed connected in a path of glowing energy.

He pulled back as if to inspect his handiwork and then pursed his lips to blow a stream of cool air onto the other nipple until it puckered like its twin.

"Hmmm, Callista," he purred, "such beauty you keep hidden under your strict façade. It's like cutting open the pages of a new book, cracking that leather binding for the first time and unexpectedly finding the secrets of naughty French erotica inside. Look at you!" he said in a tone that sounded strangely like awe.

She had but a moment's hesitation, as she wondered if he used such lines with all the women he seduced. The thought was a painful one, but stopping now for the sake of her pride would be more painful still.

He slipped both hands inside the pink silk of her loosened corset to cup her breasts and push them up together. Then he bent his head anew to lick both nipples at once. The contrast of his large, warm hands with the library's cool air on the moistened tips of her breasts sent a ripple of pleasure down her back. The feeling of need between her legs grew more insistent with his attention to her breasts, as well as with the pressure he maintained between her thighs. She moaned again and felt herself start to pant at the layers of sensation he was lavishing across her body.

She needed more of something, and soon. But with her arms bound tight to her sides in her silk sleeves, she could do no more than grip at the fine black wool of his trousers. Suddenly, he seemed to be wearing far too much. Wasn't there supposed to be more nudity involved in these matters? Her fingers itched to feel his flesh, to smooth and caress their way across his skin the way his were doing at her neck and bosom.

"Dominick . . ." she began, but got no further as he nibbled again at her lips.

"Mmm . . . yes, love?"

His use of the term caught her off guard, with an odd stinging pang. "Don't call me that," she whispered. Surely he couldn't mean it in any sense other than as a seducer's blithe throwaway. "That's what you call them. Please, just Callista."

She had to steel herself to the effect of such endearments, delivered in that honeyed drawl and coming from such a man as he. She didn't want him to play the seducer with her, but simply to be himself—the man who loved books and liked to write and who was, at the moment, introducing her to more pleasure than she'd ever imagined.

"All right," he agreed easily. "I'll call you Callista. As long as you keep calling me Dominick. Or"—he flashed a crooked grin—"just call me wicked."

"Yes, my wicked lord Dominick." She wasn't yet fully comfortable with the intimacy of his given name, any more than she could see he was ready to give up the mask of seducer.

She was, however, prepared with mounting urgency to seek another kind of intimacy. "Please, umm. . . ." How did one ask for this? She tried plucking at his trousers and waistcoat, which was all she could reach. "Please."

"Ah, Callista, in fairness to you, I want you to be sure." He cupped her face in both hands and brushed back the tresses from her cheeks. "Is this truly what you want?"

She knew Lady Barrington and the others from the society page stories still hovered in the distance, that he offered no more than an evening's dalliance, that by the dictates of society's morality she should say no. Perhaps even more to the point, to protect her heart she ought to stop things right here. But she couldn't. Oh, she just couldn't. Not tonight. Not with the contrast this slow lovemaking presented to the nightmares she still had of Garforth's hands on her and the threat of bills coming due sooner than she could pay them, and the daily fatigue and struggle of keeping her motley household together. This man treated her with respect and tenderness. It was not for her to judge him or to expect the impossible. They had now, and tonight.

She'd made her decision.

"Please," she whispered to him again.

Desultory applause follows Catherine LaRoche's reading as the fourteen bored students in attendance go back to plotting their weekend bar plans over mochas and cappuccinos.

One person, however, does step up to LaRoche. This woman is too old and frumpy to be a student. An introduction clarifies the situation: She is a professor. Catherine Roach teaches gender and cultural studies in New

College at the university. She explains that she's writing an academic book about the function of the romance narrative in popular culture. La-Roche had noted this woman in the audience, listening attentively to the reading but with a smirk on her face. When the professor invites her to sit for an interview, LaRoche is intrigued.

"I'll buy you a coffee," offers Dr. Roach.

"Make it a skinny extra-hot venti latte," says the novelist, "and I'm all yours."

The professor rolls her eyes as they order from the barista. "Must you cast everything in terms of seduction and romance?"

"Why not?" The novelist smiles. "I like romance. It makes me happy." The author peers at cake pops on the glass counter and selects a chocolate one sprinkled with pink hearts. She hands it to the professor. "Here—you look like you could use a little happiness and romance."

"I'm perfectly happy!" the professor counters, although she accepts the cake pop and nibbles on it as she launches into a mini-lecture on the perils of false consciousness in sex-positive feminism while the barista froths their milk. "I'm just busy," she mumbles defensively, brushing crumbs off a battered briefcase that overflows with red-lined student essays and dog-eared books.

"Come on, let's treat ourselves to a shot of whipped cream vodka in that coffee," says LaRoche as they slide into a booth with their drinks. She discreetly hikes up her skirt and pulls a slim silver flask out of a holster on a black lace garter. "You *also* look like you could use a little loosening up. And after reading for these students"—LaRoche shudders delicately—"I could use a reward." The novelist pours generously into each of their cups. She picks hers up to salute the woman opposite her, noting as she does that the professor looks oddly familiar. "Ask away, sister."

What follows is a faithful transcript of the talk between LaRoche and Roach that fateful day at the Ferg Starbucks.

*   *   *

Roach: Let me dive right in and start out with the virgin trope. Your central protagonist—or what you people call "the heroine" [sneering tone]—is the Honorable Miss Callista Higginbotham, an inexperienced virgin seduced by your "hero" [more sneering] Lord Rexton. Why is the romance genre awash with this endless parade of passive virgins seduced by the more active and powerful male? My God, you even titled your novel *Master of Love*! What about consent and mutuality and an egalitarian partnership model?

LaRoche [sighing]: Must you be so tendentious and one-sided already? First of all, there are lots of romance novels where the heroine isn't a virgin, where the sexual relationship is more egalitarian from the beginning. But in order to have the conflict and character arc necessary for plot development, you have to start with disequilibrium between the characters. A sexual disequilibrium is an obvious starting point, especially for a heterosexual nineteenth-century romance, where such a setup would be expected.

Roach: But this seduction motif can be such a trap! Don't you think it's a dangerous storyline: that he will settle down, commit, love her forever if only she sleeps with him? Hasn't this stupidity sunk many a woman, a girl? She throws her love away on an unworthy man, on the foolish hope that her love will heal the bad boy or reform the rake and get him to settle down with her forever. What is the power of this crazy myth? It gets us to chase love in self-destructive ways, stay in doomed relationships, ignore good men, and waste our time trying to crack open emotionally distant men. And why do these books have to be so "lovey-dovey," as my sister-in-law calls them, as if romantic love is the only thing a woman cares about? And for God's sake why, once she's happily-ever-after seduced, is everything all flowery and impossibly romantic and cosmically orgasmic, instead of who's-picking-up-the-kids-at-carpool-today and I'll-clean-the-litter-box-if-you-fold-the-laundry!? That's what real life is like! [Sound of coffee cup slamming down]

LaRoche: Wow, you *are* on a roll! Do you wordy academic types think steamrolling others is the way to go? [Sounds of slurping coffee]

Roach: Stop dodging my questions! Why don't you just read me that mouth-nibbling part again? There's something fishy going on there.

LaRoche: With delight!

As his mouth nibbled at the corners of hers, she knew she
would freely give all he asked, greedily take all he offered, and deal with the damn consequences tomorrow.
Tonight she wanted to be—*for once in her life!*—impulsive
and improper and wayward and loved. Some back part of
her mind, where rationality sat banished but not silenced,
warned her there lay the rub. This wasn't about love, but
about bedding down; she would forget that distinction at
her peril.

Roach: See! He's seducing her, but really she's seducing herself with
the fantasy of the romance narrative. In real life, this fantasy often doesn't
work out "happily ever after" for a woman. In real life, he'd probably sleep
with her, get her hopes up, and then dump her, right?

LaRoche [more sounds of slurping]: Could be. Or she could dump
him. Neither of which would make for a romance novel, now would it?
The genre doesn't seek a proportionately accurate representation of relationship outcomes, any more than suspense thrillers end without the
whodunit explained or the bad guys brought to justice. Of course lots of
cold cases are unsolved by police departments. But you don't read about
them in the suspense novels, do you? Why don't you get your drawers in
a knot about that?

Roach: Try to focus; we're talking about romance, not suspense. And
there's a related problem here, which is that the genre tells its women readers not only that they *want* this bad-boy seduction romance narrative but
that they *need* it. I had a young woman student in my office last month,
sobbing, because she and her boyfriend had recently broken up. It wasn't
that she missed *him* so much. I asked, "Was he really such a great guy?"
"I don't know," she said, waving her hand dismissively. "But we were going to move in together and get married and I was going to settle down
and that was going to be my life! And now I haven't taken the GRE or the
LSAT or the MCAT or applied to any graduate schools or law schools, and
now it's too late and my life is over. My life is over!" she wailed. Her upset
didn't seem about losing this one particular guy but about losing GUY,
the archetype of HUSBAND or ONE TRUE LOVE, about not having
that required aspect of her life figured out and sewn up, ticked off the

to-do list. I'm concerned that such coupling-up is made mandatory by the romance genre, as if women aren't complete and happy unless they're pair-bonded for life.

LaRoche: The poor girl. I agree entirely that the romance narrative becomes an imperative in the culture, especially for women. And the narrative *shouldn't* be an imperative. Of course, a woman doesn't need a man to be complete—just like a fish doesn't need a bicycle, as those magnificent second-wave feminists taught. Nor does a man need a man, nor a woman a woman, nor a werewolf a vampire. There are other satisfying life options for love, connection, community, and fulfillment. There are other answers to the central question of how to live a good life outside of romantic pair-bonding.

Roach [bewildered]: But the romance genre seems not to admit the existence of these other options. As you say, it makes the romance narrative into an imperative. Do you mean that as a criticism of the genre? Do you agree with me that the seduction narrative that ends in the genre's mandatory coupling-up (or ménage-à-trois tripling up) is a problem for women?

LaRoche: No, I don't agree, or not exactly. Let me try to be clear. The romance narrative as imperative *is* a problem, but I don't see this problem as the fault of the romance narrative itself or of the publishing genre of romance. It's not because of romance novels that the imperative to find true love exists in the culture. In other words, I agree that the notion we all need to be coupled up is a problem, but I don't see the romance genre as the *cause* of this problem. You and I are looking at this issue from different angles. The emotional satisfaction of a happy ending is central to the pleasure of genre fiction. As I said, it's not just romance; in Agatha Christie, Hercule Poirot always solves the murder mystery. Is this a criticism of romance fiction—that life doesn't always end with happy resolution? I don't think so! EVERYONE knows that. You'd have to critique a wider human desire for completion or wholeness in our narratives as in our lives, including the notion of moral justice and afterlife reward in various forms of heaven, paradise, or good karma. We're addicted across the board to that happy ending, sister.

Roach [annoyed]: You're not really answering my question.

LaRoche: That's because you've seduced me into talking your language, the language of academic speculation! Let me try again. Certainly, the romance story can be a trap. Love in all its forms can be a trap. Any sane person knows that. Any newborn baby knows it: The mother or caregiver will not always be there, exactly when needed, to satisfy all your desires for love and warmth and food and security and pleasure. The one you love will inevitably fail you to *some* degree. And you'll screw it up yourself by being unable to intuit or articulate your own needs, because who truly knows their own heart, let alone the heart of someone else? It's the first Noble Truth of Buddhism: All is suffering or dissatisfaction, imperfectly fulfilled desire. Even on a good day, in a good life, the underlying truth is that love and its goodness are not perfect and unchanging but unstable. Even if the one you love and lust after does prove worthy, one day that person *could* still dump you and, if not, that person *will* ultimately die. So really it's heartbreak ever after. Life and love are a time bomb waiting to blow up in your face. Even if you *are* happily in love.

Roach: Wow—you're even grimmer about love than I am!

LaRoche: I am not grim! I'm happily in love, married twenty years to a wonderful man.

Roach: I know, you crazy woman! I'm married to him, too!

LaRoche: Isn't he a sweetie? And so sexy! Oh, look! [Squealing noises] There he is now in line, getting the blonde roast! [Sounds of chair scraping]

Roach: Stop waving and get back here—you're making a spectacle of yourself! We are *not* inviting him over, missy! Would you please stay focused on the discussion!

LaRoche [pouting, sounds of sitting back down]: Don't you ever have any fun?

Roach: I *am* having fun, debating a goofball like you! Now, your Buddhist take on romance is all very *enlightening,* I'm sure. But what really concerns me about "the end" is something else entirely. As you are pointing out, romantic love is a complicated bet for life happiness. For a lot of people, it doesn't work out and they don't even *want* such a hot-house setup, with someone in your face all the time. For no one does it work out with the deceptive ease of a fairytale's happily-ever-after ending. So why insist on romance as the be-all and end-all of life strategies, as the prime narrative of popular culture, when it's so fraught and risky a path? Many people clearly don't hew to this party line, that they have to find true love in order to live happily ever after. A whole lot of people live quite contented lives alone or in serial romances or various configurations of fluid domestic arrangements with partners, lovers, housemates, family, and friends, moving in and out of relationships more or less happily over the course of an adult lifetime. What about such alternate, more fully realistic narratives of the vagaries and varieties of love?

LaRoche: You're missing the point, you nerdy egghead! Genre fiction offers mythic fantasy and escapist pleasure. IT IS NOT SUPPOSED TO BE FULLY REALISTIC!!

Roach: Fine, fine, calm down! Even if it's not supposed to be realistic, I think a lot of people still take it that way.

LaRoche: Readers aren't stupid. People know how to read these books: They read for fun, not because they're being brainwashed about how they should live their lives. Readers know and are fine with the fact that in real life romance doesn't always happen like in the books. It doesn't need to. There are, of course, many pleasures to the single life.

Roach: Exactly! We need to pay more attention to these pleasures of the single life! Given the risks and drawbacks of erotic love, living life without a romance partner seems a pretty good bet. Have you heard about the statistical rise of singledom these days and the new analysis of "singlism" as a form of discrimination and stereotyping against people who choose to live life solo? You should read the psychologist Bella DePaulo on it, as well as her analysis of "matrimania."

LaRoche: Maybe one solution is to have secondary characters in the novels who live fully realized and contented lives without romantic pair-bonding. In *Master of Love,* I deliberately give a large role to a character who isn't interested in romance. Celeste, Lady Rexton, is the glamorous widowed mother of my hero; she happily juggles a string of young lovers but wrinkles her nose at the mention of love. She calls romantic love "a new-fangled notion, and a dangerous one in my opinion. One loves children and dogs. One enjoys a lover. And if one is lucky, one gets along with a spouse." I must admit that Lady Rexton is one of my favorite characters in the novel. I like the perspective she brings: her self-confidence, her mature sexuality, her unashamed embrace of pleasure.

Roach [sanctimoniously]: I'm not at all sure that woman is a good role model. But if we're talking about characters and plot, let me ask you this: Why are these books sometimes so badly written? From a literary perspective, the quality can be horrible—clichéd writing, repetitive plots, cardboard characters, unrealistic endings.

LaRoche: There are lots of wonderfully crafted romance books out there. But literary-quality writing takes time. Successful romance authors generally publish two or more novels a year. Their publishing houses push them to this level of prolific output in order to keep fresh titles in front of voracious readers. Authors don't have time to think about their every word. And that's not the point of this type of book anyway. The point is emotional engagement.

Roach: The point nowadays seems to be lots of vampires and weird sex. What's up with that crazy bondage and spanking business? How is that any good for women? If some guy hit me with a riding crop I'd call the police!

LaRoche: And if you hadn't negotiated consent first, you certainly should. But otherwise, your problem is just that you're vanilla and boring. In a context of informed consent—adult, safe, and healthy—love and pleasure come in many flavors.

Roach: How *progressive* of you, and yet still—those heroes and heroines are all paired off and matched up by book's end, whether same or opposite sex and no matter how "flavorful" they are. That seems a very uniform and vanilla conclusion to me. They're living their happy ending and implying that we should, too!

LaRoche [sighing]: You're on such a high horse you're not even listening. I think we hit up here against one of the constraints of the genre. They are, after all, *romance* novels. If you don't want the matched-up lovers, go read women's fiction or chick lit or full-on erotica without the romance. Go read detective fiction. Go do whatever you want, but stop expecting the genre to be other than what it *by definition* is.

Roach [whining]: But the romance narrative has such power, such dominance in storytelling and in the culture. Young women can end up feeling like failures if they don't achieve their one-true-love-happily-ever-after. There is *such* pressure on them to find Mr. Right early on and to not let go, as some badge of successful womanhood. I hear it all the time in my seminar on Gender, Sexuality, and Popular Culture. They come into class with counts of how many women got engaged the week before: "Three new girls got a ring this week!" Another exclaims, "I know *four*!" The romance and marriage imperative then feeds straight into a cultural repro-centrism that says a woman needs to be a mother in order to be complete. "First comes love, then comes marriage, then comes baby in a baby carriage." I chanted that ditty on the school playground over forty years ago! Has nothing changed? The romance narrative is so omnipresent, it can be destructive. We need other models.

LaRoche: And yet people continue to *choose* romance, partnership, family—in life as in their fiction. No one is *making* them do so. Most of us are better off—happier and more complete—with love in our life than without love. E. M. Forster offers that glorious epigraph "Only connect…" in his novel *Howards End*. It's a central insight. It's hard to be alone. You say we need other models; I say we need other people.

Roach: I get that loving and being loved is a good thing, that we're better off with than without love, that love makes one healthy and happy. But why does love have to be defined in terms of a romantic partner? Does a woman—or any adult—need sex or romance or erotic love to mature as a person and to find happiness? What about the new asexuality movement? Could love not be defined as the love of family or children or friends or supportive work colleagues? Could it not be the love provided by community? Or the love of just one good friend? Or simply a beloved pet? Perhaps the love relationship could be to an ideal: art or science or social justice— as long as there is some worthy other that pulls one outside the solipsism of one's self toward something more, toward *connection*. The romance narrative becomes problematic when it portrays romantic love as the only or the best pathway to soul-binding, to the happy and well-rounded life.

LaRoche: I think it's fair to say that a fundamental conviction of the romance genre is that romantic love—being loved passionately and well by a worthy partner who is devoted to your well-being—makes you a happier person. The romance genre wishes such love for us all.

Roach: So maybe *this* is the question: How much space, how much power, do we accord to the romance? And what alternatives do we provide? Let me put it to you this way: Have you ever heard of the Bechdel test?

LaRoche: Named after Alison Bechdel, from her long-running comic strip *Dykes to Watch Out For*? Why, yes, I have! I've often thought it poses an interesting test for romance fiction.

Roach: As do I. And I think you fail it.

LaRoche: Do you really? I'm sure that makes you happy. I see you're gloating already.

Roach: Let's review the test's criteria as a way to evaluate the genre, shall we? When applied as an indication of gender bias in a work of fiction or TV/film, the test asks whether a storyline features scenes in which at least two women, preferably named, talk with each other about a topic other than men. The test suggests that fiction should portray fully fleshed-out women characters who have female friends with whom they share a broad range of interests.

LaRoche: Yes, yes—I know. In other words, a woman shouldn't be portrayed as the gratuitous lone female thrown into a male-dominated storyline, nor as interacting with other women only in catty and competitive ways, nor as engaging solely and obsessively in "boy talk," as if women have no other interests than getting a man.

Roach: Exactly! And according to these criteria, I'm not sure much romance fiction passes the test. The heroines sometimes, but by no means always, have strong women friendships. But I would wager that most of the dialogue among the women characters has to do with a man.

LaRoche: In *Master of Love*, one of my favorite chapters is the one where Callista sits drinking sherry and talking with three other women: her housemate, a girlhood friend recently returned to Callista's life, and Lady Rexton—that fashionable older woman with the young lovers.

Roach: But these four women talk about men, don't they?

LaRoche: Yes, but they also talk about philosophy, fashion, notions of beauty, childhood memories, an upcoming philanthropic ball that they're planning, various anxieties, the nature of aging. . . .

Roach: But it's a conversation dominated by pleasing and getting men! According to Bechdel, it fails the test.

LaRoche: You're quite the little bulldog, aren't you? Look, I agree that women characters in romance do talk and think about men a lot, but I must say that the genre makes me wonder about the value of the test itself. The test implies that it is trivial or limiting for women to talk about men and romance. But in truth, questions about love and partnership are not trivial at all. I think most people would agree that such questions are actually among the most central, for all of us.

Roach: But—

LaRoche: Before you get yourself all worked up, let me agree that women should certainly be talking about more than just men (as should men and queer and transgender people about their respective lovers). We should all be concerned with more than just romance and sex and partnering-up. And none of us needs to do any of that in order to be complete or fulfilled human beings. *However,* even agreeing with you on all of that, I still think most people would say that figuring out such issues and continuing to think them through is an important and engaging and enjoyable activity. We are sociable creatures. Many of us like to talk about other people and our relations to them—romantic and sexual relations included.

Roach [grudgingly]: Okay, I'll grant you that.

LaRoche: For many heterosexual women, getting a good man to love and having him commit also addresses issues of financial stability and protection—even literally physical protection in a world where women live within the shadow of rape culture.

Roach: Oh, please—I draw the line there! When a woman is sexually assaulted, it's usually by a man she knows. It's the boyfriend or husband or ex or acquaintance who poses the greatest threat to a woman in terms of rape—not the faceless guy in the alley.

LaRoche [mockingly]: Okay, I'll grant *you* that.

Roach: All right, then. So let's talk about this issue of rape and domination. Why in God's name is the romance hero so impossibly dominant—the "alpha male" you call him, right?

LaRoche: I think we hit another defining feature of the romance genre here. Some books feature a "beta hero," a gentler, more everyday, less macho man as the leading male character. The genre debates the desirability of such beta heroes, but typically, perhaps stereotypically, the romance hero *is* the alpha male. He's powerful in key ways upheld as masculine ideals within traditional patriarchy: He's tall, big, strong, capable or masterful in various ways, sexually skilled, successful, and often downright dominant.

Roach: But I'm worried about the extent to which the seduction by this dominant and powerful alpha male can sound like a rape. Consent is so central to good sex, and can go so wrong. Do you know the figures on college campuses about the prevalence of unwanted or coerced sexual contact, all the way up to full rape, usually by someone known to the victim? Students talk about it as "bad hook-ups" or sex gone wrong, but it's still rape.

LaRoche: In romances—straight or gay—the hero is typically some version of the quintessential male but with the assurance that he is a figure of honor who will do no harm. So, yes, the heterosexual romance with the alpha hero upholds the patriarchal ideal of masculinity but with the feminist twist that this hero's power is never used against the heroine. In fact, his power is never misused at all, for any unjust purpose of exploitation. The historical hero, for example, might mutter over the heroine's décolletage being too low and throw his cloak over her when some other man ogles her, but he never bars her from social events, and he always supports her autonomy.

Roach: But how realistic is that? That this tycoon-billionaire-duke-sheik-alpha male is, underneath it all, a feminist boy scout?

LaRoche: Are you back to that realism bugaboo? Your problem *again* is that you're assuming the novels are realistic portrayals of the possibilities of human relationship. Don't get me wrong: I believe in romantic love and good men—I live it with that man of ours—but romance as a genre derives its power and pleasure from the extent to which it operates in the realm of fantasy.

Roach [sarcastically]: Yeah, like didn't we just agree that the alpha male protecting his woman from other males is a fantasy? Fantasy is a *bad* thing, a problem. We need to live with each other and work out our relationships in the realm of *reality*!

LaRoche: Fantasy is not a bad thing at all! It plays a crucial role. People talk about romance as an escapist fantasy genre that women read in order to get away from the drudgery and stresses and dissatisfactions of their lives. But I think the role of fantasy is much more profound. It's where we work out deep conundrums of the culture, like the problem of female desire in a patriarchal world.

Roach: So the novels *are* about domination? About women wanting to be dominated by men, in their fantasies if not in reality? They are "bodice-rippers" after all, right?

LaRoche: Are you being deliberately obtuse?! I'm saying it's more *complicated* than that. The problem of exploitative domination is out there—it's all over the culture, for both men and women. Genesis has God punish Eve—and all women—with this curse: "Your desire shall be for your husband, and he shall rule over you." I love that line for the beauty of its clarity. *There* is the problem, so neatly encapsulated right in that line. For me, romance doesn't create this problem. (Interestingly, in the Genesis story, it is God who creates the problem.) What the romance story creates is a safe, imaginative space to think through this problem. How can desire ever work out, without falling into exploitative domination, for any of us? In romance stories, by the end, there is no domination; instead, there's safety and reprieve from domination. The alpha male, dominant in the society, specifically does *not* dominate the heroine, not in the sense of being oppressive or demeaning. The story may flirt with such in the beginning—the hero may be bossy and arrogant and may even be a Dom like Mr. Fifty Shades who wields control in BDSM play—but by book's end, the hero submits himself to her. He avows, in one form or another, that she is everything to him, that he can't live without her, that she is his one true love. Romance novels are fantasy responses to the *problem* of domination. Women authors and women characters *control* the alpha male.

Roach: But isn't this fantasy nature of the genre ever a problem itself? Like, what's up with the incredible sex women experience in these novels? Is that why people call it "mommy porn"?

LaRoche: Do you have a problem with great sex?

Roach: I do when it creates false expectations! One student told me that her mom said, "Honey, you can read those books all you want, but don't you go thinking sex is anything like that! It just ain't so." In that seduction scene you started reading, don't you go on to some vaunted fifty-page, triple-orgasm, *tour-de-force* defloration of poor Callista? No, no—stop!! Don't pull it out! We are *not* going to read that part!

LaRoche [pouting again]: You are such a spoil sport. [Sounds of shuffling paper] What about this exchange, then? It illustrates the point of how there can be layers of fantasy at work within a love scene:

> As he laid her across the settee, he traced a finger over her cheek. "For a prize such as this, I would carry you over the Khyber Pass and across the endless trek of the Silk Road. I would tie you up in my tent night after night, seducing you with love words and caresses until you opened your heart to me and accepted me as your lord."
>
> "At which point you would add me to your harem of a thousand other conquered ladies and forget all about me?" [she asked.] It was a question a little too close to reality to fit into the fantasy he spun.
>
> His smile grew bemused as his gaze swept down her length. "Callista, deeply unworthy of you as I am, I will never forget you." He stood up to toss more coals on the fire and then gathered pillows and a cashmere throw from the armchairs.
>
> It was a line he'd surely used before to ward off the affections of a lady inclined to want more than he cared to give. "Yes, I'm sure of it," she answered lightly. "Now come and prove how wicked you are."

Roach [with more sneer]: Fantasy within fantasy, where it all works out, both romantically and sexually. And yet Wilhelm Reich famously referred to the "sexual misery of the masses." Leo Bersani's superbly titled 1987 essay "Is the Rectum a Grave?" opens with the even better line, "There is a big secret about sex: most people don't like it." Human sexuality research shows that only about 25 percent of women reliably reach orgasm from vaginal penetration alone. Despite all that, mainstream romance novels—to say nothing of erotic romance or erotica—routinely portray women panting with passion and climaxing from intercourse at the drop of a hat. It's ridiculous!

LaRoche [laughing]: Wild passionate orgasms don't sound ridiculous to me. They sound pretty darn good! What romance novels offer in this regard is the fantasy that women do have orgasms, as you say, at the drop of a hat. In one erotic historical romance, Jess Michaels's *Taboo*, the heroine talks herself to orgasm with the hero watching; she doesn't even touch herself. And it's "worse" than that, honey! Part of the fantasy is also that all good men are incredibly talented lovers—often trained by an earlier French mistress; I use that trope myself with Dominick—patient, generous, guilt-free, and inventive. These are men who are happy to forsake their own pleasure since their truest satisfaction comes from pleasuring their woman.

Roach: All you're doing is repeating myths about sex that put pressure on women and make them feel inadequate.

LaRoche: I don't think you get it. Yes, part of the fantasy is the ease of mind-blowing sex. Obviously, sex is complicated, especially for women, who are in many ways the more vulnerable and disadvantaged in regards to it. Women can suffer more from coercion and rape, sexual harassment, unintended pregnancy, the burdens of childcare, greater pressures to be sexy and slim and coupled (like the student you mentioned), but also greater shaming from cruel double standards when they *are* sexually active. And you're right: Women's sexual pleasure is less assured in much heterosexual coupling, where the master narrative favors vaginal penetration despite the fact that, as college sex educator Dr. Emily Nagoski puts it, "The clitoris really is the hokey pokey." Women are trained to seek, to want, to expect sexual love. But it's hard in all these ways. And that's not even to get into the difficulty for women of knowing and expressing what they want sexually when they are still conditioned into the greater compliance and passivity of the "nice girl" stance. Nor the ability of desire to derail reason for all of us.

Roach [bewildered, again]: So how do romance novels make it easier?

LaRoche: Listen, this is what I've learned from writing romance fiction. The genre is a fantasy play space to explore and try to work out this conundrum: that to be human is to seek connection and love, and yet love entails great vulnerability. It entails risk and loss and pain. So how can love ever work out? In the romance novel, writers and readers play the script through in endless permutations within the big story line. Heroes and heroines meet—in various combinations of gender, species, and number—desire flares, conflict bubbles, they work out their differences, they commit, they're happy. The genre becomes a fantasy breathing space of reprieve, even of amnesty or freedom, from the dissatisfactions and tragedy of love that everyone knows—that, yeah, you may have found someone to love, but that person isn't perfect, and sometimes drives you crazy, and either way, you're not going to be together forever because one of you is going to die. Reading a romance is like respite for the caregivers, a break from harsher realities of life. One reader told me a story of a man she knew who read romance novels at the bedside of his dying wife, for his comfort.

Clearly the genre isn't for everyone. Not everyone likes reading Agatha Christie, either. I do think that more women than men enjoy reading romance because the stakes are higher for women. Many of them enjoy a safe place to think through these problems of female desire. That's one reason why the ending, where it all works out, is so sweet. It's a fantasy of relief.

Roach: Hmm, I think those dynamics are more problematic than you realize. But let's talk about this ending and the abasement of the alpha hero in terms of your *own* novel.

LaRoche: I wrote the last scene deliberately. It's where Callista and Dominick get to that place of mutuality and the egalitarian partnership model that you wanted. He's not seducing her anymore; now there's equality in their love play. Dominick starts off as the "Master of Love," as you note, but by the end, there's a reversal and Callista masters him.

Roach: Is this not in the love scene where your *Publishers Weekly* review says you "push the boundaries of good taste"?

LaRoche: Yes! I laughed out loud in my office when I read that. I've decided that the last chapter of my romance novels should feature some form of anal play. Because, you know, it's the end.

Roach: Please—that is pitiful! Why don't you just read the passage?

LaRoche: Gladly! I also would like to take this opportunity to acknowledge inspiration for this scene in a hot fanfiction about *Miami Vice*, a guilty pleasure of mine featuring that oh-so-slashy pair of detectives Crockett and Tubbs.

> A thick braided cotton rug cushioned the floor, along with the towels they'd strewn about. "Lie down on your back," she ordered, pillowing his head. She drizzled another of the oils—a potent aphrodisiac of bergamot, jasmine, and cedar—over his chest, belly, and thighs. And rubbed it in everywhere with long slow strokes. Then she nudged him onto his side, grasped his length in one hand, and reached under his thigh to cup him in the other. He was slick with oil everywhere, hot and hard. As he stiffened further in her oiled hand, his puckered opening relaxed at her massage. She slid one finger slowly in and out, pressing firmly.
>
> "Don't stop," he groaned.
>
> "I won't. I am your Mistress of Love," she breathed in his ear. "I am yours, forever. And you are mine." She bit on his earlobe and sucked.
>
> The oil was thick and redolent with its spiced aromas and Dominick's own magical scent as she palmed him faster in one hand and rocked into him with the other.
>
> He hardened even more. "Callista, beauty!" His cry was a plea, a promise, a pledge.
>
> And then he climaxed, with a roar of openmouthed pleasure.
>
> When it was over, he lay panting on the bath chamber floor, twisted in the towels, satiated.
>
> She curled behind him, draped one leg over him, and kissed him on the temple.
>
> He was hers, and she was his.
>
> Love had mastered them both.
>
> And it had set them free.

Roach: Well. So. [Paper-rustling noises that sound suspiciously like a woman fanning herself] Is this the new height of feminist liberation?

Anally penetrating a man? I see what *Publishers Weekly* had in mind! This is pornography!

LaRoche: Why not? She takes charge. She's no longer passive in their lovemaking. Isn't that what you wanted? In my reading experience, mainstream romance doesn't feature anal play. But mainstream magazines have taken to describing it as "the new oral." You want some interesting pornography? You should check out the annual Feminist Porn Awards! Now, there's a celebration of possibility and pleasure in *all* forms—for women, men, and trans!

Roach: It's not the porn quality of your writing that I care about. You're just kidding yourself if you think a kinky hand job qualifies your heroine as any sort of feminist liberator! But go ahead and push your boundaries, you shameless hussy.

LaRoche: That's the language that's kept women down. I've come to believe that the politics of respectability has its limits. I find I like being shameless.

Roach: Would you please wipe that smug smile off your face! Didn't your agent initially discourage you from including this scene?

LaRoche: Yes, she suggested substituting something more banal, more traditional and predictable for a mainstream historical romance. I asked her whether romance novel love scenes must always be banal. May they never be anal?

Roach: Oh, that is *terrible* wordplay! You *should* be ashamed!

LaRoche [laughing]: My editor just said, "What's up with the butt play?" She and my agent actually both had good ideas about how to strengthen the sex scenes and Callista's arc of development as a woman coming into her sense of sexual selfhood. And they let me proceed. Here, let me read you something else. What do you think of this passage?

> *The woman:* Restless in bed and sleepless through the night, I longed for my lover. I wanted him desperately.
>
> *The man:* The sweet, fragrant curves of your body, the soft, spiced contours of your flesh invite me, and I come. I stay until dawn breathes its light and night slips away. Your full breasts are like sweet clusters of dates. I say, "I'm going to climb that palm tree! I'm going to caress its fruit!" Oh

yes! Your breasts will be clusters of sweet fruit to me, your tongue and lips like the best wine.

The woman: Yes, and yours are, too—my love's kisses flow from his lips to mine. I am my lover's. I'm all he wants. I'm all the world to him! Come, dear lover—let's tramp through the countryside. Let's sleep at some wayside inn. And there I'll give myself to you, my love to your love! And when my lover sees me, he knows he'll soon be satisfied.

Roach: Did you write that, too? Sounds like an early draft of more cheap porn.

LaRoche: Honey, you are so conventional—that's the Bible! It's religious love poetry. It's a compilation of verses from the good ol' Song of Songs, or Song of Solomon, in an idiomatic contemporary translation of the Bible entitled *The Message*.

Roach [humph]: That's rather steamy for the Bible.

LaRoche: Human sexuality, erotic desire, romantic love, and marriage have millennia of history as models for the relationship to the divine. Sexuality can be understood as a manifestation of cosmic creative energy, as a pathway to transcendence of individuality, as interdependence. Religious traditions provide varied examples. Think of Tantric practices, the Jewish Shekinah, Hindu Shakti, the land as fertile Mother Goddess, the Christian church and the soul both cast as the bride of Christ!

Roach: Calm down, woman! Now you're claiming the romance genre is divinely inspired in its stories of men and women falling in love with each other?

LaRoche: Why assume a heterosexual stance? You sound so old school! Don't you have that rainbow-shaded Big Al mascot sticker outside your office door? As if the University of Alabama and the Crimson Tide are bastions of queer positivity? The romance genre nowadays, even increasingly mainstream romance bestsellers, embrace gay and lesbian love stories. And with the growth of romantic erotica, women can claim sexual desire and pleasure in many forms without being ashamed.

Roach: Oh, please! You think you're so edgy and sex-positive with erotic love cast in all these grand cultural terms, but you know what? I find the whole romance genre very conservative. Even E. L. James's story, with

Ana and Christian's "kinky fuckery," is really quite conventional, isn't it? Gay/lesbian isn't queering much and neither is BDSM kinky fuckery when all the stories wrap up and settle down to a traditional happy ending of love and commitment. In Ana and Christian Grey's case, the same repro-centrism that I mentioned earlier even turns those two lovebirds into poster parents for the standard nuclear family! Doesn't this bother you?

LaRoche: "Oh, please!" right back at you, *Dr. Roach*! Are you saying all your romance narratives have to pass a left-wing political correctness test? That you can only accept a romance story that adheres to some pro-gressive egalitarian vision of side-by-side sex? No one on top! No one on the bottom! Everyone must remain free and uncommitted at the end! What about feminist pornography? What about the woman who longs to be the sexual submissive? What about people who like to play with rough sex or storylines of nonconsensual sex? If you want to "queer" the romance narrative away from conservative conventionality, how far are you willing to go? I bet you'd lose your nerve in that game of chicken long before me.

Roach [defensively]: Well, if so, it would be because I don't see that the stakes are high enough to make the game worth winning. What do we really gain in these romance narratives? What do the heroines and the largely women readers *get* that makes the risks, the complications, of the genre worth it?

LaRoche: Now that's a *great* question! One could answer that what one gets, in the best of the genre, is wonderful storytelling and the en-gaging pleasures of the text. But personally, I'm not that interested in the literary quality or experience of these books. Sure, they're fun to read. But I find these novels fascinating because, in my humble opinion, the genre does deep work in the culture. I think what is at stake, as you put it, is no less than knowledge and its concomitant of power.

Roach: That's rather a grandiose claim, isn't it?

LaRoche: Perhaps. Nevertheless, the fantasy space opened up by the genre can lead to self-knowledge for readers, as it does for the heroine.

Roach: Or it can lead to ongoing self-deception, complicity, and com-placency about how power really works in the gender dynamics of ro-mance and society.

LaRoche: Make your judgment as you will. I believe that sexual knowledge is a key pathway to self-knowledge and to personal empowerment,
as well as to greater cultural knowledge. Have you heard of the mixed-
media American conceptual artist Sophia Wallace? Heard of her show
Cliteracy? You should go see it; it's so brave and brilliant! Her central idea
is the paradox that female sexuality is constantly used and objectified,
but with almost no accurate knowledge or celebration of how women's
sexual pleasure works. Her installation consists of one hundred "Natural Laws," such as No. 57, "Democracy without cliteracy? Phallusy," and
No. 39, "The world isn't flat and women don't orgasm from their vaginas."
People can get T-shirts emblazoned with her tagline, "Solid Gold Clit." In
other words, sexuality is an important source of knowledge. For a woman
to know how her body works is a good thing, as is for her to know how to
make it work for her own pleasure—and for partners, male and female, to
know how to pleasure a woman (hint to men: No. 46, "Viagra won't make
you cliterate"). Such literacy about the clitoris may be a fundamental human right; the gender distribution of orgasms may be a measure of freedom in society, as Wallace says. To return to your original question about
why virgins, this is a big part of why heroines often start out sexually inexperienced or sexually unfulfilled. Through a good and pleasurable experience of her sexuality, a woman not only comes, she comes into knowledge.

Roach: Oh my God! I hope you don't have all of these horrible sex
puns in your novel—no wonder it's selling so badly! And are we back to
the virgins again?!

LaRoche [sounds of slapping the table]: Apparently we are! The virgin
seduction story allows the reader to experience that moment of a woman gaining greater knowledge about herself, about how her body works,
about how relationships and society work, and thus gaining more power
than she had before. Remember this line? "She felt a fluttering within
her breast, an opening up and release of a new self beginning to stretch
wings." The heroine's defloration becomes a moment of equalizing the
power relations with the hero. As she discovers more about herself and
develops as a sexual being, she grows in self-confidence and power.

Roach [goadingly]: But you're saying she needs him, right? To grow
and become whole? So we're back to that again, too?

LaRoche [angrily]: To discover the full power that her sexuality grants to her—yes, but also it's sometimes because she needs his social power to compensate for the discriminations of patriarchy! They find each other, and find themselves, together!!

Roach [loudly]: They'll find out they're idiots when the lust wears off and the happily-ever-after wears out!!

The Starbucks manager comes by at this point to interrupt, as voices rise and the women hoist paper cups for lobbing.

Manager: Ladies, ladies, please! A little decorum, if you will! Last week, two football players started a brawl with a young man from the dance department, and I don't want any more broken chairs in here.

*   *   *

If only I could reassure you that LaRoche and Roach resolve their differences and walk out arm-in-arm into the bright Alabama sunshine. Alas, despite the manager's intervention, they soon sink back into fractious debate until the baristas have to kick them out for disturbing the students.

So, let us leave Starbucks. In fact, let us duck out before the football players come back to start a different brawl over free advance copies of LaRoche's *Fifty Shades of Crimson*. I hear it's Book I in her new gay-bondage-erotica-football-romance trilogy set amid the practice fields and locker rooms of the Alabama Capstone, with its too-hot-to-handle follow-ups *Bama Bound* and *Roll Tied*.

In this section, I've resisted a theoretical turn. Instead, I've played around in goofy narrative mode—deliberately, as a different way of presenting an academic argument. Despite my blithe attempts at forsaking the more restrained and temperate norms of academic convention, I remain aware of them, wary of what gods and muses I might provoke with my play—for everything has a cost.

So let me end with a quick and sober summary.

There are clearly transgressive and progressive possibilities offered by romance fiction, as well as constraints and complicated questions posed by the genre. There is as well the strange and seductive pleasure of *this* question: How to understand the creative and fruitful possibilities of ludic research, of play and performance, of a wholehearted engagement of the self—Roach and LaRoche coming together—pointing toward another model of the academic life? And what new possibilities of academic writ—

At this point, LaRoche pops back in, fluttering a handkerchief, choked up and clearly unable to help herself:

LaRoche: Sister! You're going to make me cry, that's so beautiful: all that language about "creative and fruitful" and "wholehearted engagement"! I sense a happily-ever-after ending coming up for us!

Oh, dear. I advise you, reader, to turn the page on that woman. And to tiptoe out quickly before anyone gets too weepy.

Although . . . perhaps LaRoche *is* correct. Maybe even within the bounds of hardboiled academic criticism, we may allow ourselves room for hope in the happy ending.

Why, you ask? The conventions of academic writing involve no happily-ever-after ending for scholarly books and their authors.

And yet, a good ending seduces us all—even us nerdy academics—with its faith in the powerful thrust of a firmly argued thesis, its promise of rhetorical climax, and its fantasy of satisfying resolution.

So, yes, let us dare hope: for happily-ever-afters, for us all.

4

Sex

*Good Girls Do, or, Romance Fiction as
Sex-Positive Feminist Mommy Porn*

L isten to this *cri de coeur* by romance heroine Lishelle. She is one of the
main characters in the 2007 novel *Getting Some* by *USA Today*–bestselling author Kayla Perrin, and Lishelle is royally fed up:

> See, this is what I don't understand. If guys fuck a hundred women,
> they're heroes. They feel no shame in bedding a woman they've just
> met. But if a woman has a one-night stand, my God, she's a dirty whore.
> How dare she like sex? This is the twenty-first century, honey. It's high
> time we women embrace our sexuality and bury the shame. We have
> needs, the same as men do. Why do we feel so friggin' bad about going
> after what we want?[1]

Lishelle's passionate endorsement that women embrace their sexuality
highlights how the story of romance is rapidly changing, perhaps especially for young women. Contrary to traditional notions that "good girls
don't do things like that," today's good girls do. A new era has opened
up wherein women can write or read such erotica, hook up with multiple
partners and different types of partners, make amateur porn or post pin-
ups of themselves on sites like *Suicide Girls,* attend home-sale sex toy parties, wear porno-chic fashion, take pole-dancing classes at the local gym,
revel in TV's *Girls* or *Sex and the City* reruns, and, of course, read the *Fifty
Shades* trilogy. Or consider the phenomenon, much reported in the press,

of heterosexual women, well-educated and of upper-income levels, having sex without wanting long-term boyfriends. For the younger woman, she may feel she has no time or need for a serious male partner amid the demands of education and career moves; for the older woman, the children may be grown and flings provide more fun. Both like sex but prefer to enjoy male company without the compromises of full-time commitment.[2]

In all of this, we see that the category of what's culturally acceptable in love and romance has in many quarters grown much bigger. The slow but ongoing success of the LGBTQ movements on legal issues of same-sex unions and partner rights is part of opening up this romance narrative, as is increasing social acceptance for difference and diversity in gender expression and sexual orientation based on a notion of informed consent. New words have entered the vernacular to track these changes. In 2003, the American Dialect Society declared *cliterati* the "Most Outrageous Word of the Year." A wonderful mashup of clitoris, glitterati, and literati, the term refers to "feminist writers or leaders" or "influential women" and evokes an image of sexy, glamorous women interested in writing and the arts and not shy about the role of sexuality in all such.[3] This phenomenon of new, potentially liberating and open attitudes toward consensual sexuality, including women's sexuality, is what commentators and scholars have characterized as sex-positive culture, sex-positive feminism, or, in a different spin, "pornification." In romance fiction, we hear its boldly playful echo within Romancelandia writing groups and reader blogs that adopt such names as *History Hoydens, Word Wenches, Word Whores, Historical Hussies,* and the *Smutketeers*. Its effect is seen in the publishing prominence of erotic romance and the concurrent intensification of sexual content in much mainstream romance fiction. As sociologist Eva Illouz posits in *Hard-Core Romance,* "If the nineteenth-century novel was about the self-discovery of a young woman through love, contemporary popular texts aimed at women now ask, what is to be discovered about oneself when engaging in an active sex life, free of matrimonial goals and constraints?"[4]

In the thirty-five years that I've been reading romance novels, this development is one of the most fascinating changes within the genre. Like the wider romance narrative that operates throughout the culture, romance novels are in the midst of a sea change as they mirror shifting sexual norms for women. We see these changes in such areas as the novels' levels of explicitness, their underlying attitudes toward sexuality and sexual diversity, and the consensual sex practices in the books. The novels are affected by and in turn shape sex-positive culture and new societal ideas about what is acceptable sexually. The development of the market for erotic romance is also related to the explosive growth of digital publishing. For those buyers still shy despite this new openness in the cultural zeitgeist, the anonymity of sales and the privacy of the reading experience mean that anyone with an e-reader can enjoy the spiciest of stories in full discretion on a bus or park bench. In 1993, the pioneering UK imprint Black Lace launched as the first publisher of erotic fiction written by and for women with stories focused on female sexual pleasure. In 2000, American e-book publisher Ellora's Cave combined romance fiction with erotic content to launch the first-ever erotic romance imprint. One of the earliest digital publishers and one of the few from that period still thriving, Ellora's Cave succeeded in creating a new and popular "romantica" brand. (In erotica the characters come together in couplings that don't necessarily end with monogamous pair bonding; in erotic romance such love bonding does occur in at least a happy-for-now ending for the characters.)

During my early years at the Romance Writers of America conferences, this rise of erotica was a big and controversial topic. Debates abounded in RWA's monthly *Romance Writers Report* and at the conferences' annual general meetings about erotic romance and the extent to which the annual industry awards should recognize it as a separate subgenre. Erotic romance opened up publishing opportunities and provided an exciting, imaginative space for many writers who felt liberated and empowered by this turn. Fans flocked to erotic romance as never before. Some writers were clearly delighted by the possibilities posed by this new fictional exploration of women's sexuality, even if elements of shaming and closeting still shaped their own writing lives. In an interview, one author of short story erotica told me she was "out" to her parents but laughingly added that she'd informed her father he wasn't allowed to read her fiction; "I'm still daddy's little girl," she explained. For her, the rise of erotica was an example of how the culture had become more sexually open and how women had more sexual freedom and power. Other authors deemed the erotica "not their cup of tea" and expressed concern that the new spiciness could reinforce prejudices against the genre. One agent whom I interviewed said, "I'm seeing publishing houses increasingly put pressure on writers to ratchet up the sexual heat level in their manuscripts, even in mainstream romances."

Although these developments preceded the *Fifty Shades* trilogy, it is E. L. James's 2011 controversial megahit, of course, that really brought this woman-oriented, romantic erotica to mainstream attention. In 2013, James was the world's top-earning writer, with an estimated income of $95 million. From her series' beginnings in fanfiction and digital publishing to its transition to print book format, it has sold over 100 million copies in 52 languages. The trilogy's first book, *Fifty Shades of Grey,* set records for the fastest-selling paperback ever. Illouz takes this mega-bestseller status of *Fifty Shades* as indicative of an "immense change in values that must have occurred in Western culture—as dramatic a change, one might say, as electricity and indoor plumbing." Perhaps representing this change in values, Hollywood producers chose Valentine's Day to release the movie version of *Fifty Shades of Grey* in 2015: American pop culture's new date movie to celebrate romance. James's stratospheric sales have emboldened publishers to increase their offerings of erotic romance by other authors, such that the subgenre enjoys a level of almost mainstream popularity. A bit naughty perhaps, seems to be many people's take on it, but really, what's the fuss?[5]

This mainstream growth of erotica signals important changes in American cultural attitudes toward women's sexuality. It may point toward a loosening of double standards and an opening to a consent-based (safe, healthy, informed, adult) model of sexual expression. And yet ambivalence around sexuality and especially around issues of women's sexual choice and pleasure remain central in American culture—indeed, worldwide. Accordingly, there is risk as well. These new ways intended as sex-positive come fraught with their own dangers. Part of the risk for women is that of turning themselves into what author Ariel Levy termed "female chauvinist pigs" in her 2005 book of that same name, through the internalization of a sex-bunny sensibility and aesthetic that repeats and gives flesh to old sexist stereotypes. Women may also experience the type of losses that Laura Sessions Stepp laments in her 2007 book *Unhooked* about the American campus hook-up culture. Another part of the risk is the early sexualization of the "porno-tot" phenomenon (seen in controversies around little girl beauty pageants and thong underwear for preteens) and the loss of innocence and health risks feared by the abstinence movement. A British romance novelist whom I interviewed, a sex-positive feminist in her own right, warned of these risks in taking the new sales of erotica as indicative of any deeper change in the culture: "It would be naive," she said, laughing, "to conclude that we now live in an era of sexual equality and openness."

Without wanting to be overly optimistic about the real possibilities for change, I see the rise of women's erotica as indicative of an important cultural moment of possibility and counter-resistance. Just what is at stake about sexuality in the romance novel's complex nexus of shame and pleasure, hurt and healing, vulnerability and protection, pleasure and anxiety, risk and reward, bondage and freedom? How can we evaluate the ambiguous implications of this change as a current large-scale cultural experiment, with potential for liberation but with risk for re-inscribing traditional and limiting norms of women's sexuality as passive and subordinate? How does contemporary, sex-positive feminism challenge and change—or not—the standard romance narrative? Does today's romance fiction help move women's sexuality from margin to crossroads to center, or does it re-marginalize women's sexuality anew? And how does the trend toward more explicit sexuality in romance novels and more sexual choices in lifestyle relate to such apparently opposite cultural trends as, for example, the premarital abstinence movements of the conservative Christian group True Love Waits and father-daughter Purity Balls, as well as the publishing growth of inspirational romance novels with little to no explicit sexuality? In all of this, there is a daunting challenge for the new erotica to pull off, but—perhaps—real potential as well, to help us all live in ways that are richer and ultimately more loving.

So what happens when women start depicting sexual desires and fantasies, as well as dissatisfactions and anxieties, in forums outside traditional "male-stream" or male-oriented mainstream pornography?

Here's one answer: They *do* sex-positive feminism in their writing. Many romance novelists today *are* the cliterati.

ROMANCE AS PORN

For about ten years now, I've been teaching the undergraduate seminar "Gender, Sexuality, and Popular Culture." For several years, I've included a unit on the romance genre and most recently I added material on pornography. I bring books into class with titles such as *Jane Sexes It Up* and *Whores and Other Feminists*. We look at the website of the Feminist Porn Awards. We look at queer porn; the class tends to appreciate the depictions of what one student deemed "real-ass women enjoying themselves." We debate the Annie Sprinkle quote that "The answer to bad porn isn't no porn. . . . It's to try and make better porn" and Tristan Taormino's claim that making porn can be a valuable act of feminist activism. We read Carol Queen on "whore stigma." We study implications of the sex-positive ethic of full consent. We discuss how to evaluate this material in terms of Carole Vance's well-known axis of pleasure and danger in the exploration of sexuality.[6]

In the fall of 2012, by some accident of registration, for the first time ever the class consisted entirely of women. All year long, the *Fifty Shades* trilogy dominated the bestseller lists and the term "Mommy Porn" was in the headlines. Also new that year was an exercise we invented of an online romance narrative. I started the students off with a scenario that I made up about Whip Dickens, a good ol' boy architect from backwoods Alabama, and his rival in architectural stardom, Rotunda Dupré, a curvy sophisticate from Atlanta. The students dived into the writing task with gusto and began posting scenes and commentary on a collaborative storyboard website. One question that came up in our writing experiment was whether to include sex scenes in our romance fiction and what parameters we should adopt for doing so. Through our fiction exercise and our readings in feminist theory and popular romance, we ended up talking a lot about depictions of sexuality in romance novels as well as in the sex-saturated corridors of popular culture. We revisited that timeless question: What exactly is pornography anyway? And we asked how sex scenes in romances differ from those in full-fledged erotica or pornography.

Here is my take: Romance fiction *is* pornography. The more obvious version of this point is, as I have mentioned, that the genre is getting sexier all the time, with erotica, BDSM, non-heterosexual, ménage, and paranormal romance stories increasingly diversifying the genre and turning up the heat. But I want to argue for the less obvious and more radical version of this claim, namely that the romance genre as a whole is pornographic, including even religiously themed inspirational and sweet romances with neither on-page sex nor overt sexual references. My argument has a second part: Yes, I cheer, romance is pornography for ladies! Or "mommies," if you will, as the media reports have it, titillated by the vision of respectable ladies and nice suburban soccer moms lining up in droves to get their copies of *Fifty Shades.* The point is that romance, from the sweet to the spicy, appeals to mainstream women readers of a wide demographic spectrum including those who see themselves as fitting into traditional feminine roles and styles (whether they be actual "mommies" or not). I cheer, because in my take, this status of romance as porn is a good thing. I find fruitful the notion that romance fiction functions for its largely female readers as a type of feminist pornography, very different from standard male-stream porn. Romance offers instead a woman-centered space of sexual fantasy, in many ways feminist, that functions as good porn for its readers.[7]

Let me explore some terms here, since much depends, of course, on how one defines pornography. It's a notoriously tricky word. Its original Greek etymology means "writing that is about prostitutes." The *Oxford English Dictionary* explains the root πόρνη or *prostitute* as a "variant of the base of περνάναι to export for sale . . . as prostitutes were often bought slaves." The *Online Etymology Dictionary* further notes that the "main modern meaning 'salacious writing or pictures' represents a slight shift from the etymology, though classical depictions of prostitution usually had this quality." Thus, a value-neutral definition of *pornography* refers to a depiction, either printed or visual, of sexual subjects or activity.[8] But the term frequently carries a more negative connotation. This sexual depiction is judged as degrading or exploitative in one way or another, especially toward women; as unhealthy for the consumer, no matter how entertained or eager that consumer may be; and as unseemly and detrimental for the larger society, in no small part because of the unintentional exposure or overexposure of young people to porn and because of the horrors of child and other nonconsensual pornography.

Partly because of these negative connotations, many authors, readers, and romance academics may counter that the genre isn't about sex *per se* and that it embraces a much wider story about relationship, love, and the arc of character maturation that makes a person worthy of happily-ever-after romance. All true: There are lots of ways in which the romance genre is *not* about porn. But still, I want to insist, the genre deals with mature love relationships *that involve sex*. Another way to make my point would be to say that a porn framework can help us to understand the romance narrative. It's not a romance story if the relationship is platonic and without desire. (I think of the title of Jean H. Hagstrum's sweeping history of the couple, *Esteem Enlivened by Desire*.) Perhaps the lovers are star-crossed and can't come together, such that there is no sexual consummation or no happy ending, as with Humphrey Bogart and Ingrid Bergman at the end of *Casablanca*. But still there is desire, there is longing, there is eros. If the characters love each other but do so as best friends, comrades-in-arms, siblings, or parent and child, all without that charge of eros, then the story is not a romance. It's a love story of a different sort, although tellingly, not one that our culture deems a "love story." Love story, from this angle, is a polite euphemism for a tale involving sexual love. This point holds true for romances without explicit sex, where such consummation happens outside the written scenes or after the story's ending. Really, I'm simply suggesting that we might as well call a spade a spade. Romances, no matter how clean or sweet, are stories about sexual love. Even when and if the sex is deeply off-page, the reader knows that it is happening.

Nevertheless, I suspect that many people will still find the label "mommy porn" an unpalatable one for romance fiction—needlessly provocative, sensationalist, misleading. My argument may seem to play into the very hands of those who seek to dismiss and discredit the genre on precisely this basis that it *is* porn, by which they mean badly written stories about smutty sex, with an unwholesome effect. An example helps to illustrate this concern. In early summer 2011, a blog debate raged highly critical of romance novels, from a Mormon and evangelical Christian perspective, on exactly this charge, that the genre functioned as "pornography for ladies." The novels, went the claim, are addictive to women readers and destructive of their marriages because the stories create unrealistic expectations in women's minds about love, marriage, and sex. In truth, ladies, your husband is never going to look like the Fabio alpha male on the cover, your marriage is never going to be quite so happily-ever-after, and the sex—sorry, gals—is never going to be so cosmically, cataclysmically awesome. A conservative fear here is that genre romance will make "good women" sexually unhappy and demanding: disappointed with their standard-issue husband and incited to run off for hot sexcapades elsewhere. In constructing their arguments, commentators drew heavily on the work of Julianna Slattery, a psychologist at the evangelical Christian organization Focus on the Family and author of *Finding the Hero in Your Husband: Surrendering the Way God Intended*.[9] From this perspective, generally aligned in America with social conservatives and the Christian right, if romance fiction is porn then it must be bad, in the double sense of lacking both moral rectitude and literary standing. Ergo, women should not read it. My argument may seem only to add fuel to this fire in which the romance genre gets burned and its reputation tarnished.

My response is twofold. First, I don't doubt that romance fiction can be unhealthily addictive for some readers, as can any form of media engagement or consumer consumption if taken to an extreme, such as playing computer games or buying designer shoes. Romance reading may even make some women discontented with their lout of a spouse. And if he's too loutish or if he's abusive, she should indeed be discontented. On this point, many authors whom I interview claim that part of the function of the genre is to assure women that they deserve respectful and supportive partners; there is in this way an educative aspect to their stories. One erotic romance writer who also serves as president of her local Romance Writers of America chapter said to me, "Part of why I write is to support and expand women's sexual choices and fantasies." Another author who wrote mainstream African American romances explained that she saw her books as "teaching how to love well." Her readers reported back to her that her books showed them "it's okay to ask for things in the bedroom" and that a hero is a man who supports a woman's choices and autonomy.

The genre may equally strengthen marriages by helping women who are distracted and drained by the unending demands of mothering and house care to reconnect with their sexuality and their husbands. A new writer sitting beside me one year at a Romance Writers of America awards luncheon told exactly this story; she had three girls under the age of twelve whom she homeschooled in the South. She said that romance novels helped her marriage "by turning it around 180 degrees." "Love and romance need to be central to marriage," she said thoughtfully. "I had sort of forgotten about myself as a woman and a wife because of my role as mother and teacher and house-cleaner. When I discovered romance novels, I rediscovered that part of myself." She was still unpublished but working hard on a manuscript. "The genre helped me to remember love and romance and to reconnect romantically with my husband. He noticed right away that I was different," she added, laughing, "and wondered what he'd done right!" Social conservatives and the religious right have nothing to lament in this story.

Second, I am disturbed by the alternative of *not* considering romance to be pornographic. Let's say that we adopt instead the term *erotica* for the spicier forms of the genre. Indeed, second-wave feminist theory often took this stance. Gloria Steinem, for example, made much of the difference between the two terms in her influential 1977 essay "Erotica vs. Pornography." To Steinem, porn is bad, based on "an imbalance of power that allows and requires sex to be used as a form of aggression," even violence. Erotica, by contrast, "rescue[s] sexual pleasure" with the inclusion of "love and mutuality, positive choice, and the yearning for a particular person." The romance genre certainly meets Steinem's criteria of mutuality, love, sexual pleasure, and a yearning that values the individuality of the beloved. The genre's sex scenes can be erotic but are not pornographic in the sense of degrading, subjugating, or lacking in affection. But some of the third-wave feminist and sex-positive material that my students and I considered in class views this linguistic move from *pornography* to *erotica* as a little euphemistic, a little precious and apologetically ladylike, in not fully acknowledging or accepting women's sexual agency and desire.

Why not embrace the reality that these romance stories are about sex and that there's nothing wrong with that? Indeed, second-wave feminist theorist Ann Snitow—to complicate the historical trajectory that I just traced—made a version of this point in 1979. She, too, rejected the distinction of "erotica" as good from "pornography" as bad and provided a fine and rousing exploration of the romance novel as porn for women.[10]

From this perspective, self-confident women who are comfortable with their sexuality can legitimately enjoy the naughty, escapist pleasure of fantasy stories about love and sex—either visual or verbal—ranging from the most delicately sweet to the most raunchily explicit. Additionally—and here sex-positive advocates and BDSM aficionados further part company with Steinem—these stories may even feature power differentials and dominance-submission dynamics, as long as these stories are framed within a fully consensual and overall healthy relationship. The pornography may not even have a story or any overlay of romance to it; it may be "pure sex," so to speak. In all cases, a sex-positive feminist perspective suggests that there is nothing wrong with the term *porn,* nor with considering aspects of the romance genre as porn. We can playfully, honorably, reclaim and redefine that term—as fat studies does with *fat,* as queer studies does with *queer.* Many people might have found *bitch* to be a demeaning term before Sarah Wendell reclaimed it in the context of romance reading in her persona as Smart Bitch Sarah and her 2012 essay "You Call Me a Bitch Like That's a Bad Thing." If we are to call ourselves bitches—as in intelligent, sassy, self-confident women—why can't we call what we read porn—as in intimate relationship stories with sexual pleasure at their core?

I'm interested in this project of reclaiming porn and rehabilitating its definition in feminist and queer directions. I place this project in a context where women—young women, most acutely—suffer from impossible contradictions and double standards. *Be sexy but also demure,* demands the culture. *Don't be a prude but don't be a slut. If guys sleep around it's a valued sign of mastery and control, but if you do it you're a whore.* I see this project as central to breaking down the pernicious and enduring double standard that a woman is nasty and vulgar if she revels in sex. In the characters and sex scenes that they write, romance authors are opening up restrictive sexual taboos in ways that have real potential to lessen social injustices for women, for sexual minorities, and for men too long restricted to a narrow macho role. As Snitow puts it in relation to the Harlequin romance novels, "These are sex books for people who have plenty of good reasons for worrying about sex."[11] Romance stories can give people permission to explore love and sexuality and ultimately themselves in new, liberating ways that emphasize consent and pleasure.

If there is risk here, it may be that the genre is not pornographic *enough*, in this liberating sense that I am developing. Feminist scholars of popular romance, for example, have long been engaged and troubled by this paradox: Many women love to read novels in which they are seemingly bound to men. Germaine Greer famously wrote of the romance hero that "the traits invented for him have been invented by women cherishing the chains of their bondage."[12] By "bound," I intend meanings ranging from partnered or married all the way up to literally tied and shackled in consensual BDSM play, or kidnapped and forcibly seduced in grand old-school "bodice-ripper" style. Thus, the genre limits women (but does it?), yet the genre empowers women (but does it?). Much influential scholarship by critics such as Janice Radway, Sally Goade, and Susan Ostrov Weisser has and continues to prod along these lines. Interestingly, feminists and conservatives have both expressed ambivalence about the romance genre, but in opposite directions. The feminist concern is that romances make women happy and pacified so that they don't take action against the limits of traditional gender relations, and the conservative concern is that romances make women discontented and restless so that they do.

From a feminist perspective worried about romance novels' takeaway message for women, I agree the question is legitimate. It is reasonable to wonder whether readers, perhaps especially adolescent girls whose sexuality and female identity are still under formation, derive something from their reading experience in terms of a "moral of the story," and whether this moral has ramifications. As I've noted before, authors commonly do talk about the genre's positive message and influence in women's lives. The question perhaps comes down to this: Does the romance genre tend to encourage women's compliance with narrow notions that women should aim to be in romantic relationships with men and to be happy as wives and mothers? Do the conservative Christians have it wrong, in other words, and instead of being against romance novels they should hand them out to girls at Sunday school? How does the genre support a patriarchal status quo and how does it support women in their resistance—sometimes subtle, passive, compensatory, or fantasy-based—against such a status quo? I approach this question from other angles in chapters 6 and 8, but I want to answer it here in relation to the category of pornography.

In my view, the romance narrative enables more expansive possibilities for healthy sexuality to the extent that it embraces and fulfills its pornographic potential. Pornography has power to transgress and disrupt tired norms for how women, how people, should live their lives. Snitow, for example, celebrates pornography's breakdown of barriers, its infantile emotional gusto, its embrace of the joys of passivity and of helpless abandon. Note here that much mainstream porn (conjure whatever stereotype you may have of men furtively renting or downloading clips of busty blondes busily servicing male pleasure) does not live up to this potential. The romance genre, it must be admitted, does not or has not always fulfilled this potential either. The risk when Snitow was writing lay in the heroine's passivity: "She must passively wait, must anxiously calculate" in order to get her good man. Today's heroines, like Lishelle in my chapter opening, are gaining more freedom to articulate and pursue their romantic and sexual pleasure: "It's high time we women embrace our sexuality and bury the shame." But the fuller transgressive potential of pornography still lies unrealized in the genre's traditional emphasis on heterosexual coupledom and on parenthood, what feminist and queer theory call hetero-normativity and repro-normativity. (There is also the genre's bugaboo of penetrative sex, but I'll get to that later.) In the majority of romance novels, by story's end the central female character is partnered with a man—whether happy for now, soulmate bonded, or traditionally engaged and married—and often pregnant or heading toward that state. Almost by definition, a romance novel ends in some version of this monogamous pair bonding. In contrast to the second-wave feminist slogan "A woman needs a man like a fish needs a bicycle," to live happily ever after in a romance novel, that fish and bicycle *do* need each other.[13]

To the extent that romances push a vision of a woman's life as incomplete unless she ends up with a man—a vision of women's mature fulfillment necessarily achieved through monogamous, heterosexual marriage and motherhood—this vision would certainly be a limited one. The romance narrative becomes problematic if and when its stories imply that a woman must be a heterosexual wife and mother in order to be happy. Note that the problem is not with these choices *per se*. I am a monogamous, heterosexual wife and mother (of two boys, no less; I've ended up living with *three* males with nary a female in sight except for the cat) and I dare to believe myself happy and fulfilled, on the one hand, and to be a queer-positive and sex-positive feminist, on the other hand. The problem is when these stances become norms that are enforced by the culture as more or less mandatory. The narrowness of these norms ignores the potential for happiness and fulfillment from the single life through celibacy, divorce, widowhood, serial romance, or casual consensual sex. Of course, this narrower vision is *not* all of what today's romances are about. Romances written in recent years feature, almost universally, strong and empowered heroines who work for their living and stand on their own two feet in storylines that buck patriarchal conventions mandating male leadership and female submission. Equally, romances are full of plotlines requiring characters to earn their happy ending through emotional risk and commitment, as well as through a career plan and self-sufficiency. Today's heroines, in other words, even after falling madly in love, remain strong female alphas in their own right: high-achieving professionals or kick-ass vampires.

And while readers do sometimes consume these novels in voracious quantity and with great attachment to the genre, fans are by no means uncritical in their reading practices, when and if storylines seem lacking. The advent of online readers' communities exposes the rich interplay among readers, texts, and authors. Far from accepting characters' choices and any views implied by authors, readers often argue back. They write challenging evaluations of individual books and of the overall genre and its trends.[14] They post comments deriding the "too stupid to live heroine" along the lines of, "Why would any sane woman act like that?" or "Why would she fall in love with a jerk like him?" (My own novels have garnered such critiques in readers' reviews, such as one wittily titled "Master of Love, not Common Sense" on Amazon: "The common sense quota was so far below understandable I found myself constantly being taken out of the story [who goes alone to a creeper's apartment for a business deal? Callista does!] and wondering how any of these characters managed to survive.") Furthermore, romances do not universally mandate a life choice of man-and-children as a woman's path to happiness. The growing gay, lesbian, and erotic romance markets (to say nothing about the sex lives of lycanthropes and immortals in paranormal romance) portray sexual diversity in a wide and positive light. I am heartened by the growth of erotica and paranormal, with their happy-for-now endings and non-vanilla sex scenes, and by the new publishers of lesbian, gay, asexual, and queer romance (e.g., Bold Strokes Books and Riptide Publishing).[15] The counter-note of reservation, however, is that even in erotica, the take-home message can sometimes read as "Kinky play is fine and good to let the little lady have her jollies, but we've got to get her settled down and safely married off with kids by story's end," as indeed the relationship resolves in *Fifty Shades*.

In defense of the genre, however, and to risk a tautology, these romance novels *are* all romances. By definition, they tell a story of an intimate relationship with an optimistic ending, and the majority of the genre's offerings will follow the common-enough life path of heterosexual motherhood. As one novelist who is a published academic scholar on romance studies explained to me, romance is not a counter-cultural genre but a "literature of the center. It celebrates the values and lifestyle of the center: marriage, love, children, home, and security." Accordingly, we can't fault romance stories for being, well, *romantic:* tying happiness to enduring love partnership in line with standard cultural scripts. But these stories do add pressure to the omnipresent cultural narrative that one needs to be coupled up as proof of a successful life. And we *can* fault the culture for not offering more validation to alternate pathways toward fulfillment. Even the self-made millionaire is pitied if he (or she) ends up alone in a mansion with no beloved, no family, and no children with whom to share it all. A more "pornographic" romance genre, with a wider depiction of life paths and of consensual sexual lifestyles and choices, could lessen this aspect of the genre. It could redirect the cultural impact of the genre away from a high-stakes and laser-vision quest to find your one true love or else, and toward a more expansive goal to find loving connection with other people and with worthy values. And, as the next section explains, here is what else a reconceived notion of pornography could do for the romance genre: *It could improve our cultural cliteracy.*

CLITERACY: WRITING AND READING WOMEN'S PLEASURE

In this discussion of a pornographic romance genre, I obviously have in mind a wider and more positive vision of pornography than the term may conjure up for some. Call it feminist pornography, or queer porn, or sex-positive porn. It would be a mistake, however, to call it softcore porn since these alternative productions quite happily include hardcore, kinky, and fetishistic storylines. "Feminist" here does not mean soft-focus with lots of loving dialogue and a plot that tries to be meaningful. Whichever term is used, the point is to distinguish this alternative from standard, mainstream porn. To make this point, witness the enlightened advocacy of the Feminist Porn Awards, a gala event produced annually by the Toronto sex-toy shop Good For Her. The year that I attended this fascinating event the awards ceremony was held in conjunction with the first-ever academic conference on feminist pornography and the book launch of Tristan Taormino and colleague's *The Feminist Porn Book: The Politics of Producing Pleasure.*

This Canadian awards competition bills itself as "the largest and longest running celebration of feminist porn in the world." Organizers seek to recognize and encourage the increased production of high-quality porn for women, for sexual minorities of all stripes, and for heterosexual men tired of the limitations of conventional porn. With this annual award competition, Good For Her rebelliously celebrates an alternative to stereotypical pornography: They celebrate "feminist smut." Note that their choice of terms such as *porn* and *smut* deliberately goes in the op-

posite direction from a cleaned-up literary term like *erotica*. Through
the deliberate use of loaded language, the Feminist Porn Awards seek to
challenge stereotypes about sexuality and sexual depictions as dirty, de-
graded, and unladylike, and to highlight women's genuine sexual agency
and pleasure. As their website professes, "We believe the world is inun-
dated with cheesy, cliché, degrading, and patronizing porn. But we also
believe that erotic fantasy is powerful, and that women and marginalized
communities deserve to put their dreams and desires on film, too." This
sex-positive sensibility delights in erotic media but looks for media representations that showcase diverse expressions of consensual sexuality and
honor diverse body types. Fat women, scrawny guys, trans bodies, older
people, and differently abled folk all have their own sexy beauty. In particular, and going against the grain of traditional porn, Good For Her's
award-winning films tend to feature active female desire and women's
real orgasms.[16]

This point about women's sexual pleasure is crucial to the argument
that I am developing. If feminist porn is first and foremost about highlighting women's sexual pleasure and about the politics of producing
this pleasure (as the subtitle and introduction of *The Feminist Porn Book*
underline), then no cultural production better matches this mandate
than romance fiction. From this perspective, the romance genre fits
squarely within the label of feminist porn as one of its main exemplars
(although generally also one of its tamest). Central to romance fiction,
as to feminist porn, is the depiction not simply of sexual activity but of
women's *sexual satisfaction*. This is an aspect of the romance genre that I
find under-examined: the extent to which the heroine's sexual pleasure
is guaranteed. Even in non-explicit romance novels devoid of all steamy
love scenes and in the genre's nineteenth- and earlier twentieth-century
precursors, which, by the conventions of their day, did not feature on-
page sex, readers can safely assume that the heroines are sexually satisfied. To be blunt, we believe that the women are happily orgasmic. In the
romance genre, by the books' end, readers feel assured that the lover's
embrace and the marriage bed are always pleasurable for the heroine.
Women *like* sex in romance novels. Their desire is taken as a good—not
a shameful—thing.

This assumption of sexual desire and sexual pleasure is partly what I mean by the claim that the romance genre as a whole is pornographic. If this off-page sexual pleasure is crucial to the happily-ever-after satisfaction of the novel even in the sweet romances, then "porn"—in some sense—is central to the genre.[17] This sexual pleasure, I have come to believe, is one of the most challenging and potentially transformative aspects of romance fiction for the culture. As the co-editors of *The Feminist Porn Book* note in their introduction, "Society's dread of women who own their desire, and use it in ways that confound expectations of proper female sexuality, persists."[18] The controversy around romance novels is partly explained by the fact that these are books about women wanting and getting great sex from partners who know how to deliver. This is an anxiety-provoking message indeed for a culture more comfortable with male arousal and satisfaction than its female counterparts.

Addressing that anxiety head-on and naming it as a pernicious cultural blind spot is a recent art installation that aimed to improve our *cliteracy*. This brilliant term is not my own. It is the title of a 2012 large-scale mixed media art exhibition at a New York gallery by the American conceptual artist Sophia Wallace subtitled "100 Natural Laws." As described in the installation's accompanying website, "A provocative work about citizenship, sexuality, human rights, and bodies, CLITERACY explores a paradox: the global obsession with sexualizing female bodies in a world that is maddeningly illiterate when it comes to female sexuality." Wallace's exhibit features one hundred "natural laws," or truths and aphorisms, about the clitoris and, more broadly, about the role of women's sexuality in culture, designed to make viewers more "cliterate" or knowledgeable about female sexuality. These natural laws include

- No Justice, No Peace, No Orgasm, No Liberty
- Freedom in society can be measured by the distribution of orgasms
- Penetration with a penis is just one of innumerable ways to have sex
- Democracy without Cliteracy? Phallusy

- The World Health Organization estimates between 130–140 million women have been brutalized by female genital mutilation in the last ten years

- 99% of porn is a monocrop of rapid penetration gratuitous ejaculation 1% plot and 0% cliteracy

Through her art, Wallace's goal is to correct ongoing misconceptions about sexuality, expose media misrepresentation, highlight the horrors of female genital mutilation, create open dialogue—and amuse. I often found myself laughing out loud. Her work, as is true of the genre of romance fiction, offers a way of reading and writing about female sexuality that is woman-centered, sex-positive, and cliterate: informed about the particularities of female sexual pleasure.[19]

It must be acknowledged, however, that the cliteracy of romance fiction is not that of full realism. In the romance novels that my students read for class, the women quickly noticed that the sex depicted was fantasy sex. By "fantasy," I intend dual senses of "really great" and "unrealistic." One of my students reported her mother's comment, "Honey, you can read those books all you want, but don't you go thinking sex is anything like that!" Women in romance fiction experience incredible sex. The heroes are masterfully sensitive, skilled, and attentive lovers, with complete control over their sexual response (no erectile dysfunction or premature ejaculation for these men). The heroines enjoy guaranteed orgasms, often through penis-in-vagina intercourse. "That only happens in 20% of cases for women!" yelled out my students. (Male characters have incredible sex, too, but that seemed less fantastical to my women students.)

As human sexuality and relationship researcher Emily Nagoski pointed out in her presentation at the Feminist Porn Awards' academic conference, quoting nearly a century's worth of replicated scientific studies, only about 25 percent of women reach orgasm from vaginal penetration alone and over 90 percent of women who masturbate do so with little or no vaginal penetration, concentrating on clitoral stimulation instead. She wonderfully concluded, "The clitoris really is the hokey pokey, and I mean like woah." Or as the Black Lace website guide to author submissions dryly notes, "Multiple orgasms through penetration alone are not most women's experience." Penetrative sex is not the height of sexual pleasure for most women, and yet penis-in-vagina sex remains the norm in hetero-sexual romance novels. Hand and mouth on breast and clitoris all provide foreplay—often delicious pages and pages of it—but penetration is the hokey-pokey in romance's sex narratives. Ironically, as Nagoski pointed out at the conference, it remains the norm in the majority of feminist, lesbian, and queer porn films as well, even when the penis is displaced by substitutes such as a dildo. We cannot seem to think ourselves beyond the convention of phallic penetration, even in woman-centered romance and feminist or lesbian pornography, despite its limitations as a pathway to pleasure for women.[20]

At least two conclusions are possible, both of which I find persuasive. One is that these depictions of sex in woman-centered erotica function as a compensatory fantasy space. Readers, viewers, and writers all know that the sex on offer in both romance novels and porn flicks is not fully realistic. Frankly, they prefer it that way. Popular press headlines have been touting recently how "Sleep is the new sex"; in one survey, 80 per-cent of Britons preferred the choice of "a good night's sleep over a night of passion."[21] A busy life can lead one to the point where sex feels like a both-er for which one has little time or energy. In such a context, there is an appeal to the imaginative play of an escapist romp wherein sex is easy and good. The fantasy here is that desire lights women afire at a mere touch or glance. That her body melts, that pleasure consumes her, that climax is automatic. Unlike the sad truth of *Tootsie*'s 1982 now-iconic line where ac-tress Teri Garr accepts ownership of her sexual knowledge—"I'm respon-sible for my own orgasms!"—in romance novels women do not bear this responsibility. The genre sees to that orgasm for women, thank you very much, through a partner who knows the ropes and through the fantasti-cally responsive sexual physiology with which nature endows the hero-ine. And the genre makes sure it's a damn fine climax, with plenty more where that came from. In this way, romance novels compensate for real-ity in fantasy scenes of endless foreplay, true love seductions, and earth-shattering female pleasure. And the feminist porn flicks, with their active female desire and non-faked orgasms, allow for the fantasy of climaxing like an Olympic-caliber porn star who can give and take it all.

The second possible conclusion is that woman-centered porn still has work to do in order to get past a male-oriented preference for penetrative intercourse. Here, I see romance novels both unwittingly participating in and consciously reacting against the cultural illiteracy about women's sexuality. It is telling, I think, that such penetrative intercourse functions more or less as the standard cultural definition of sex: PIVMO, a friend of mine called it, for "penis-in-vagina-male-orgasm" sex. We need to queer—to question and transform—this penetrative norm as the be-all and end-all of sex by offering alternatives. Feminist pornography, including romance fiction in all of its subgenres, could explore more diverse depictions of what gives most women more pleasure: clitoral stimulation with or without penetration, the solo joys of masturbation (still rather a taboo in the genre outside edgy contemporaries or erotica), and a wide range of body pleasures, experienced in a safe and supportive context. Romance fiction shares in Wallace's project of cliteracy, but too much of the genre shies away from the project's fullest embrace. The genre continues false master narratives wherein the heroines easily reach climax through penis-in-vagina sex, including, rather improbably, the genre's legions of untried virgins. I implicate my own romance fiction as guilty here as well; the master narrative is difficult to escape.

In connection with this discussion of pornography, I am inspired by the notion that "a feminist is a woman who writes." The French feminist author Hélène Cixous issued a rousing and influential call for women to write in her 1976 essay "The Laugh of the Medusa": "Write!" Cixous urged women. "Writing is for you. . . . Write, let no one hold you back, let nothing stop you. . . . Write your self. Your body must be heard." Writing, she said of the woman author, will give "her access to her native strength; it will give her back her goods, her pleasures, her organs." By this definition, a woman becomes a feminist by putting words on paper or screen in order to "break out of the snare of silence," to develop her voice, to become a person of power and individuality, to work her will in the world, to pursue her pleasure.[22] "Do not underestimate the power of your words!" a keynote speaker urged us at the Romance Writers of America conference one summer. Another speaker on a panel of new authors told her story of being a young military wife with two kids who had learned to always put the needs of others before her own; she credited writing romance with helping her to find herself, to mature, and to grow as a woman. "My heart became braver when I wrote" is how she put it, as she advised us, "Don't let fear hold you back." From this perspective, words and books have force to transform both self and world. But wielding this force is not easy. It takes courage and involves risk. As George Orwell had it in this feisty sentiment, "Good novels are written by people who are not frightened."[23]

In the publishing contract that I signed for my two romance novels, a clause appears that is apparently standard for major commercial publishers. It states, "The book is not obscene and will cause no harm." By signing the contract, I was supposed to agree not to submit a book manuscript that was obscene or harmful. On my agent's advice, I added an amendment that is apparently also standard: "*To my knowledge,* the book is not obscene and will cause no harm." It got me thinking: What is my knowledge about obscenity and the harm that it or any other aspect of a book may cause? I was a generally happy and well-adjusted teenager and yet I remember feeling mildly suicidal after reading Sylvia Plath's *The Bell Jar* in high school. Many books that I've read have made me weep. Halfway through reading Ann-Marie MacDonald's luminous novel *Fall on Your Knees,* I threw it to the floor. The story so disturbed me with its themes of incest and death that I gave up reading the book for six months. Eventually I had to finish it, but it is one of those books that haunts me to this day. Reading *does* cause harm. And so it should. Books should unsettle us. Author Franz Kafka expressed the notion with Germanic angst: "We need books that affect us like a disaster, that grieve us deeply, like the death of someone we loved more than ourselves, like being banished into forests far from everyone, like a suicide." Now *there's* a vision of reading: the book as disaster, death, banishment, suicide. Kafka concluded, "A book must be the axe for the frozen sea within us."[24] If a novel is an axe hacking away at the frozen sea inside us, then, baby, that's going to hurt.

Applying this perspective on the power of books and on the author's writing task to the genre of romance fiction, I see this picture emerge: A feminist is a woman (or person of any gender) who dares in writing to explore thoughts, desires, and fantasies that run contrary to traditional descriptions of how a woman is supposed to be. This contrariness relates in particular to patriarchal scripts for normative feminine docility, sub-missiveness, and sexual passivity. Such scripts are still very much alive in the culture's demands that my students regularly report. Women are supposed to look sexy but not seek out sex, to be both whore and virgin at the same time. Women—"ladies"—do not traditionally go on the hunt for sex or overly enjoy it; such licentiousness is the province of their fallen sister, the soiled dove, the campus slut. The college girl's walk of shame back to her dorm room the morning after a party or hook-up—hair mussed, mascara smeared, tugging on her microskirt and tottering incongruously on her stiletto-heeled shoes in the morning sunshine—endures as today's legacy of these notions. It is a point almost too obvious to make that no equivalent walk of shame exists for college boys.

Amid such enduring cultural scripts, the simple act of writing can be transgressive and liberating by granting voice to the writer and by putting stories into the hands of readers. This is especially the case when such exercise of voice and story has been denied or poisoned by cultural stricture. As a way to work against the grain of oppressive cultural messages, I find courage and poignancy and beauty in women writing lusty sex scenes. Precisely because such writing and reading is still not considered entirely seemly, these acts can become feminist by opening up new space. To me, it's a "You go, sister!" moment. Indeed, most things not considered ladylike nominate themselves to me for their transgressive potential. As I get older, the politics of respectability increasingly loses its appeal. In this sense, I cheer on all the women reading their *Shades of Grey*—or writing their own.

To say that romance fiction is porn is to say that it is all right for women to be unafraid and unashamed in their sexuality. That's what I see behind *Shades*'s multimillion sales figures: Once the bandwagon started, the safety of numbers meant it became acceptable for other women, curious and amused, to jump on as well. It's okay for women to read and write about sex, even if the literary quality isn't that great (sorry, E. L. James, but don't worry about it). It's okay for romance fiction to be porn, different from traditional male-oriented porn, with a great diversity of woman-centered sexual fantasies of desire and agency: fantasies in which the lovers are always attentive and a woman's pleasure is guaranteed.

"I LOVE YOU," HE SAID: THE MONEY SHOT

One last point, to pull these strands together. There is a key, climactic narrative moment in the happily-ever-after ending of the popular romance story. This is the moment where the hero declares his love for his beloved. You probably know the moment I mean, when plot and character conflicts, both internal and external, are resolved, such that the hero now says—where conflicts are often resolved precisely *because* he says—in one form or another, "I love you." Here is the moment when our hero declares, I can't live without you—even if I'm a duke and you're a courtesan; I'm a vampire and you're a human; I've devoted my life to vengeance and you're my sworn enemy; I used to love you years ago but you cruelly betrayed me and broke my heart; I'm from the eleventh century and you're from the twenty-first; I'm a dragon and you're a wolf; I'm a pirate and you're my captive; I'm a feline alien sex-slave and you're my spaceship captain slave-owner—despite all such trivialities, I am incomplete without you. Be my mate, be my wife, be my husband (gender and sexual orientation don't matter here). My heart beats only for you. I am yours, at your feet.

So, here's my fullest argument: Romance fiction is porn, but it's a particular type of woman-oriented feminist porn with a *telos,* or narrative goal. Romance fiction is teleological, building and driving toward this climax of the narrative. This narrative goal, I argue, is the happily-ever-after moment best encapsulated in the hero's declaration of love. In other words, the moment where one most sees romance fiction as pornography is, paradoxically, not in the sex scenes themselves. As I've already noted, these sex scenes aren't even on the page in some of the books. Instead, one sees romance fiction as porn in the happily-ever-after ending, especially in that key moment of climax when the hero declares his love. This is the moment when the hero is won, when he proves himself to be finally and fully on the side of love. In the fantasy play space of the novel, this moment is the woman-centered triumph—even, I argue in chapter 8, in gay romances. This moment is equally the porn triumph, the erotic consummation of the story, the point of the sex.

In this sense, sex is foreplay in a romance narrative. A book's earlier scenes of sexual desire may range from a mere unfamiliar fluttering in our virginal heroine's stomach to full-blown multi-orgasmic sexual encounters. What these various erotic scenes do is serve as build-up and lead-in that prepare readers for the true literary and sexual climax of the narrative: the hero's open-hearted "I love you." The real erotic tension lies not in whether the protagonists have sex but whether and how their desire blooms into a life-changing love. The sex is important—very important, as I have argued—but in genre romance, as opposed to feminist or queer porn without a romance plotline, the sex has to lead to this "money shot" or verbal proof of the hero's passion. For those of you not familiar with this term, which has entered at least semi-polite vernacular from mainstream porn, the money shot is that climactic moment in the porn flick when the male actor ejaculates outside the body of his partner, such that viewers can see his semen spurting out in all its glory, preferably it seems over a partner's face or chest. The money shot is the viewer's guarantee that the actor isn't faking his orgasm. It's the cinematic shot for which viewers pay money. This is REAL SEX, is the visual message, because there lies the sticky evidence. Similarly, this is TRUE LOVE, romance readers know, because the hero is on his knees, heart in hand (sometimes more or less dramatically, in one literary form or another). Lisa Fletcher argues that "I love you" is the defining speech act of the romance novel; I'm arguing further that the hero's declaration of this phrase is the money shot of romance porn.[25]

After I drafted this chapter, I serendipitously found almost exactly this point in a romance novel. *Here's Looking at You* is a contemporary romance released in 2013 by bestselling British author Mhairi McFarlane. In the book, the main character, Anna, answers love-interest James's question about why she likes the romantic novels stocked on her flat's bookshelves. She gives this explanation:

> It's the climax—no, don't be cheap—of the big gesture scene. *That's the romance money shot.* In ordinary life, no one ever declares their passion. You get a few signals, get pissed [drunk], end up in bed, it becomes a habit. I love the hero saying all the things to a woman you want to hear but no one ever says. . . . It has to be about why she's so remarkably special to him and she finally finds out all her feelings of obsession are reciprocated.[26]

At a Romance Writers of America conference a few years ago, the late Kate Duffy, at that time editorial director at Kensington and an influential figure in romance publishing, similarly insisted that every romance novel must contain exactly this element of the hero's willingness to make this declaration of passion. No matter how taciturn he is at the beginning of the book, how much of an emotionally closed-off "strong and silent" type he is, by book's end, for him to be a worthy romance hero, and for readers to trust that the characters' love relationship is deep and lasting, that cowboy has got to say "I love you." And it can't be too subtle or indirect. He can't just slide by with a mumbled "Me, too," when the heroine says, "I love you." He's got to have the courage to go out on a limb, to risk exposing himself emotionally, and to proudly declare, "I love you." Such a declaration is all the more powerful if his beloved hasn't yet declared any love in return, so that the hero is unsure whether his declaration will be well-received and reciprocated. It's even better if he has to perform this risky speech act in public and in front of witnesses. That's his verbal semen spurting out, his vulnerability, his proof of authenticity, our guarantee that this is the real deal. For the hero, it's a speech act but also and primarily an enactment of emotion: love, passion, desire, commitment, protectiveness, possessiveness, pride. For readers and authors, I see a feminist act of woman-centered imaginative play—the fantasy of the potentially dangerous alpha, stand-in for all his tribe, rendered in this most vulnerable and potent moment of narrative climax impotent to committing further harm, neutered, tamed, made safe, won. This moment is the culmination we read for, the climax toward which the love and seduction and plot and character arcs have all been leading.

The words spurt across the page. We gasp.

"I love you," he says: speech act, emotion act, feminist act, porn act.

5

Notes from the Field

Romance Writers of America

Goddamn, I love my job.

I'm sitting in the thirty-eighth floor bar of a swanky Dallas hotel, eating a solitary late supper and listening to lounge music. The hotel is one of the sites hosting the annual national conference of the Romance Writers of America. After a long day of interviews and workshops and keynote addresses, I'm quaffing champagne and watching an older couple on the parquet dance floor. They are dancing to the stylings of the piano player, who is a little schmaltzy but endearing nonetheless. The man and woman are laughing, cheek-to-cheek, he in a suit and she in a chic black dress. They are beautiful and sexy in their seventy-year old bloom. I watch them in the reflection of the floor-to-ceiling windows as the big Texas sky sheds the last of the day's light.

The city skyline stretches as far as I can see, streetlights twinkling on to forever. Dallas is the home of Southfork, of brothers Bobby and J. R. Ewing from the eponymous *Dallas* primetime TV soap opera. I grew up watching the show. Visitor brochures in the hotel lobby offer tours to Southfork. I wonder briefly about going but decide that dining in this top-floor lounge is similar enough: over-the-top, self-indulgent, a wonderful guilty pleasure. The *Dallas Morning News* on the loveseat next to me tells stories of the war in Iraq and a man charged with killing his eight-month-old son with a cocaine overdose. But still, on this dance floor and at this conference is celebrated the possibility—the reality—of love. I am fascinated by this romance narrative and its hold on us, by the extent to which the narrative deals so voluptuously in both fantasy and truth.

I move on to calamari and a Texas merlot so dark a purple that it's almost black, served in the biggest glass I've ever held. I'm a happy woman, although I alternate between self-satisfied pleasure and self-conscious doubt. Coincidentally, the International Women's Peace Conference is meeting in the same hotel as the Romance Writers of America. When I checked in for the romance conference, I caught sight of one of my former professors from Harvard in the lobby. She wore the nametag of the peace conference, and I found myself ducking. Tomorrow evening I'll have another dilemma. It's the RWA awards ceremony, the dress-up grand finale of the conference. I'll have to cross the lobby to catch my shuttle bus to the event. What if I see my old professor again? What would I say to her? My plan is to be strapped into a long velvet gown in midnight blue. It's got sparkles on it. I'll be wearing a padded push-up bra to hoist my breasts into place and my mother's diamond bracelet. Concerned about panty lines and thinking about going all out, I was even flirting with not wearing underwear.

No academic conference that I've ever attended—and in twenty-eight years of academia, I've been to quite a few—has ever been this much fun. I am overwhelmed and bemused by it. Am I allowed to enjoy myself so much while researching an academic book? Shouldn't I be doing something more serious? I feel no guilt over leaving my husband and kids behind for four days of this Shangri-La. I am discomfited, however, by a sense of wrongdoing in leaving behind some part of my professional identity. Long sparkly velvet? Academics—scholarly intellectuals—aren't supposed to wear velvet, especially without underwear. The presence of my professor makes this point acute. She's a kind woman and a well-respected scholar, author of multiple books and articles on ethics, peace, Christianity, and community. For all I know, she may read romance novels in her spare time. Maybe she's a closeted romance writer wannabe like myself; maybe she's not wearing panties either. My cowardly ducking is certainly not fair to her. But seeing her stirs up my guilt and confusion. At Harvard, I was studying feminist ethics, as she did, and working on issues of sustainability and antiviolence in the context of Christian religion and culture. In one trajectory of my professional identity and career, I would be here with her at the International Women's Peace Conference, doing the righteous work of antiwar protesting. Instead, I'm hanging out with the RWA. I'm up in the sky lounge, gorging on some damn fine chocolate bread pudding.

But—and here's the rub—I don't *want* to be at her conference. I want to be exactly where I am, excited and engrossed by mine. Does that make me a failed feminist ethicist? A lousy academic? A bad girl? Surely not, I reason with myself. My friend Alexis teaches at a university here in Dallas and takes me out for Mexican cuisine one night. When I lay out for her my tangle of emotion and response, she assures me that the two conferences are but flip sides of a coin. Romance is all about peace, she says; go for it! There are certainly intellectual puzzles galore to work through here and new writing challenges to test and expand my craft. A project on the romance narrative raises questions about norms of femininity and masculinity, changes in the portrayal of female sexuality, stigma and empowerment in publishing's only woman-dominated genre, and so on. Issues germane to feminism and ethics and world peace abound in romance fiction. I *know* all of this. So why do I still feel awkward, even a little embarrassed? It's not the novels or the genre of popular fiction itself that causes my discomfiture; I've read romance novels without shame all my life. I *know* that women's fiction has nothing to apologize for. Probing my feelings in the sky lounge between licks of crème anglaise off my spoon, I decide that it must be the pleasure of it all that has me flummoxed. The velvet. The midnight chocolate buffet. The feather boas. It takes an academic gal some getting used to.

I recognize one deep root in my struggle over the meaning of my new research enterprise and my newly emerging researcher self. It's an old conundrum, really. As a girl, I fretted about how I could enjoy my family's Sunday roast when children were starving in Africa. As a young professional, I worried over how I could celebrate getting tenure—that gold ring of the professorial career path—when other graduate students, through no fault of their own, didn't get tenure-track positions. It's an uneasy awareness of good fortune. Yes, I know—I am sheltered, privileged, no doubt spoiled growing up with loving parents in my quiet Canadian suburb. That *Dallas Morning News* is still beside me; I sit next to war and death and child abuse. But somehow my reality counts also, and I am safe, loved, tipsy, and fascinated by the romance narrative. What to make of it all? Desire, love, ambivalence, confusion, pleasure. I am drunk on the wine and the romance of this place.

One thing I do know—I am entranced by my dancing couple. The piano player goes on break, and the woman and man sit side by side on a couch, to drink wine and nod their coiffed silver heads in sedate, WASPy enjoyment of the lounge soundtrack. Billie Holliday sings now, so much better than Piano Man, bless his heart. The couple are chatting, smiling, holding hands. I want to be them, want Ted and me to be them when we reach their age, still heading out on hot dates, dressed up and flirting all night long. It takes luck to have such love. I imagine myself going up to them as I leave: I would lean in, touch the lady's arm lightly, and smile as I murmur, "Thank you for reaffirming my faith in love." They would laugh and offer some charming southern rejoinder, the man gallantly insisting that "It's Sara Belle who makes us look good; I'm all left feet." But even apart from the invasion of their privacy and the risk of sounding like a stalker, I know that I wouldn't do it. In our age of cynicism, the sentiment of faith in true love seems entirely too corny to articulate out loud. Yet I confess to believing in it. I believe this woman and this man are in love. I believe in deep and lasting romantic love as a force that can change lives for the better, heal wounds, bring peace and fulfillment, and make sex hotter.

Yesterday, I got back to my hotel room late in the afternoon. After the nonstop excitement of the day's program, when I'd valiantly crammed in every conference event that I could, I'd missed lunch and was now hungry and burned out. I knew I should get something to eat, but I was too tired to move. Instead, I picked up a book that I'd received at the conference (one perk of registration is armloads of free romance novels). Flopped on my bed, I read the last two chapters to the book's end. I often do this with books: start reading in the middle, or only read the end, or begin the book but deliberately don't finish it. I get a sense of more novels that way, although admittedly I miss out on the full arc of the story. The ending of this story was particularly poignant, a tear-jerker wherein the hero finally realizes he loves the heroine but not before she almost dies in childbirth. I sat up on the bed, my eyes and nose a disgusting teary mess, and said out loud to myself, "What is the pleasure here?" I was hungry, worn-out, and crying, alone in my hotel room. Why? Why was I doing this, instead of having a nap or a nice hot bath or a decent meal? The answer has something to do with the pleasure of love. There is an emotional appeal to vicariously experiencing romantic love at its most intense, with all the concomitant suffering and risk, and then safely emerging through that pain to a point where everything works out for the lovers. There is a pleasure to seeing the author pull off the magic trick of crafting a happy ending out of impossible conflict. The enjoyment lies partly in the affirmation of love itself. Love, happiness, peace, security, fulfillment—although hard-won, these goods are real, and they are possible. In the books, certainly; in life, potentially. Such is the romance novel's reassuring promise.

Part of this promise has to do with women's sexual pleasure and satisfaction. Women's sexuality is a powerful theme in the genre of romance. If not always fully articulated, this theme exists as an undercurrent. It is played with in the flirty and gorgeous get-ups worn by conference attendees at the Romance Writers of America awards ceremony, in the jokes cracked at many panels, and in the stories I hear from the women with whom I talk. I am coming to see that at these conferences—as in the larger romance fiction community of writers and fans, and in the pages of the genre itself—one thing that women are doing is creating a safe, permissive space of sexual fantasy and imagination. And make no mistake, this fantasy play space is made by and for women. Although there are some men in attendance at the conferences as escorts to wives or girlfriends or participating as editors, agents, and the occasional author, the conference is overwhelmingly female. No other segment of the publishing industry is so heavily dominated by a female presence. Indeed, I start to wonder whether there is any other woman-centered professional sphere that is larger or has more cultural impact than romance fiction. Where else do you find such a cohesive working community of women in such a popular and lucrative industry? Romance fiction is a powerful woman-space of female professional identity and accomplishment, of female fantasy and desire. By creating this space, women gain a unique freedom to imagine and play.

For example, at another RWA conference, I sit in a large hotel convention hall waiting for a "How to write the romance novel" talk to begin. The speaker is Susan Elizabeth Phillips—SEP, to fans—a *New York Times*–bestselling author of contemporary romantic comedies. A crowd of women, a couple hundred of us at least, is quickly filling the rows of chairs facing the speaker's podium where SEP is due to arrive at any moment. The room hums and buzzes with excitement. A few men are in the ranks, including a tech guy plugging in cables and making adjustments to the podium's microphone. Suddenly, a high-pitched shriek from the AV system rockets through the room. Hands fly to ears as the deafening noise threatens eardrums and electronic circuitry alike. Tech Guy leaps into action. He runs at top speed across the convention room to some control panel against the far wall. Arms outstretched, he leaps into the air and dives headfirst for the cables like a batter sliding into home plate. The banshee screech of the feedback cuts to blessed silence as he yanks loose the offending cable from the speakers.

Into the sudden quiet comes one woman's yell, "Can you do that again with your shirt off?" Sound explodes once more: women laughing, cheering, applauding. Our blushing hero climbs to his feet, smiles shyly, and sketches us a charming bow.

Another time, I am in a smaller conference room, listening to a panel of authors and editors talk about the treatment of women's sexuality in current romance novels. "Sex and the Single Title" is the panel title, and "hotter all the time" is the general agreement. There is much enlightened talk about the greater permission and freedom that writers now have to explore non-heterosexual storylines and to include more sexual material. One top-selling contemporary romance author happily reports that five years ago she would only have been able to allude to masturbation whereas today she can write a full scene of self-pleasuring. Another writer on the panel, however, sees the present moment of sex-saturated popular culture as a burden. Two and a half scenes of standard sex have been her traditional limit (the half being a partial seduction or interrupted intimacy). Now her editor strongly urges her to throw in a couple more to stay on trend. And she is warned that she might need to start thinking "beyond the vanilla." She feels pressured to include more sex than she is comfortable writing and finds herself resenting the gratuitousness of it.

But it is the sole male speaker on the panel who sums up the tone best. He opens his comments by reading from the novel of one of his authors, an edgy but still mainstream dark comedy set in the present day. The author, J. J. Salem, couldn't make it to the RWA conference herself, but this handsome, middle-aged man seems happy to sit in for her. He introduces her work, *Tan Lines,* and turns to the first page from which he reads her hook line, surely worthy of nomination for Best Opening Sentence in a Romance Novel: "There are 8,000 nerve endings in the clitoris, and this son of a bitch couldn't find one of them." As with Tech Guy, laughter erupts in the room. Smiling nods and amused glances pass among the women in the audience. Yes, men can be blundering and clueless in bed, the poor dears, incapable of performing a simple act of clitoral stimulation. Either they can't find it or else they're not looking because they are too distracted by the vagina. But J. J. knows the score. In a way, it's better to have her male editor read the line, at least the way that he delivers it— laughing along with the joke, a knowing, self-deprecating grin in place. He gets the complaint, seems to agree that he and his tribe are guilty, but proves by his presence on the panel that he's there to learn.

All of these moments help me to better understand the sexual dynamic at work in these conferences, as in the romance fiction community itself. There is a heady sense of frolic here, a freedom to enjoy and play with all forms of female pleasure. As one speaker at a conference awards luncheon says in her opening remarks, "It's so awesome! RWA is such a woman-centered, girl-power thing!" These woman-centered pleasures range from the fundamental satisfaction of a woman finding her voice through writing, to the theatrical play of adornment, to the hedonistic delights of food (chocolate is *huge* in the romance community), to the satisfactions of sex. An editor at a conference panel, using the example of the novels' covers, encapsulated these pleasures as "women in beautiful dresses and men in not much of all: What's not to like?!"

Through this frolicsome play, romance writing and reading supports the fantasy exploration of women's sexuality. In a culture where women are advised to look sexy and young but are also easily shamed or dismissed when they do so, this impossible bind of double standards and contradictory messages—"be hot but pure"—is intense. How to figure it out? What is the role of sexuality in personal identity, romance, and relationship? What brings women pleasure? How to navigate this treacherous terrain? As it turns out, the romance fiction community of writers and readers is a prime cultural site for the exploration of these questions. With a conservative estimate of ten thousand new novels published yearly (not to count novellas and short stories) at a rough average of, say, sixty thousand words each, that's a community of women collectively engaged in the production and consumption of well over half a billion new words every year devoted to the story of romance.

This freedom or permission to explore issues of sexuality through romance fiction is not, however, absolute or simple. As noted, some authors feel pressured by it, with this pressure then functioning as yet another way that the romance narrative can become an oppressive imperative. What if you are perfectly happy with your two-and-a half vanilla love scenes, thank you very much? What if you find full-blown erotica distasteful? What if you worry that the growth of erotica could harm romance fiction by mischaracterizing an already stigmatized genre? One erotica author, not unkindly, described to me her colleagues in the sweet camp as "those nice ladies in pink and pearls" and acknowledged a certain tension between them and her sister writers of sexually explicit romance on exactly these points.

A big question in all of this was how spicy the genre can and should get. When I was in the Dallas sky lounge, *Fifty Shades of Grey* had not yet appeared on the scene, and the future of erotic romance was—as it is now—unclear. The subgenre of erotica seemed to be taking off, but some authors believed that the trend was about to die a quick death. "Too many badly written books are killing reader appetite," one top historical romance author told me. She predicted that "once the titillation factor wears off, readers will tire of it." But I must say, the attendees at my Dallas RWA conference didn't seem tired of anything. They seemed energized. A mood of revelry prevailed, and some part of it clearly had to do with sex. Don't misunderstand me: I don't mean to imply that these women

were *having* sex. This place was no orgy. As conferences go, it was probably unusually celibate. From the conversations I had, most of the women
seemed to be heterosexual, with lots of stories of supportive husbands at
home. But this sisterhood was definitely sexually energized; they *owned*
their sexual power.

One prime area where I saw this dynamic at work was in the annual
awards ceremony. The highlight of every national conference of the Romance Writers of America is, without doubt, this gala event. In my four
years of attending their conferences, the Dallas awards night was my favorite, if only because it was followed by a truly epic dessert and chocolate buffet celebration. I have never witnessed such sugary extravaganza
in my life. Texas is, indeed, the land of bigger and better. And sometimes,
in the land of romance fantasy, bigger truly is better. Shot glasses of cap-
puccino cream with brandied berries. Caramelized fruit skewers. Coco-
nut flan with blackberries.

And then there are the dresses. The ceremony is black tie, and the wom-
en seem to relish the chance to dress up, in line with the flirtatiousness of
the genre. Whether young or old, large or slim (and this being America
and Texas, there are a lot of luscious big gals in attendance), tonight is
glam night. Silver and black, red and purple, sequins and lamé, velvet and
silk. Thigh-high slits, strapless bustiers, and plunging necklines. Evening
wraps, matching purses, stilettoes and platform heels. Body glitter and
up-dos. Some looks are more Goth, with black tulle and lace, although
most are soignée and glitzy. Tattoos are in evidence, winking at us from
a cushion of cleavage or tucked into the hollow of a collarbone. There's
even the occasional corsage, provided, I assume, by the few tuxedoed
men in attendance. These women look *fab*. And for the vast majority, they
are not dressing up for a partner but for themselves and for each other.
There's a sense of celebration of each other's beauty, of play with female
adornment and aesthetics. I'm grateful that my own velvet lamé helps me
to fit in. Having no long gowns in my wardrobe, I had procured my midnight blue from an upscale Salvation Army shop near my parents' house
in Canada. Secondhand becomes a tradition for me at later conferences
as well. My favorite source turns out to be a consignment boutique in
Tuscaloosa where an endless wall is packed tight with cast-off pageant

dresses. (The Deep South is the beauty pageant capital of America.) I attend subsequent RWA awards ceremonies dressed in silver sequins or draped pink chiffon, channeling third runner-up in last year's Miss Collard Greens.

The Romance Writers of America awards show is choreographed much like Hollywood's Academy Awards, with slick production values, comedy bits, industry profiles on romance publishing, and a top author serving as emcee. Recognition is given out to the year's best published novels—the RITA awards—and most promising unpublished manuscripts—the Golden Hearts—in categories such as "Best Long Historical Romance," "Best First Book," and "Best Inspirational Romance" (Amish is hot right now). As with the Oscars, RITA award winners receive a much-coveted small golden statue. In our case, "Rita" is a seated woman writing a book. A solo attendee such as me is less common at these events; most women seem to come with friends from their local RWA chapter or with partners from a writing group. As presenters announce the finalists and open the winner's envelope in each category, women scream and whoop for each other, clapping and cheering wildly. Not since I researched my previous book on exotic dance and spent a happy evening in a club where men stripped naked for an appreciative female audience have I been part of such a jubilant and raucous group of women.

In their acceptance speeches, winners often thank their husbands—and occasionally a girlfriend (there are only women up for the awards). "He taught me the meaning of romance" and "He is my hero" are phrases uttered more than once. We hear of a husband who "postponed heart surgery so that I could be here tonight, which tells me that there's nothing wrong with that man's heart." The audience lets out a collective "Aahh" at these moments; romance clearly plays well with this crowd. One woman gets big laughs by offering her "thanks to [her] husband . . . for great sex." Even more than the male partners, however, it's the female friends who get the thanks. Clutching their awards, winners graciously avow they couldn't have done it without their sisters in the Moody Muses, the Playground, the Magic Sweet Crew, or the Success Sisterhood. My seatmate during the Dallas award show, a lovely middle-aged mom writing her first manuscript, tells me that the romance community isn't at all competitive because anyone can get published if she writes a great book. With those ten thousand romance titles coming out yearly, there's always room for one more new author.

After the ceremony, we spill out of the ballroom into the reception area where the dessert buffet is laid out and the bartenders are popping champagne corks. So many women—about two thousand in total at the conference—all dressed up, talking and laughing, happy. The festive mood is infectious. I look down at myself, in my secondhand velvet and borrowed diamonds, strolling through an acre of gourmet dessert with a glass of champagne in hand. I laugh, too. I am glad for tonight's winners, delighted in the support surging through the crowd. Sisterhood is strong here tonight. Woman-Power flows. As one winner said in her speech, "It's amazing to have all this estrogen in one room!" Another thanked the RWA itself, "for empowering women."

At the buffet, I meet such interesting women. Over miniature chocolate éclairs, I chat with a mother and daughter in attendance at the conference together. The daughter is a college student working on a paranormal romance manuscript (*Twilight* came out recently and broody vampires and werewolves were sizzling up the conference corridors). Her mom is an avid reader. When I ask them about the pleasure of reading romance, the older woman tells me about her husband. She describes him as a good man but a bit of a benign oaf who rarely bothers with romantic gestures; she has to beg him to dance at their annual company Christmas dinner. Although he spends much of his leisure time watching TV, he gets exasperated when she is engrossed in a novel. He'll yell at her from the bedroom, "You're still reading at 3:30 in the morning? When are you coming to bed?" This woman's three-word answer to why she reads romance? "Escape from reality," she tells me, rolling her eyes. Romance reading affords her harmless, compensatory pleasure for the lout on the couch who's not at all a bad guy, but still, let's admit, no Fabio.

In a story that runs in the opposite direction, another woman with whom I talk is a twenty-something mother whose husband gave her the trip to the conference as a gift. (A very generous one, as registration, transportation, hotel, and meals can easily add up to well over a thousand dollars. Many of these women make a significant dent in family or personal budgets to attend.) This young woman tells me that her full-time responsibilities for two small children had left her feeling that she was "all Mommy" and little else. But she stumbled across romance novels and began to read them during the kids' naptime. She decided she wanted to try to write such books. Her husband told her she should go for it. But it was Romance Writers of America who taught her that she could.

I think about how the feminist and gender theory to which I am committed pushes us to ask questions about subversion, about social justice and change. How are romance writers subversive of standard norms that can stifle women in terms of how they should be (compliant, sweet, nurturing, groomed) and what romance should look like (male-lead, heterosexual, monogamous, reproductive)? In one sense, the community of romance aficionados does not seem very subversive. They want to change the male boor into the romance hero but they primarily do it on the page, in fiction. How political an act is that, in terms of improving women's real lives? And yet, in another sense, romance stories model and teach what a strong woman and a good man look like and what a healthy romance should be. One aspiring romance novelist whom I meet at the conference tells me that she sees romance as "a subtle soapbox that teaches women about egalitarian relationships"; in her case, she says, reading romance has made her more self-aware and confident, more willing to speak up for herself, and more alert to what to speak up about. In a workshop talk, multi-published bestseller Suzanne Brockmann echoes this language. She derides the notion that romances are "mind candy" and says that her goal in her novels is to provide "recipes for fabulous equal partnership romance." These are strong feminist lessons indeed, sweetened by the obvious pleasure and relaxation that the books offer to millions of women, busy with work and family and home and dealing with life's inevitable stresses. From this perspective, a woman who claims time for herself to do something that makes her happy *is* committing a subversive political act. "Leave me alone: I'm reading, I'm writing" is a feminist battle cry that resounds from Aphra Behn to Virginia Woolf to today.

I order one last item from the waiter—coffee with cream, perhaps simply because I'm enjoying directing a man to serve my pleasure. I don't want that pleasure to end. It's also an attempt to get some of the tipsy out

of me before I have to teeter back to my hotel room on my heels. The waiter is an attentive and polite young man with a fine Texas drawl. Tuning
into the many varieties of pleasure swirling around me at this conference,
I realize that one of them is the fantasy of a man devoted to his partner's
desire. Having escaped from the daily grind of job, kids, errands, and the
laundry pile, I revel like an unrepentant despot in the sheer pleasure of
ordering the waiter to bring me course after delicious course and of him
doing it with a smile, a polite nod, and a snappy "Yes, ma'am." I can't help
but feel that this male acquiescence is part of the appeal of the romance
genre for women readers socialized into the caretaker role. It is the appeal of the genre noted by Janice Radway studying her romance-reading
housewives. The stories are all about men serving women's pleasure. The
heroes love their women with such devotion that these men will risk their
lives and forsake their own orgasms to see their beloveds safe and sati-
ated. These guys know where to find the clitoris and what to do with it.

Sinatra is singing "Witchcraft," and my couple heads back out on the
dance floor. One after another, the songs on the playlist are all about
romance. I'm scribbling away in my field journal, sneaking peeks at the
dancers and playing well the part of a mad woman. But these Texans have
a generous heart, and I've tipped well. They leave me alone to giggle to
myself and write. Another tune by Ol' Blue Eyes comes on, and I sip at the
last of my coffee to listen to the lyrics. Sinatra lingers on the word *forever*
several times in the song, but more as a question or a fear than a promise.
The song pierces through my booze- and pudding-soaked sentimentality
as very poignant and so beautiful. I might even wipe at a tear with my
cocktail napkin.

Later, I look up the song. It's called "How Do You Keep the Music
Playing?" Originally written for the 1982 movie *Best Friends,* with music
by Michel Legrand and lyrics by husband and wife songwriters Alan and
Marilyn Bergman, it was nominated for a 1983 Oscar in the category of
Best Original Song. Sinatra recorded the tune on his last studio album,
L.A. Is My Lady, in 1984, when he was almost seventy years old. It's a
great song for later in life and for my older dancing couple. Like a million other love songs, it riffs on the motif of find-your-one-true-love-and-
live-happily-ever-after, but the genius of the lyrics lies in turning this

romance imperative into an interrogative. The song opens with a long series of questions—doubts and anxieties, really—about the nature of romantic love:.

> How do you keep the music playing?
> How do you make it last?
> How do you keep the song from fading too fast?
> How do you lose yourself to someone and never lose your way?
> How do you not run out of new things to say?
> And since we know we're always changing, how can it be the same?
> And tell me how year after year you're sure your heart will fall apart
> Each time you hear her name?

The song is about the fragility of love. It's about the lover's fear that love might not last, that love is a delicate and rare and precious thing. And Frank's right. You need luck to make love work, as well as commitment and courage and patience and a list of other fortitudes and virtues. Lots of singers have covered the tune—Tony Bennett, Barbra Streisand, Celine Dion—and back home I listen to a few of them. But there's a special poignancy in Sinatra's version. You can hear the age in his voice; he's not belting it out like Barbra or Celine do in their covers. There's a quaver to his singing on some of his lines. He's an older man, asking questions about how to make love last a lifetime, worrying that maybe it doesn't, supposing in the end—it's the best answer he can come up with, the most he can hope for—that maybe love can last, with work and faith and the goodwill of the gods. "With any luck," croons Sinatra, "then I suppose the music never ends."

Love *is* a mystery. Maybe it is an illusion, at least in the sense of One-and-Only-True-Love-Sailing-into-the-Sunset-Forever. So many of us chase love, all our lives, to our detriment, even to our abuse and death, and only sometimes to our benefit. You are right to wonder, Frank: How *do* you lose yourself to someone and not lose your way? How *do* you make love last? With divorce rates sky high, it seems a magic trick indeed. And then comes the confession of this beautiful line: "The more I love, the more that I'm afraid that in your eyes [Celine changes it to "in his arms"], I may not see forever." Love makes us afraid, because it makes us vulnerable. Your partner may say to you one day, "You know what? I'm done."

Maybe she runs off with someone else. Maybe he dies. Maybe you die. Either way, your love is over. You don't get to see forever.

Love *is* fragile. As is life. The couple in their seventies surely knows that death can happen at any moment. Everyone knows it, although we do our best to hide from the knowledge. A good friend my own age died in an instant, on her way home from shopping one sunny Tuscaloosa afternoon, when a motorcyclist struck her car head-on. She left a loving husband and two children. So how do you keep death at bay? Tell me, Frank, how do you keep romantic love alive? How do you keep desire lusty amid the laundry heaps and the squalling children? How do you keep alive the faith in love and happy endings that gives hope and purpose to life and that allows us to believe, despite such painful evidence to the contrary, in the goodness of this world?

Friends, here is one answer.

You read romance novels.

And—if you're really lucky—you write them.

6

Love

Bondage and the Conundrum of Erotic Love

This chapter springs from a question mark.

In April 2009, Princeton University hosted an academic conference on romance fiction and American culture entitled *Love as the Practice of Freedom?* The gathering's interrogative title is a quotation from literary and feminist theorist bell hooks. Conference organizers adopted hooks's key notion of "love as the practice of freedom" to serve as an interpretive framework for thinking about romance fiction in American culture. In order to indicate the open-ended, analytical nature of the conference's project, they appended to hooks's phrase a question mark.[1]

In this chapter I consider the meaning of this question mark. We've arrived at a key question, one that lies at the very heart of this book: What exactly *is* the nature of love depicted in the romance narrative that plays such a central storytelling role in the culture? This narrative insists that love is a good thing, a practice of freedom, as hooks suggests. But, clearly, we love badly as well, to our disadvantage, our loss, our heartbreak, sometimes tragically to our death. Blinded and besotted, we waste our love, throwing it away on unworthy partners. All this is love, too.

So, *is* love the practice of freedom? And, if so, in what sense? What does it mean to "practice" freedom? When, under what conditions, does love become the practice of the opposite, namely some type of bondage?

Can one distinguish *good bondage* from *bad bondage* in the practice of love? How do these issues play out in the narratives about romance in the popular culture and in genre fiction, including in BDSM erotica novels that feature literal bondage?

Against the backdrop of these questions, here's what I think: Romantic love is an ambiguous—and sometimes dangerous—practice of freedom *and* bondage. The romance narrative that directs us to find love and happiness risks turning into a practice of "love as bad bondage," but it can also model and teach the ideal of "love as good bondage" in all of its complicated glories and pitfalls of commitment and constraint. Furthermore, this romance narrative, as it plays out in its infinite variations in romance publishing and the wider realm of popular culture, constitutes the prime cultural site for working out the meanings and dangers of this ambiguity of love that entails both freedom and bondage. Thus the massive popularity of genre romance fiction. This ambiguity of romance holds particularly true for women in a culture still marked by patriarchy, but also, in different ways, for men who risk such labels as *pussy-whipped* simply by acknowledging love.

LOVE AS FREEDOM: "TO BE NEAR HER I WOULD CARRY WATER IN HELL"

At the Princeton conference, acclaimed romance novelist Beverly Jenkins read and discussed the prologue from her 1996 historical romance novel *Indigo*. The moment was a powerful one, followed by much engaged discussion with the audience. *Indigo's* prologue is an epistolary narrative functioning as backstory to the novel as a whole. It recounts the how and why of a man literally giving himself into slavery in order to be with the woman he loves.

David Wyatt is a free, land-owning black man in 1831 America, working as a merchant sailor. In the two letters that constitute the novel's preface, David writes to his sister Katherine to explain that he's given up his freedom in order to marry his pregnant lover, an enslaved woman on a southern plantation: "For the love of a woman named Frances Greaton, I have forsaken all I am and given my freedom over to her master. I am a slave now, Katherine." He feels deeply the incomprehensibility of what he's done, "but Katherine," he tries to explain, "to be near her I would carry water in hell."[2] Jenkins's story, after this preface, follows Hester Wyatt, the grown daughter of David and Frances. Hester has become the Michigan owner of a freedom house on the Underground Railroad and a conductor of escaping slaves. She harbors a wounded man who turns out to be Galen Vachon, a famous conductor and fabulously wealthy free Creole black man, handsome as sin. Romance ensues, including an eventual reunion of Hester with her long-lost mother, Frances, all on the eve of the Civil War, with its promise of liberation for all African Americans.

In regards to this prologue's text of terror, its plot of horror, Jenkins sympathetically defended her character David's action, with great rhetorical persuasion, based on the notion of *love*. Love can be a practice of freedom, even when it occurs within—sometimes precisely *because* it occurs within—a culture viciously tainted by the violence and dehumanization of racism. Given David's love for Frances and given the institutionalized slavery of their time period, David *had* to give himself into slavery. His love and the situation, Jenkins implied, led him inexorably to that choice.

Jenkins evokes here bell hooks, a renowned theorist and cultural critic on issues of race and feminism in America. Hooks, in the much-cited and reprinted chapter from her 1994 book *Outlaw Culture* entitled "Love as the Practice of Freedom," argues for the political and healing power of love: "The moment we choose to love we begin to move against domination, against oppression. The moment we choose to love we begin to move towards freedom, to act in ways that liberate ourselves and others. That action is the testimony of love as the practice of freedom."[3] In the following decade, hooks went on to write a "Love Trilogy" about the pressing need for love, in its many forms much wider than solely romantic love, amid what she decries as a culture of lovelessness: *All about Love: New Visions* (2000), *Salvation: Black People and Love* (2001), and *Communion: The Female Search for Love* (2002). This concept, however, of love as the practice of freedom is a complicated one, as exemplified in this narrative of David and Frances. What I want to examine are the dynamics of both freedom *and* bondage at the heart of romance narratives that can lead to a nexus of liberation and domination, of empowerment and loss of self, all in the name or service of love.

We may begin with the etymologies of the words themselves. Intriguingly, *to free* and *to love* share common roots. They are among the very oldest words in the English language, with forms dating back to the ninth century. According to the *Oxford English Dictionary*, the original, now obsolete meaning of the verb *to free* (Old English stem *freo-*) is "to love" and "to embrace, to caress." The meanings of *free* in its early Germanic cognates are "to love," "to woo, court," "to have intercourse with," "to marry." These cognates are probably related to the Sanskrit *pri-*, "to please, delight," and *priya*, "beloved," "dear," and "wife." We see these roots in the similarity, for example, of the German *frau*, "woman" and "wife," and *frei*, "free." In English, this linked sense remains in the old-fashioned colloquial expression *to make free with*, as in to take liberties with someone, to treat that person in an intimate or sexual manner.

The *Oxford English Dictionary* conjectures that these cognates and related meanings stem from a common Indo-European base word with the original sense of "one's own." This intertwining word history of *free* and *love* "perhaps arose from the application of the word [*free*] as the distinctive epithet of those members of the household who were 'one's own blood', i.e. who were connected by ties of kinship with the head, as opposed to the unfree slaves. In the context of wider society only the former would have full legal rights, and hence, taken together, they would comprise the class of the free, as opposed to those in servitude."[4] To be *free*, in this sense, is to be loved by others who share with you common membership in a family or clan or tribe, as opposed to the unloved slaves outside that inner circle. One is loved because one is free and not a slave but also—the paradox begins to develop—because one is tied firmly by and within bonds of community to others.

LOVE AS BONDAGE: "THAT LOVE IS AN AWFUL THING"

If love and freedom are tightly related in these ways, how is it that love seems so often to lead us astray into some of life's worst binds and heart-breaks? Does, for example, *Indigo*'s backstory regarding David count as such heartbreaking tragedy, when his love for Frances leads him to forsake his own freedom? How can David's act of giving himself into slavery be compatible with true love? Jenkins herself raises these questions in her author's note at the back of the novel, when she quotes the factual slave narrative that inspired her own fictionalized version. In an oral history recorded as part of the Federal Writers' Project from the 1930s a former slave told the story of an acquaintance, a free man named Wyatt who gave himself into slavery in order to marry a slave girl: "He was crazy to do that. That love is an awful thing, I tell you. I don't think I would give my freedom away to marry anybody."[5] Jenkins has her heroine Hester echo this assessment in the novel, after Hester recounts her parents' story to Galen: "Love must be a terrible thing," Hester concludes. Later, she adds that love "brings only sadness," as she lists all the examples she knows of tragic and unrequited love, including a local mixed-race couple unable publicly to live out their love.[6]

The clichés tell us that love heals all wounds, that love conquers all, and yet an obvious opposite truth, captured also in cliché, is that love blinds. Love can blind us to our own best interests, to our very self-preservation. We can love, to our detriment, someone unworthy of our love. "Love is a battlefield," warned American rocker Pat Benatar in her 1983 hit single. "I can't tell you why," she sang, "but I'm trapped by your love, and I'm chained to your side."[7] A longstanding philosophical and theological tradition, with fifth-century church father Augustine as its representative, warns against the bondage of sexual desire: Concupiscence, that excess of lust for sensual gratification, blinds our rational will against proper orientation to the higher good. But it's not only sexual lust that can lead us astray. Even love, purportedly the nobler emotion that purifies lust into committed romantic attachment, brings trouble as well. Bondage themes of both desire and love as trap and chain and battle, cause of immobility and blindness and confusion, are perennial themes spun out about the darker side of romance.

As early as the late seventeenth and eighteenth centuries, British amatory fiction writers cautioned how erotic love could breed illusion. Eliza Haywood—a precursor of today's popular romance novelists, along with Aphra Behn and Delarivier Manley, known collectively as the "Fair Triumvirate of Wit" or, even better, the "Naughty Triumvirate"—particularly championed this theme. Haywood was a top-selling author of her day, along with Daniel Defoe and Jonathan Swift. Her writing gained her a tagline from the contemporary poet James Sterling, later oft-repeated and grand enough to breed envy in any twenty-first-century bestselling romance author: Haywood was the "Great Arbitress of Passion."[8] The cover of Haywood's 1725 publication *Fantomina; or, Love in a Maze* bears as an epigraph the couplet by the English poet Edmund Waller: "In love the victors from the vanquished fly. / They fly that wound, and they pursue that die." In these lines, love is literal battlefield, a space where victors wound and then flee and where any left-behind lovers foolish enough to mount pursuit can only fail. No second chances or happy endings here.

In *Fantomina*, Haywood warns readers (women readers, in particular) of these dangers of love—of vanquish, wounding, and death—through, for example, her heroine's angry musings when she learns of the faithlessness of her lover Beauplaisir: "'Tis thus our silly, fond, believing Sex are served when they put Faith in Man: So had I been deceived and cheated, had I like the rest believed [her lover's story of his constancy]. How do some Women (*continued she*) make their Life a Hell, burning in fruitless Expectations and dreaming out their Days in Hopes and Fears, then wake at last to all the Horror of Despair?"[9] This protagonist is herself engaging in a highly elaborate series of charades and deceptions to entrap the wandering attentions of the fickle Beauplaisir, so the lady holds no moral high ground. False expectations, fruitless hope, endless waiting, despair, deception, betrayal, cheating, and lies—along with plenty of lusty "Happiness as the most luxurious Gratification of wild Desires could make" and the passionate Bliss of the "strenuous Pressures of his eager Arms." Such is the mixed lot of those who love.[10]

All too frequently, literature suggests, we are deluded by sexual and romantic passion. An earlier paradigmatic example of this theme of love as bondage comes from the English Renaissance poet Edmund Spenser's 1595 sonnet cycle *Amoretti*. In sonnet 37, Spenser plays with layer upon layer of imagery about the female beloved as beguiling trap:

What guile is this, that those her golden tresses,
She doth attire under a net of gold:
And with sly skill so cunningly them dresses,
That which is gold or hair, may scarce be told?
Is it that men's frail eyes, which gaze too bold,
She may entangle in that golden snare:
And being caught may craftily enfold,
Their weaker hearts, which are not well aware?
Take heed therefore, mine eyes, how ye do stare
Henceforth too rashly on that guileful net,
In which if ever ye entrapped are,
Out of her bands ye by no means shall get.
Fondness it were for any being free,
To covet fetters, though they golden be.[11]

Note Spenser's use of *fondness* in the last couplet, which shares with Haywood's use of *fond* an older definition of "foolishness." In a usage now archaic, *fond* originally meant silly, infatuated, foolishly credulous, and in an even stronger sense, idiotic, weak-minded, mad, and dazed. All of that, Spenser suggests, it is for a free person to covet fetters, even if they are beautiful and golden. The golden wedding band, the golden hair net, the young beauty's blonde tresses: Spenser fuses together all three images to represent the bedazzling trap of love. All are snares, nets, fetters used by the woman—craftily, with guile, sly skill, and cunning—in order to entangle, catch, enfold, and entrap weak and frail men, who are made to gaze boldly and rashly through woman's guile. In other words, we are blinded to truth by love—or at least by passion and desire. Even more harshly, suggests the poem, only an idiot exchanges freedom for the band/bond/bondage of marriage.

And yet, Spenser composed sonnet 37 as part of a complex and glorious poetry cycle commemorating his courtship and marriage to Elizabeth Boyle, a young Anglo-Irish beauty who became his second wife the year before the poems were published. The overall cycle celebrates not only his love for Elizabeth but the notion of the Protestant love-marriage itself, as a sacred covenant—a bond—uniting spiritual and physical love. And so we may read his sonnet's warning against the fetters of love ironically, as gentle self-mockery, as play with standard literary conventions, perhaps as an instance of his equivalent of the contemporary romance novel's "dark moment" of discord and breakup, and even as indicative of this paradox of love itself—a practice that entails both binding and freeing, both blinding and seeing.

So, the great conundrum: Is love worth the risk? Embodiment entails vulnerability for all creatures. In some ways, this holds true especially for women. Sexuality is perhaps the messiest, the most complicated and dangerous, aspect of human embodiment. It raises complex psychosocial issues: anxiety over losing control; fear of relationality and the vulnerability of opening oneself to another; male fear of women's sexuality rooted in childhood fear of the mother; the instability of male gender and sexual identity in mother-reared patriarchal societies; women's fear of men's assault—and men's fear of such assault—in a world that bears witness to the willingness of so many to use rape to humiliate and control; and, finally, the sheer chaotic power of the sex drive and the ability of desire to derail reason. All this creates a conundrum in the culture, a type of trap in the messages fed us: *You want to love, you must love, love is good for you, and yet love can also be bad.* This puzzle of erotic love is portrayed and explored in the endless permutations arising from the pop culture wells of genre fiction, Hollywood films, advertising, and more, which people consume in massive quantities across the culture, in fantasy exploration of how the puzzle can ever work out.

Here's a notion: *Erotic, romantic love may be the most dangerous thing we do to ourselves.* Romance entails the risk and vulnerability of opening your heart, as well as letting another person into your body or take in a part of your body. It is an ominous commonplace, continue the clichés, that "All is fair in love and war" and in "the battle between the sexes"—or, more simply put, that "Love stinks," as sang the J. Geils Band on their 1980 album title song. A more recent number-one hit single video offers up pop sweetheart Taylor Swift acting out every stereotype of the jealous girlfriend turned crazy violent: "'Cause darling, I'm a nightmare dressed as a daydream," she sings in "Blank Space" as she attacks the boyfriend and his car.[12] Love can and does go dreadfully wrong. Dates turn into rape. Domestic partner abuse batters and kills people—mainly women, but men also—every day. The romance novel rake, in reality, rarely re-forms, even though the culture makes such bad boy scoundrels look darkly appealing. The cruel truth is, love can break your heart; shred your self-esteem; ruin your finances; leave you with unwanted pregnancy, dis-ease, and social shame; get you killed by a stalker who won't let go.

Such examples of love are clearly not in the practice of freedom. Such examples do not liberate ourselves or others, to recall hooks's words; in-stead of freeing us *from,* they involve us *in,* actions of domination and op-pression. These dark and tragic stories of love—and Haywood's, Waller's, and Spenser's literary depictions of deception, blinding, and battle—are in fact the opposite: love as the practice of bondage, or, more precisely, what I propose to call love as bad bondage. Such love can entail bond-age to an unworthy partner, bondage within cycles of abuse, and bondage to low self-esteem such that one feels undeserving of anything better in one's love life.

Hooks helps us here in *All about Love* by insisting love is a practice by which she means we should always think about love as "an action rather than a feeling." Adopting M. Scott Peck's definition from his classic 1973 self-help book *The Road Less Travelled,* hooks says that love as practice is "the will to extend one's self for the purpose of nurturing one's own or an-other's spiritual growth." She explains this definition by stating, "When we are loving we openly and honestly express care, affection, responsi-bility, respect, commitment, and trust."[13] According to this definition, love as bad bondage is clearly not love, or not what the romance narra-tive would deem "true love," as in that narrative's mythic imperative to find your one true love and live happily ever after. A "one true love" is one who loves you truly, along the lines hooks develops, instead of falsely, as in love as bad bondage. As a true love, I must be willing to *act,* in an extension of self, in ways that are caring, affectionate, and respectful, in order to nurture my beloved's growth. Such true love also implies that, as I nurture my lover's growth, I nurture my own as well. We cannot, do not, love another truly if we abandon the duty to love ourselves and to act in our own best interests. True love, in other words, does not make one into a martyr or a doormat. If such loss of self happens—if I extend my-self to the extent of loss of self—the relationship is not true love. A true love would never request from the beloved, nor allow of that beloved, any practice not in the beloved's best interest. Such practice would be false love and bad bondage.

If, therefore, false love is a practice of bondage, then true love is its opposite, a practice of freedom, as indeed hooks says. And yet it's not so simple, because true love, or good love, entails its own type of bondage as well. Love is never a simple joy or pleasure, if for no other reason than the sure and stern knowledge of the beloved's eventual death. In every moment of love is this proleptic experience of loss, making all deeply felt love poignant and tragic. Such is one cost of love. Pushing further, we arrive at the heart of this chapter's thesis: *Romantic love—as a life practice among lovers and as a literary-cultural narrative—is a conundrum of freedom and bondage.* Love presents the enigma that it simultaneously both binds and frees the lovers. Put another way, the bonds of love entail love as a practice of avoiding bad bondage while learning to accept—and even to revel naughtily in—good bondage.

So, point one: Love *is* bondage. But it's a good bondage. Love as the practice of freedom results in good bondage. We can even map this claim out mathematically:

romantic love = the practice of freedom = good bondage ≠ bad bondage

This bondage or binding involves a restriction of freedom that is key to popular culture's vision of romantic love. To love is to forsake all others, to cleave to a one and only, to tie the knot, to settle down, to give up any other possibilities for romantic or erotic love in a monogamous pair-bonding that will last unto death. The culturally iconic Christian marriage vows, for example, bind two partners together: "I take thee . . . to have and to hold . . . forsaking all others, as long as we both shall live." Returning us to the words' original etymological roots, love becomes an act or experience of freedom precisely *because* that love binds you to one very specific and special other. "By binding me, you set me free," as another songster rhymes.[14]

Romance fiction portrays true love as both binding *and* freeing, and, ultimately, as freeing *because* it is binding. This paradox is a tricky one and raises the complicated questions of empowerment and self-deception at the heart of much suspicious feminist analysis of the genre. *Indigo* continues to provide illustration, since David's decision to enslave himself makes this point about love so acutely: He makes himself a literal slave for love. In this vision of the romance narrative, love is a self-slavery in which you bind or shackle yourself to another and give up certain freedoms, but willingly, forsaking such freedoms as lesser in significance and appeal and as ultimately forfeitable. Yet, we can ask, did David's disposition of himself into slavery in order to be with Frances go too far, into the earlier described problematic loss of self? It's not hard to argue yes. David gives up self quite literally: the self-determination of legal freedom for the political, economic, and social bondage of slavery in the antebellum American South. Frances herself protests David's decision: "To her credit," he writes his sister in the novel's preface, "Frances was furious upon learning what I'd done and refused to speak to me for days." David has given up too much to be with her and should not have gone so far, Frances argues.[15]

David's defense, however, is that he only gave up his outer self in order to gain his heart's true desire. To put it another way, as a black man living in a time when slavery and racism curtailed the physical, political, economic, and social freedom of so many African Americans, David chose to define freedom for himself. The one freedom whose exercise he refused to give up, the freedom he staked his life on and declared most precious to him—most central to his personhood and sense of self—was the freedom to love. While hooks argues love is the practice of freedom, in composing her novel Jenkins offers the twist that the ultimate freedom is the practice of love. The blurb on the novel's back cover details the challenges Hester and Galen must overcome before they "can find the freedom only love can bring." Love makes possible a very special and precious type of freedom—the freedom to give one's heart to a worthy other, to fulfill one's being in fully partnered union, to achieve one's highest and most complete self through the practice of true love. When it comes to love, romance novels suggest that there is no difference between the practice of freedom and the practice of good bondage. Love as the practice of freedom is a bondage one chooses freely, a bondage one accepts and embraces, with full consent. True love equals freedom equals good bondage. David was right, in other words, and so is Jenkins: *David becomes most free when he sells himself into slavery to be with his beloved Frances.* It is a paradox so contradictory as to be absurd. And yet it is true, or else love means nothing. Such is the conundrum presented by this vision of romantic love.

Perhaps surprisingly, precisely because of this conundrum, the literal bondage stories of the recently popular BDSM erotica subgenre can work particularly well as romance fiction. True love, since it entails this binding of two bodies and souls at its very narrative core, lends itself to literal bondage scenarios—as in the tale of David and Frances; as in the kidnapping, captivity, and "bodice-ripper" stories that have long formed a controversial part of the popular romance oeuvre, going all the way back to Samuel Richardson's 1740 *Pamela* in which the hero confines Pamela to a country estate to force her agreement to his pursuit; and as, of course, in the 2011–12 blockbuster *Fifty Shades of Grey.*[16] This BDSM erotica subgenre illustrates the extent to which romantic love intersects with both literal and metaphorical bondage and often dramatizes explicitly the difference between good and bad bondage.

Hooks used the terms *domination* and *oppression* synonymously and in opposition to her central term, *freedom.* A BDSM fan or practitioner, however, would see things differently. For example, at an academic romance fiction conference I picked up a brochure by the National Leather Association, a pansexual BDSM/fetish education and support network with the mantra "Safe, Sane, and Consensual." The brochure distinguished between domestic violence, which it defined as "non-consensual dominance and control," and healthy BDSM, in which "two or more consenting adults consent to exchange energy, power, sensations, or experiences (however extreme) in ways that fuel their mutual happiness and increase self esteem." Importantly, the definition further insists that "in a healthy BDSM relationship all parties involved are actively invested in the well-being of each other and themselves."[17] Accordingly, literal bondage practice—the practice of dominance by a master over a submissive—can be either good or bad, either liberating or oppressive, depending on whether or not it is done *lovingly*—that is, practiced with full consent by all partners as, in hooks's terms, an expression of "care, affection, responsibility, respect, commitment, and trust." When depicted within a narrative of true love, the practice of BDSM bondage often serves the narrative function of freeing one or both of the lovers from some metaphorical bad bondage: bondage of self to shame or doubt or insecurity or old trauma or stultifying conventionality.

One example is James Buchanan's 2009 romance novel *Hard Fall*, a fascinating gay, Mormon, rock-climbing, detective mystery, BDSM love story. The hero, Joe Peterson, is a Utah sheriff's deputy and committed Mormon; he's also deeply closeted in a homophobic rural and conservative church community. Lust flares and then love blooms between Joe and Kabe Varghese, a daredevil climber working at a local ranch on parole. Some mild flogging, bondage, and dominance—with the aid of harness and rope from rock-climbing rigs—make this point about the difference between good and bad bondage. As the more dominant Joe puts it, "I don't know how to explain the difference, but I knew. He fought *against* me, but he didn't fight *me*. The point of all the writhing and squirming wasn't to get away. Naw, he just didn't want to make it easy on me." Later, his lover Kabe says, "You take control and make me feel things. . . . You're doing it 'cause you want to enjoy it and you want me to enjoy it, not because you wanna push me around." By the end, readers have no doubt that true love is what these two men share—respect, commitment, trust—and that liberation is what they experience as a result of the bondage and dominance in their love play. The novel's closing paragraph seals that certainty. The happy-for-now and potentially happily-ever-after ending employs as its central metaphor a rope that ties Joe and Kabe together. This metaphor combines the lovers' favorite sport of rock-climbing and their enjoyment of bondage practice with the perennial trope of the bonds of love. Joe, now publicly out, is in "free fall"—in trouble with his Mormon church, exposing himself and his family to shame, dragged through a court case as defendant, and on disciplinary suspension—but because he has true love (and hot sex) with Kabe, the reader can trust that all will be well. Joe muses, "My rope was playing out at fifty miles a minute, but there was this hard slip of nothing boy anchored solid to the face and he had me on belay. So I figured it was about time to let myself fall, fall real hard, so long as I landed in his arms."[18]

Such BDSM narratives help romance authors make the point that romantic love is most definitely, unabashedly, a form of binding or bondage, but that a definite difference exists between good and bad bondage.
For worthy souls willing to do the hard work of practicing love, this good
bondage—whether of the Dom variety or Spenser's golden fetter of the
wedding ring—can be very good indeed.

MEN AND BONDAGE: "AT LEAST I'M NOT PUSSY-WHIPPED"

Building on this point about love as a type of bondage is a second important point, namely that this good bondage aspect of romantic love can
be much more transgressive and risky for men than it is for women. Romance renders men vulnerable to accusations of unmanliness simply by
their acknowledgment of love for a woman.

There are different models of manhood at work in literature and the
culture. The contemporary men's movement, for example, traces out
archetypes ranging from the warrior to the king to the minstrel to the
lover.[19] The combined archetype of the warrior-king is the model of manhood most often adopted in the romance novel. We call him the alpha
hero: the patriarchal ideal of a man who is socially and culturally dominant, physically large and powerful, handsome or at least striking in his
looks, capable of violence, rich and successful, self-confident and tending
to arrogant. Romance alpha heroes embody these characteristics in ways
that vary with the conventions of the particular subgenre or publishing
imprint, the details of the storyline, and the skill of the author. In clever
romances, an alpha hero can be strong in unexpected ways, stretching stereotypes while still meeting reader expectations. The hero might become
more alpha through the development of his character arc: more professionally successful or wealthy and gaining in social renown, for example,
as love enables his growth. Some romances feature a hero less fantastical
and more everyday in his realism, more of a regular run-of-the-mill good
guy, or what the genre calls a beta hero. But even in romances without a
typical alpha, the male protagonist rarely strays too far from this model of
masculinity. He may not be a full-blown warrior-king, but he is never, for

example, presented as a short, ugly, obese, dirt poor, and unskilled social outcaste. In the romance, he is still and always hero material. A central irony of the heterosexual romance novel is that the hero ends up queering this ideal of alpha masculinity by calling into question the values of control, domination, and self-sufficiency on which this notion of manhood is based. As hooks writes, "To choose love is to go against the prevailing values of the culture."[20] When the romance hero chooses love, he goes against the prevailing values of patriarchal culture.

Our hero typically starts out needing no woman and dallying in games of *eros* merely for pleasure. Yet according to the true-love narrative, for a man to love a woman, he must be willing to make himself emotionally and physically vulnerable to her. To love truly—for man, woman, and gender queer alike—is to *fall* in love, to lose your position and equilibrium. It is to give someone else power over your heart, your happiness, your very sense of self. When a woman grants such power to a man, she leaves intact traditional norms of masculine dominance and feminine submission. However, no true alpha male would give such power to a woman. He would not, cannot, entrust so much of his self to someone who should be inferior to him and in his control. When a man does—when the warrior-king opens his heart, when the rake reforms, when the hero is domesticated—from the point of view of patriarchal culture, love makes him less of a man. Love emasculates the hero. Love restricts his freedom in ways that the culture describes in negative bondage metaphors. We call him leg-shackled, tied to apron strings, married to the old ball and chain, henpecked, and, in perhaps the most dramatic and telling label of contempt, pussy-whipped.

A key task of the popular romance narrative is to negotiate this dilemma for the hero. How can he still be the alpha male if he has given someone else power over him? How can he be dominant if he is submissive to his beloved and to the power of love itself? As an example of this dilemma, J. R. Ward's bestselling paranormal romance series *The Black Dagger Brotherhood* features a scene in the first novel *Dark Lover* (2005) where the hero vampire-king Wrath—described as "six feet nine inches of pure terror dressed in leather"—can lust after Beth, the half-breed heroine about to transform into vampire herself, but must fight his growing love for her. In this scene, Wrath goads a happily mated brother, Tohr-ment, that Tohr is weak because he's "a male who's dumb enough to love his *shellan*." Tohr responds, "I'm lucky to have found love." Ward writes of her vampire hero's inner struggle: "Wrath's temper surged, set off by something he couldn't put his finger on. 'You're *pathetic*. . . . At least I'm not pussy-whipped,'" he tells Tohr.[21]

Although the king of the vampires lacks the self-awareness at this point in the story to identify what sets his temper "surging," readers easily rec-ognize the dynamic at work. Wrath's budding romance throws him into an impossible dilemma: By making him reliant on a woman, the relation-ship threatens to weaken him according to the codes of patriarchal man-hood by which he has lived his life, but by completing and maturing him through love, the relationship also promises to strengthen him according to the codes of the romance narrative. Wrath will need to work himself out of this dilemma by developing a new understanding of manhood that defines strength not in terms of emotional distancing from women but instead in terms of his love for Beth and his eventual complete surrender to her. This surrender and acceptance of female power is symbolized in their marriage ritual, overseen by the vampires' ruling goddess figure of the Scribe Virgin, when Wrath kneels at Beth's feet, head bowed, and al-lows his vampire brothers, including Tohr, to carve Beth's name into his back.

A similar example, although in a lighter vein, comes from Robin L. Rotham's 2008 erotic romance *Big Temptation*. In the epilogue—happily-ever-after in place, the hero and heroine now married, their first child safely delivered—the hero Barrett is teased by his brother when the hero-ine pulls Barrett away from a football game, that iconic sport of tough-guy manhood. "You're whipped, man," the brother mocks. But then the brother's fiancée calls him over to address wedding invitations: "'Speak-ing of whipped,' Barrett grinned at him."[22] These two men are both hap-pily enough in love that this scene, unlike the previous vampire passage, reads as comedic. The brothers good-naturedly laugh at each other, and us at them, about being at their women's beck and call. But from within the perspective of patriarchy, for a man to open himself to love is a deadly serious business indeed. It means he's weak, pathetic, pussy-whipped.

One can dismiss such accusations as insecurity on the part of males overcompensating for their sexual anxieties or as bitchy manipulation on the part of females who know just how to strike at the Achilles heel of patriarchy by taunting a man that he is less than manly. While *pussy-whipped* and its tamer truncated cousin *whipped* are not, admittedly, standard terms of polite conversation, they do show up regularly outside romance fiction in the hallways of pop culture and colloquial conversation, played with in this vacillation between comedy and contempt. Apps exist for digital devices to make the sound of a cracking whip, perfect for mocking a friend at just the right moment. The terms are rowdy commonplaces, upholding the rougher end of the spectrum of masculine caricature that is inhabited in the middle ground by such stock comedy figures as the leg-shackled boyfriend or the hen-pecked husband.

A recent advertising campaign by Pinnacle Vodka shows how pussy-whipped imagery resonates through the culture. Pinnacle is a top-selling brand of premium French vodka that describes itself as "innovative" and "fun." The vodka comes in twenty-nine different flavors, including the highly popular Whipped Cream offering. A series of ads in *US Weekly* and *Cosmopolitan* promotes this flavor under the tagline "Whipped so good." One of the ads, entitled "Reason to get him Whipped #3," shows a bare-chested young man—muscled and handsome—carefully ironing women's shirts at home. The other images in the series have men chopping onions in the kitchen, vacuuming the house, or juggling an armful of dirty towels while, in this last advertisement, a woman luxuriates in a bubble bath in the background. The message? Housework is for women and for emasculated guys who are so in love or in lust with a woman that they stoop to these cleaning tasks themselves. Women whip men into the shape of female desire (dominatrix-trained domestic sex slave?) using pussy as whip, weapon, lure, reward. The women then reward themselves with whipped-cream flavored cocktails. In all this, men become comedic and complacent dupes or, when the humor is darker or absent, pitiful and derided half-men. A man can only be pussy-whipped so far before he is no longer fully a man, before he becomes woman-like. "What are you?" the taunt then becomes: "A pussy?" None of this, of course, has anything to do with vodka but is clearly evocative enough to justify millions in advertising dollars and to win entertainment industry write-ups gushing, "It's no secret that Pinnacle Vodka has become the life of every party."[23]

This discourse about pussy-whipped males has another aspect to it: It is gay. The discourse is homo-social, even homoerotic, in its concern that men not overinvest their energy in the world of women. One man becomes peevish and jealous when he feels ignored by a male friend who was previously available and a good buddy but who now spends his time with a woman. This first man accuses the defecting brother of succumbing too deeply to the lure of women, of allowing himself to be drawn too far into their orbit. The brotherhood fears the defection of this man to the world of women and heterosexual romance; it tries to rein him back in through shame, by calling into question his manhood. To be pussy-whipped is to be in thrall to a woman, to be not *in control* but instead *controlled by* her and her sex. The anxiety behind the pussy-whipped accusation serves to keep intact the bonds among men. It maintains the primacy of male-to-male allegiance over any claims levied by females.

In romance novels, this trope of the whipped man is evoked and acknowledged as the nightmare anxiety of patriarchy. But the cure is simple: true love. Love is the crucible in which a man refashions his sense of manhood in order to gain immunity from derision. Genre romance portrays the patriarchal heroes—in various ways dominant and even domineering—as made open, vulnerable, emotionally forthcoming, and soft through their bonding and surrender to a woman. Once these men experience true love, they heroically refuse control and leadership in the romantic relationship. Their love is strong enough to defy traditional requirements for manly dominance and to break them free from their emotional straight-jacketing. Love defeats the need for strong-and-silent self-sufficiency, as our hero now willingly confesses "I need you."

Within a patriarchal framework, as long as the man retains control, his domesticity has traditionally been acceptable. Domesticity has, in fact, routinely been celebrated in "Father Knows Best" plaudits of a man's rightful tender regard for wife and children, his devotion and duty to family. But if, in his emotional openness and devotion, he gives up autonomy and his role as leader in the home, he then becomes less of a man. Note that the opposite scenario in which a woman gives over too much of herself to a man—straying into the territory of love as bad bondage—paints her as a fool or dupe but doesn't make her less of a woman. In this way, heterosexual romance endangers patriarchal masculinity: "You're whipped, man," teases or sneers one man to another, from across this divide of love. At the same time, the romance story refashions such masculinity into what it views as a different and better model of manhood. The hero *willingly* shackles himself to a woman. He accepts the label pussy-whipped without shame and turns it into a badge of honor: "I'm lucky to have found love," as vampire Tohr put it. Or as the Pinnacle Vodka men signify, going calmly and contentedly about their household chores, they are "whipped so good."

LOVE AS THE PRACTICE OF FREEDOM AND BONDAGE

All of this leads to a final point. Romance novels present love as an important key to making a man good: to reforming the rake, softening the alpha, maturing the playboy, settling the man down. They do so by presenting a different vision of a strong man, one that allows for an egalitarian model of partnership love shared with a strong woman. But herein lies another conundrum: *This romance story, in breaking down patriarchy with its toxic norms of masculinity, may also be a key prop in maintaining patriarchy.* While the fantasy space of the novels is one in which masculinity is rendered benign to women through this reworked definition in which a man loves truly and gives up authoritative control over his beloved, nevertheless patriarchy—wily beast that it is—may remain intact through other toxic fantasy components of the genre.

The romance hero, for example, despite falling in love, often continues as the symbolic warrior-king of his fictional world. He remains in some form master of his domain. Thus Tohr and Wrath are still violent, dominant, controlling vampires—simply not toward their soulmates. The hero's power endures unbroken, partly so that it may be used in his woman's defense. The fantasy space of the romance genre imposes these contradictory, perhaps impossible, demands on the fictional alpha hero. Journalist Norah Vincent, in an undercover experiment to study masculinity by living in disguise as a male, noted a similar phenomenon in *Self-Made Man:* "Women were hard to please in this respect. They wanted me to be in control, baroquely big and strong both in spirit and in body, but also tender and vulnerable at the same time, subservient to their whims and bunny soft."[24] Big and strong and bunny soft—a tough act to pull off in the fulfillment of women's desires, even for a fictional romance hero.

In this connection, we can revisit the traditional question of concern raised by feminist and critical analysis of romance novels: Do they tend to lead women into, or risk encouraging women to put up with, love as bad bondage? To get a man at any cost and hold onto him no matter what, since a woman needs a man to be complete? For example, what difference would it make if *Indigo*'s plot were reversed? What if Frances were the free northern black woman who met an enslaved man on a voyage south and then gave herself into slavery in order to be with him? I suspect a predominantly female reading audience would find little fantasy pleasure in such a plot. It strays too close to the worse stereotypes of a disempowered doormat woman who foolishly throws away self and pride simply to be with a man. For a woman to say, "To be near him I'd carry water in hell" sounds downtrodden in the extreme. It sounds like the voice of a woman who has internalized her oppression and debased herself. None of the cultural power that adheres to maleness protects a woman in this self-enslavement.

Romance stories both lead us into these landmines and seek to offer guidance around them. Romance novels can portray and model love as good bondage over and against love as bad bondage, with a genre-wide effect of teaching the difference between the two and insisting that women hold out for love as good bondage. The genre teaches, in other words, what a good man looks like. The hero, no matter how alpha, never domineers over the heroine in any way fundamentally harmful to her. He may sputter at her in a spat, he may tease her in flirtation, he may as a good Dom tie her up and flog her, he may even harm her in some early tragic misunderstanding for which he'll mightily atone. But the hero—by definition—will never truly hurt the heroine, for the reason that he truly loves her. In this regard, romance novels and the wider romance narrative in popular culture illustrate quite splendidly hooks's practice of love: actions of will that nurture the beloved's growth through open and honest expressions of care, respect, trust, and commitment.

But along with this positive effect—and maybe also undermining it— romance novels offer the seductive and dangerous fantasy that the heart-breaks of love will not win out in the end. As Shakespeare noted long ago, "The course of true love never did run smooth." Yet the romance story promises immense rewards for the worthy soul who risks all for love. In one form this promise often takes, the romance heroine gives herself physically and emotionally to the hero before she knows enough to trust him as deserving of her love. This hero—by definition—always does turn out to be deserving. The genre risks here the trap of bad bond-age, in the blinding glory of the fantasy world wherein the match of love is fixed and players always beat the odds. Will the commitment-phobic scoundrel ever settle down? Will the prickly wounded soul ever open up to love? Never fear, they always will. Although the heroine's voice of cau-tion warns her to beware, she can't resist the man—nor the callings of her own wayward heart and lusty loins. The romance narrative rewards her and vicarious readers for this frankly foolish move of her faith in love, and the couple lives happily ever after.

For David and Frances, however, all does not work out. Within two and a half years of David's voluntary enslavement, he falls sick and dies. He has watched, powerless, while his beloved Frances was sold to the Deep South. The child of their love had already been sold to the Carolina Sea Islands (from whence Hester will eventually get her nickname *Indigo* and the book its title). David and Frances have no happily-ever-after. In the world of slavery and institutionalized racism within which they live, such an ending lies beyond their reach. It skips their generation, although it does bestow its grace finally upon their daughter. Hester finds true love with Galen, who is even able to reunite her at book's end with her long-lost mother, Frances. The biblical story of Job comes to mind. The happy ending of that book—which can be read as a love story between Job as blameless, faithful wife and God as fitful, jealous husband—sits uneasily in the heart and mind of a reader who has suffered with Job through the death of all ten of his children, the loss of his life's wealth, and the col-lapse of his health, all due to a capricious bet between Satan and God. Is

Job's ending a happy one—"the Lord even gave to Job twice as much as he had before" (Job 42:10)—or was the suffering that preceded this restitution so horrific that no happy ending can compensate?

Similarly, the horror in Hester and Galen's backstory and in the sociopolitical story in which they live makes a fully happy resolution difficult. On the book's final page, Hester reflects, "The end of slavery would make the picture complete, but until it occurred she would be thankful for life's smaller joys."[25] There is a reason why not many romance novels, with their obligatory emotionally satisfying and optimistic endings, are set among African Americans in the antebellum South. Here, then, is a final question: If knowledge of social injustice, such as slavery, makes it difficult to maintain the fantasy pleasure of the romance novel, may the reverse also be true, that the fantasy pleasure of romance makes it difficult to maintain knowledge of social injustice? The satisfaction and pleasure of the happy ending may obscure the extent to which romance scripts for women, men, and love can become not just narratives in novels but imperatives in readers' lives. I have in mind scripts about appropriate ways to be a woman, to be a man, to be heterosexual, to mate for life, and to have children—scripts that continue to figure as norms in much romance storytelling. The real and fantasy experience of love may risk blinding us to the ongoing inequality and injustice around issues of gender and sexuality which can bind people into narrow roles that don't fit their individual needs or nurture their moral growth. At its worst, the romance narrative may risk drugging us against engaging in hooks's hard work of ending oppression through love as the practice of freedom. Again, love blinds us, as it binds us, as it frees us.

In all the ways that hooks describes, love *does* have a political edge, a healing touch. When we act lovingly, we liberate ourselves and others. We move against oppression. We make the world a better place. We practice freedom. And yet, love is also a fierce and terrible wonder. To love someone is to expose yourself, in an act of awesome vulnerability, to the pain and suffering of knowing your beloved will die and may cease to love you. You may prove unequal to the love. The world may turn against you and your love—in a bet by God or through institutional racism or war or tragedy or loss or injustice—and your love will make no difference.

Frances will still be sold to the Deep South. We all know there is, in truth, no happily ever after. Love can offer no such guarantee. Perhaps people read and write romance novels because they know this truth all too well and seek simultaneously, paradoxically, both to hide from this knowledge and to work it through, by repeated engagement with narratives about these poignant and piercing conundrums of love. In chapter 8, we see how the ending of the romance novel attempts to resolve this conundrum of erotic love in a rich fantasy of reparation and healing that holds together the tensions of this paradox.

For love *is* a practice of freedom. And love *is* a practice of bondage. Such is the tangle of the human heart and such the tragic beauty of the human condition.

Notes from the Writing

*"Between the Sheets" and Other Moments
toward Romance Novelist*

Yesterday, I visited the tomb of Aphra Behn.

This remarkable woman lies buried in the cloisters of Westminster Abbey in London, near kings and queens and the leading statesmen and literary figures of the United Kingdom. During Behn's lifetime in the seventeenth century, she attained a similar high level of regard and fame, although she also spent time in a debtor's prison. I was at the Abbey with Ted and our British friends Georgie and Ian for the annual Commonwealth Day Observance. (I got to see the Queen!) The cloisters adjoining the church were technically closed to the public for the day, but after the ceremony I asked several uncertain officials if it might be possible to visit. Finally I happened upon a young woman verger whose eyes lit up as I explained my request: "Ah, you want to see Aphra Behn! In that case, come with me." This spirited woman, with dark hair and red lips to match her swirling verger's cloak, ushered us through an ancient and arched wooden door. "Over three thousand people are buried at Westminster," she said as her heels clicked briskly over the worn stones of the north cloister. "We get lots of visitors wanting to see one tomb or another. But Behn is my favorite. In my opinion, not enough people ask to see her." She led us straight to the tomb.

Little is known about Behn's early life. It seems she married young and was widowed soon after, leaving her with the relative social independence of a widow but requiring her to earn her living. This she did in a way never before carried out by any Englishwoman: She wrote. Her output included plays, poetry, stories, and translations and met with both commercial success and critical acclaim. She helped develop the novel as a new literary form that we now take for granted. Based on her firsthand adventures in Surinam, South America, she penned *Oroonoko,* the first antislavery novel to appear in English. She wrote amatory fiction such as *The Fair Jilt,* which stands as precursor to today's popular romance novels. Behn's plays and novels contain frank and erotic plotlines about feisty women who lead bawdy lives. She composed stories about the complications and pleasures of desire for women. She doesn't resonate with every ideal of a sex-positive feminist in the twenty-first century, but she worked her will with words to earn her living, her country's respect, and her place in history at Westminster Abbey.

We stood in the east cloister and read the inscription carved into Behn's gravestone: "Here lies a Proof that Wit can never be Defence enough against Mortality." The inscription, however, is only half-true. Yes, Aphra, deemed in her day the "sole Empress of the Land of Wit," died, as must we all. But the legacy of her writing lives on, beyond her own mortality. Her role in the development of the novel and the genre of romance fiction endures. In *A Room of One's Own* Virginia Woolf states, "All women together ought to let flowers fall upon the tomb of Aphra Behn, for it was she who earned them the right to speak their minds." And so yesterday, with the verger's blessing, I did as Woolf urged. Going to the Abbey, I wore a violet orchid pinned to my breast.

Now the orchid lies on her tomb.

And today I am back at my writing.

Thank you, Aphra.[1]

*   *   *

How does a professor learn to write a novel, if all that she has ever written before are academic books and journal articles? How to go from nonfiction to fiction? How, in other words, could I get beyond footnotes, impersonal voice, and the use of evidence in the demonstration of a thesis to, instead, deep point of view, character arc, and dialogue—let alone to sexual tension and those steamy love scenes? And what is there to learn about the popular romance industry and genre in this attempt to publish a romance novel?

The answer is, I learn a lot. I learn about the revolutionary change afoot in publishing with the rise of digital e-books and self-publishing. I learn about the storytelling and craft elements of the romance narrative in a whole new way. I learn about the exceptionally supportive romance writing community. I learn about the intense love of both the genre and the writing life that animates this large and lively community. But first and perhaps most of all, I learn how difficult is the writing task—at least for me—and how daunting is the goal of publication.

The learning arc takes me years. And this despite the fact that I've read romances all my life and that the overlap between professor and romance novelist is not an uncommon one. The majority of published novelists—be they literary or popular fiction writers, and no matter what their genre—start out with a day job. Despite the *Fifty Shades of Grey* debut success of E. L. James and the fact that four out of the twelve highest-earning authors in the world write romance novels (James, Danielle Steel, Janet Evanovich, and Nora Roberts), the truth is that a minority of romance authors earn a sufficient living from their writing to support themselves or a family.[2] Instead, they keep that day job. As it turns out, being a professor is a pretty good day job. It means that you know how to do research, have easy access to a library, and possess solid writing skills (even if the intricacies of dialogue and other fiction techniques remain a mystery). You may even have a specialty area, such as history or literature, that might help with the novel writing. Several successful current romance novelists are college teachers, such as historical authors Eloisa James and Madeline Hunter, and others such as Jennifer Crusie have an academic background.

Their success stories heartened me. Ever since I was a teenager, I've wanted to write historical romance novels. My goal was always that specific: not just to be a generic author but to publish the type of romance fiction that I liked to read. I wanted to write big, juicy, swashbuckling novels whose covers featured a buxom woman with billowy long red hair in a risqué embrace with a muscled hero in black leather boots. I made an early attempt to write while in graduate school in Boston when I drafted a hundred pages or so of a historical romance set in England during the War of the Roses. The story was called *Conquered* with the epigraph—of course—"Love conquers all." It featured a spunky (American meaning) heroine trying to end a bitter feud between her family and the handsome new lord on a neighboring estate. I joined Romance Writers of America for a short while during this period. I got far enough to see how difficult it would be, both to finish a strong manuscript and to find a publisher willing to put my story on bookstore shelves. The writing was a great escape from drafting my dissertation—perhaps *too* tempting a distraction—but I didn't see how I could combine the academic career that I wanted with the giddy delights of romance writing.

For one thing, I found it tough to master the very different styles of these two crafts of writing. I was pouring all I had into drafting a dissertation acceptable to my advisors and into establishing academic credentials. I didn't feel I could succeed in both realms of higher education and fiction publishing at once. The other problem was that the job market was abysmal for humanities Ph.Ds. If I were lucky, maybe one or two universities somewhere in North America would offer me a full-time, tenure-track job upon graduation. That job offer would be my one chance at staying in the ivory tower. I couldn't risk blowing it. And I knew enough about the politics of academia and the reputation of romance fiction to realize that co-mingling the two worlds was risky. Even *I* called these books trashy novels, although I meant it with affection. How would highbrow university circles, with their proclaimed leftist and feminist principles, receive the news that one of its aspirants was trying to publish a novel entitled *Conquered*?

During my interview dinner at a Mexican restaurant in Tuscaloosa where I couldn't get a margarita to quell my nerves because it was a Sunday and Alabama had rules to keep the sinners in check, I made what felt like the daring move of stating my desire to write romance fiction. A senior male professor on the interview committee had asked me about my outside interests and how I might incorporate those into the classroom.

Because they'd told me that the New College program at the University of Alabama welcomed innovative and quirky interdisciplinary interests, I took a deep breath and told them all about romance fiction. Alabama was the only job interview where I disclosed this fact. It turned out to be a sign of the extent to which it was the right place for me.

But even once hired at New College, I still saw fiction as a project best left for the future. So I abandoned the manuscript and let lapse my RWA membership. *Conquered* became that proverbial "book under the bed"— the manuscript you keep near for when the moment is right. Eventually, years later, after sufficient academic publishing to earn me tenure and promotion to full professor, the career scaffolding seemed in place and the moment at hand. The desire to write romance fiction hadn't gone away. Far from it. And the confusion and concern over how to combine both forms of writings had disappeared. My academic work had come to focus on the exploration of gendered fantasy spaces in popular culture. And guess what? That's exactly what romance fiction is—or at least one way to understand what's going on in these books. But instead of going back to *Conquered*—it is still under the bed—I decide to start afresh. I got a new idea for a series of four interconnected novels set in early Victorian England, around the time of the 1848 revolutions that rocked Europe with their demands for people's rights and civil liberties. My novels would trace the stories of four girlhood best friends, grown now and each facing challenges—poverty, abuse, wartime spying, murder attempts— that she must resolve with the help of her friends and, of course, a tall and handsome stranger.

I rejoined Romance Writers of America as a wannabe writer, determined this time to really learn the ropes and to work my way up the writing ranks. My goal is twofold: both to do field research for an academic book on the function of the romance narrative in popular culture and to acquire the writing skills and industry knowledge to start publishing romance novels myself. In my early interviews with authors, I tell no one that I want to write romance, that I yearn to be like them. It is my secret, about which I am insecure and full of longing. I also begin to read more widely in order to broaden my understanding of the romance genre. As I expand beyond my favored historicals into the subgenres of gay/lesbian, erotic, science fiction, suspense, paranormal, contemporary, and inspirational romance, I see how the emotional dynamics across the stories are similar in terms of the characters' initial conflict, attraction, and eventual resolution of their relationship into lasting love. Many of the books appeal to me as much as the historicals do. I realize that what I really like is the emotional grip of a fast-paced story and a dramatic character arc as people find themselves through love. I start to read Harlequin romances as well. These are the shorter books that come out monthly in series lines, with titles often involving stock phrases such as *Greek Tycoon, Secret Baby,* and *Maverick Millionaire.* I'd never read these books before, out of a disdainful prejudice that quite shames me now. It's true that some of the Harlequins are weak from a literary perspective. One has characters and setting sketched out so thinly that it reads like a dreamscape. But others are tightly written with great word craft. And when they're not, it doesn't matter; the story still works. *Every one* of those Harlequins grabs me. They make me cry, and I can't put them down.

My local Romance Writers of America chapter is too far away for me to join, but I sign up for various email listservs where aspiring writers chat and trade questions and answers. Every month, I devour the informative magazine *Romance Writers Report* cover to cover. I attend four years of the fabulous RWA national conferences, held in a different city every summer. In between my interviews, I squeeze in all the how-to craft workshops that I can, taking copious notes about pacing, dialogue, character development, and sexual tension. At the industry panels, I learn about how to find an agent and what the various publishing houses are looking for these days. Lessons on deep point of view (invented by Jane Austen, says one panelist) and how to avoid head-hopping all fascinate me, to say nothing of those panels on how to create sizzling sexual tension on the page.

The community of fellow—sister—writers in the Romance Writers of America is amazingly friendly. One might think that the atmosphere at the conference would be competitive, with so many new writers vying for publication deals. Instead, the vibe is hugely supportive. I witness published authors encouraging and advising the not-yet-published, in examples ranging from formal panel presentations to random restroom pep talks. At one conference, a multi-published author whom I'd interviewed earlier kindly waves me over to join her table for lunch. Already there is an older woman who introduces herself as an avid reader working on her own manuscript and a huge fan of my interviewee: "These people are like your favorite movie stars!" the older woman tells me. "And what are you going to do when you get back home?" the author asks this woman, clearly prompting her on their agreed-upon plan. This author answers her own question, with a big smile: "You are going to write, write, write!"

Once I gather the courage to commit to my novel writing and come out as an aspiring romance author, I am supported and mentored by authors who read my drafts, provide feedback, and advise about the industry. There is a real sense of women's community in this world of romance fiction, of a nurturing space where one can learn the guild's craft. I *never* hear an author say that an aspiring romance novelist will not succeed, despite the fact that a large majority of the members in Romance Writers of America are not yet published. What I hear instead, I and the other wannabes, over and over again, are lessons of perseverance and encouragement. I wonder about all of this positive thinking: Is it fair? Does it give false hope? But you really never do know in publishing. The conference stories bear it out, with keynote speaker testimonials along the lines of "I only became a *New York Times* bestseller after twenty years of rejections when I had to borrow money for the stamp that I was too poor to afford for my last-chance submission." I meet one woman in the hotel elevator, a successful lawyer, who has been writing romance on and off for fifteen years while trying to get published; her first novel is finally coming out at the conference with another book accepted for publication next year. When I interview one successful writer about how she started her career, she replies dryly, "I was at home with three young children under the age of six and I needed a fantasy life." Although she endured many rejections, she quotes with a big laugh the Tim Allen line from the *Star Trek* knock-off *Galaxy Quest*: "Never give up! Never surrender!"

Inspired, I go home to write, write, write.

I begin to grasp the discipline necessary to live the writing life and to produce manuscripts at the rate of a successful published author of popular fiction: at least one or two and sometimes three or four finished projects of 60,000 to 100,000 words a year. The top advice that I take in? Set a regular word count for yourself and stick to it. Visualize this goal by creating a chart of some sort. Write before you let the day in, first thing in the morning, before the day job gets to you. The romance community is full of stories about successful writers who start off as moms writing at 4 AM before the kids wake up. If you are not a morning person, do not allow yourself to go to bed until you have made your daily word count. I marvel at authors with a writing schedule of 15,000 words per week who produce draft manuscripts in six weeks. How do these women do it? However they can, it turns out. Professional writers grant permission for chocolate, wine, whisky—whatever it takes to stay at your desk until you've met your word count. Somewhat conversely, those words don't have to be great. Another piece of common advice I hear is to give yourself permission to "put shit on the page." We're not talking brilliant, edited prose good enough to keep as final copy. You edit later. It's the blank screen that's the killer.

There are tools of the trade needed for this work. I start to think of fiction writing as an artisanal craft, like that of a skilled mason who builds a wall brick by brick. One key tool is the ability to torture your characters. Fiction is driven by conflict. There have to be problems driving the story: big, bad problems that look impossible for the characters to resolve. I learn the GMC model of storytelling: goal, motivation, conflict. The romance story is about central characters, each desperately motivated to achieve a crucial goal but prevented from doing so by various conflicts, both internal and external. These characters fall in deep love and lustful desire—sometimes one character before the other, sometimes the lust before the love or the love before the lust. The relationship itself often worsens the conflict and only makes it harder for the characters to achieve their central goals. So, figure out how to torture your characters. Take your initial ideas for conflict and then, make things as bad as you possibly can.

Readers must ask how—*how?!*—could these people ever be together? Gender, sexual orientation, and number of lovers pose no problem nowadays in the plethora of modern romance possibilities. Perhaps he is a duke and she is a courtesan. Or he is a vampire and the other he is a shape-shifter. Or she is duchess and he is a pirate. Or a ménage of lovers come from families who are lifelong sworn enemies. Or she is a cop and she is a criminal. Or she has learned never to trust a man and he never to risk opening his heart to love. Their attraction and budding love seem doomed by a gulf of conflicting values and plot points, but watch! Love transcends such difference and heals wounds. By the end, all is guaranteed to work out in an emotionally satisfying resolution. More than once during this project, I hear the popular prejudice that "Anyone can whip out one of these novels." Try pulling it off, buddy, and you see that it's not so simple.

While the active listservs, annual conferences, and monthly magazine are my learning ground, the Romance Writers of America contests prove to be my testing ground. RWA is organized along a chapter model with well over a hundred local writing groups scattered across the country (including six in Canada and about twenty online special interest groups). Many of these local chapters run writing contests as fundraisers and as a service for aspiring romance writers nationwide. Organizers usually ask writers to submit the opening pages of their manuscript, although some contests focus on the moment of the couple's first kiss or the mid-story dark point when the relationship seems most destined for failure. An entry fee of around thirty dollars gets you feedback on your writing sample from chapter members. The best contests also provide the chance for finalists to be judged by top industry editors and agents. I come to see that therein lies the real worth of the contests, although the feedback from fellow writers is hugely valuable as well. But it is the access to these final-round judges that is precious, because it can otherwise be incredibly difficult for a new writer to get her work read by acquiring editors and agents.

Many editors at the traditional publishing houses—referred to collectively by their geographical location as "New York" or as the Big Five (Hachette, HarperCollins, Macmillan, Penguin Random House, and Simon and Schuster) will only read manuscripts sent to them by agents. New York wants manuscripts, in other words, already sifted through and vetted by an industry professional who knows how to judge for quality, potential, and marketability. A new writer must often be "agented" in the parlance of the industry in order to get her work before these powerful editors and to avoid languishing in a slush pile. And yet these agents are themselves equally hard to access. I learn at RWA workshops that the agents' email inboxes are literally flooded with newbie queries—hundreds of requests *every day* from aspiring authors such as me seeking representation. One well-known agent reports that she received 25,000 queries last year and took on only six authors as new clients. That's how many people are out there writing and how stiff the competition is. Given these realities, the contests are a great way to gain feedback on a manuscript and, if you are lucky, to win a reading by an agent or editor who just might be willing to take you on.

It takes me a while to figure out this system and to get my first fifty pages ready to submit. I choose my contests with care; I look for ones where the final-round judges are agents or editors who acquire historical romance. I also limit myself to contests that don't require a synopsis along with the sample pages. The synopsis is supposed to summarize the book's characters, conflict, and plot in a pithy and engaging few pages. It's often referred to as the "dreaded synopsis," and I haven't figured out yet how to write it. Indeed, I haven't even figured out the full plot of my novel, so I stick with those contests that only ask for the first fifty pages.

The first contest that I enter is a disaster. My opening scene gets poor marks for pointless dialogue and no action. One judge finds my hero to be "creepy." So much for any dreams of a quick and glorious triumph in the publishing market.

I rewrite. I work on dialogue, which I find extremely tricky. I've never written dialogue before. Even such seemingly simple skills as how properly to punctuate it and how to use dialogue tags (she said, he said; she gasped, he grunted) bedevil me. My Romance Writers of America conference notes and articles from the *Romance Writers Report* provide invaluable help as I slog away at using dialogue to advance the plot, develop the characters, and reveal goals and motivations (sometimes by having characters say the opposite of what they really mean). I have an "aha" moment about love scenes when an author on a conference panel entitled "Sex and the Single Title" shares one of the best pieces of writing advice I ever hear: Make your sex scenes worsen the conflict for the central characters. Sex shouldn't solve their problems but must complicate the plot and intensify the conflict keeping the lovers apart. The sex should be great but should also make things worse. (The one exception is a love scene in the story's finale, as part of the happily-ever-after ending.)

In the midst of attempting to incorporate such revelations into my writing, I stumble upon a contest that intrigues me: the "Between the Sheets" contest, sponsored by the Greater Detroit chapter of the RWA. Two factors appeal. Entrants are to submit a love scene between their central characters, and the final round judges are an agent and an editor who both specialize in historical romance. My manuscript at this point is called "Lessons of Love." I am not penning it in a linear fashion from beginning to end, but I do have a fully drafted seduction scene that occurs halfway through the story. I resolve to enter it.

Eventually, my results come back. I not only make it to the final round, but—holy shit!—I miraculously win the contest. The judge who works as an acquiring editor gives me a final score of 36 out of 40 and praise for the novel's set-up. In answer to the score sheet question asking whether the writing is free of clichés and shows strong voice, she comments, "The only part that hung me up a bit was his dialogue. I know he's a philosopher, but it still seems a bit flowery for a man in the throes of passion." *Dialogue!* I kick myself; tricky, tricky. Still, I must be getting somewhat better because, at the bottom of her form, she writes those magic words every wannabe longs to hear: "Please email me the full at your convenience."

The second judge is a well-known agent whom I hear speak at a Romance Writers of America conference panel. She gives me a perfect score: straight fives all across the board for emotional impact, pacing, point of view, technical writing skills, strong chemistry, and even for presenting the love scene "in a fresh way." Her written comments are short but laudatory: "There is strong development of the character as well as building the emotion in this scene. Great work." She asks for the full manuscript as well. I am naive enough at this point to believe that this win and the much-coveted invitation to "submit the full" from not one but two industry professionals means that my manuscript is about to be snatched up. I congratulate myself on how easy this process is: Draft your story, enter it in a contest, win, sell it to the publishing editor on the judging panel. Voilà!

Feverishly, I finish my draft of the full-length manuscript and send it in. When I finally hear back from the judges, the truth begins to sink in. Editors and agents request manuscripts from wannabes like me all the time, sometimes just to get rid of us or to be polite or because, in an age of easy electronic submissions, they might as well request a manuscript that they can delete within seconds. But agents and editors take on very, very few of these projects. A request for a full, in other words, means little. Generally, it means squat. After receiving my submission, the editor gets back to me within two and a half months, which I later learn is startlingly prompt. The news, however, is not good.

> To: Roach, Catherine
> Subject: RE: Between the Sheets Contest
>
> Hi Catherine,
> Thanks again for submitting your manuscript LESSONS OF LOVE. We really enjoyed your writing, but I'm afraid we didn't feel the hook was strong enough to stand out in the market place. I'm sorry this project won't work for us, but we'd be happy to take a look at any different manuscripts you may have in the works.

When the agent contacts me, she is more blunt. Her earlier "great work" and perfect score has now, upon consideration of the complete manuscript, led to a decision to pass on the project.

> To: Roach, Catherine
> Subject: RE: query
>
> Catherine:
> While I am eagerly looking for quality commercial fiction . . . I found the repetition of backstory to quickly become tedious, and the secondary characters seemed rather flat and one-dimensional. . . . Other agents may well assess your manuscript differently. . . . I wish you the best. . . . Thanks for giving me this opportunity.

So much for the contest win. I admit to experiencing a moment of deflation. Many listserv postings deal with this feeling of rejection. Writers get a lot of it, and it can be hard to bear. One aspiring writer with whom I chat at an RWA workshop confesses it's precisely the rejection that has stopped her from submitting her manuscript recently. She's been working on a medieval romance but with little success. "I've entered some contests," she tells me, "but it's hard to get negative feedback. I've had some hurt feelings from it." I can certainly sympathize, but my academic writing took me down this route before. I queried publishing houses by the dozens for my three scholarly books and reworked each of those manuscripts innumerable times. My own adage about writing, the one that I badger my students with over and over every term, is that good writing doesn't come from the writing but from the rewriting. So I dust myself off. I know that I can improve my romance manuscript. I rename it *Master of Love* in an effort to ratchet up the intensity. And I rewrite some more.

The feedback in the agent's rejection letter is actually very useful. I begin revisions by cutting out my clunky use of backstory. "Avoid info dump," another contest reviewer puts it helpfully, if not elegantly. As I learn more about craft, I come to grasp how backstory needs to be worked into the present of a narrative. I am supposed to reveal key aspects of my characters' goals and motivation bit by bit and at the exact right plot point, dribbling in only as much information as needed to avoid reader confusion but enough to tantalize and maintain reader suspense. Both too much personal background about the characters and too much historical background about the time and place of the story fall into this category of the info dump. They grind story pace to a halt. So no paragraphs on how and why my heroine came to be an impoverished orphan bookseller in Victorian London or how the German Revolution of 1848 affected British politics.

I also volunteer to judge in the national Romance Writers of America contest for unpublished manuscripts—the coveted Golden Heart Awards—in order to become further involved in the RWA and better acquainted with the range of my fellow aspirants' work. Much of this work, I soon see, is excellent. This high bar explains why I get nowhere in the Golden Heart when I enter the awards competition myself the following year. Since these contests aren't landing me an agent or an offer of publication, I decide that I need a new strategy. I prepare to launch an all-out effort to contact agents directly in the hopes of finding one willing to represent my work and get it in front of an acquiring editor. By consulting various online resources such as advice columns on romance author websites, publishing industry resources including *Literary Market Place* and *Publishers Weekly*, the list of recommended agents maintained by Romance Writers of America, and databases at the sites *Preditors and Editors* and *Agent Query*, I develop a master list of more than seventy literary agencies and agents who acquire romance. I decide on my criteria: I want a reputable agent on the RWA recommended list and not warned against on any other list, one whose agency seems open to new author submissions (some websites warn only to contact the agency if you are already an established and bestselling author), who accepts email queries (faster and easier to send out), who represents my subgenre of historical romance, and who is female.

This last criterion, as a large majority of romance industry agents are female, does not cut out many potential candidates. It does, admittedly, represent a form of discrimination on my part. I try to push myself to think through this bias: Really, Catherine LaRoche, you're prejudiced against male agents? Isn't such gender bias against your lofty principles? My justification is that this project has so much to do with female reading practices and writing communities that I don't want to drag a man into it at this point. Also, I just don't want to discuss sex scenes with a man. Strange, but it seems icky. The status of men in Romancelandia is ironic in this regard. Fantasy men loom huge as a focus of much desire in the stories, but women—myself included, it seems—are less than fully enthused about letting actual men into this space. One of my earliest interviewees at a Romance Writers of America conference is a soft-spoken but keen young man who is trying to get his first romance published. He reports feeling somewhat marginalized within his local RWA chapter, all women except for him: "They are always very nice to me but it's hard to really join in the group," he says somewhat wistfully. I'm not surprised. Part of the appeal of the genre is that it offers such a supportive community for women. Even authors who could gain sales by marketing more to men are ambivalent about doing so: "I know who my core audience is, and they are women," one long-established author tells me. "I don't want

to risk losing or alienating them by also trying to bring in male readers."
A new author echoes the point in another interview: "This genre is by, for,
and about women," she tells me, as part of her explanation of the appeal
of the genre. With the market so firmly female-oriented, I reason that my
ban against male agents is justified, if not entirely enlightened.

Using my criteria, I winnow down my master list from seventy-odd
names to a shortlist of thirty-eight potential agents. I begin to system-
atically query them all with a one-page description of my writing background and my story pitch. These agent queries, along with the fact that
I have already submitted a full manuscript to an acquiring editor, qualify
me for "PRO status" in Romance Writers of America. Membership in the
PRO community of practice recognizes attainment of a certain professional status: not yet published but seriously pursuing such within the
industry. When my little PRO pin arrives in the mail, I tack it to my office bulletin board for encouragement and good luck. Of the thirty-eight
agents whom I query, twenty-seven of them eventually reply, some within
a day or so, many with two weeks, some only after months. The other
agents on my list never reply at all. Most who do get back to me send a
short rejection form, politely indicating that the project does not fit their
needs at this time. Without taking offense, I call it a PFO—a "please fuck
off." Eleven agents ask me for more material: six for the partial manuscript and five more for the full. I send those materials out to the request-
ing agents and wait again.

Their rejections begin slowly to pile up in my email box. Some agents
simply send a template PFO. To one agent who had requested my manuscript but never replied, I send a follow-up inquiry months later; she responds with an email that she thought she'd already rejected me. Others
send comments along with their rejection, which I always appreciate as
valuable learning moments. One agent writes, "I wanted less telling of
their feelings and more showing—perhaps even in simpler prose." This
point is the biggie of storytelling how-to rules: Show, don't tell. Romance
typically uses a deep third-person point of view, meaning that the reader
is inside a character's head, thinking and feeling along with the character. Describing the physical sensations of a hero or heroine's thoughts
and emotions is better than narrating these responses. "Her stomach

clenched at the thought of facing him again" is better, for example, than "She felt fear at the thought of facing him again." Showing a character's GMC through their actions or dialogue is stronger and more direct than telling the reader in a summary narration. I've been working on my show-don't-tell but evidently not enough. This same agent comments further: "For me the novel was missing the chemistry and character development I want to see in a romance: at times it read more like an academic history than a novel, such that even the flirtations and arguments between Callista and Rexton felt distant and cool." Shit, I think, I'm writing romance fiction like a professor.

I rewrite some more. My sentences, I start to realize, are often very long. Compound sentences with multiple dependent clauses clog up the text. I become impatient with my wordy prose. For God's sake, have years of academia left me incapable of writing a simple one-verb sentence? I split up sentences, ruthlessly deleting excess phrases and whole paragraphs, even when it hurts. I use the word finder feature and my thesaurus and dictionary to vary my prose and banish anachronisms. I overuse words and phrases: Apparently, I am over-fond of "titillate" and of having my hero's "golden hair glint in the light." You must be willing to kill your darlings, goes the advice, in the sense that you shouldn't become too fond of any particular descriptions or scenes. If material is not advancing the plot at a good clip, be willing to jettison it. The inimitable Susan Elizabeth Philips puts it this way in a conference workshop: "Leave out the boring parts." It's excellent advice, really. Delete, tighten, intensify, rewrite.

Another agent accompanies her rejection with the phrase that she hadn't "fallen in love" with my writing and didn't "feel the spark." Is the romance story so powerful, I wonder, that even agents use this narrative of love to frame their reactions to the manuscripts? Other agents who take the trouble to write feedback say that they enjoy the story, just not quite enough. One comments, "I really like both the idea and title and think the book has some real charm. Unfortunately however, it felt a little staid to me. There was something about the writing and the story itself that just didn't bring it that next level for me. I kept waiting and hoping it would have that extra oomph." Another agent calls the story "a little too familiar." A third links her rejection to the fact that "the explanation of the heroine's arcs and responsibilities are too trite." The plot drags, avers yet another; it needs "more propulsion." A final agent assures me that "I read your sample in full and I must admit I was a bit torn on this. Your writing is really lovely, you have a wonderful narrative voice, and the dialogue seems genuine." Hurrah on the dialogue, at least. "But my concern," this last agent concludes, "is that the story has a bit of a familiar, predictable feel to it."

I sense that I am getting closer to a strong and sellable manuscript, but how to give it that fresh drive, that extra oomph that they are all looking for? How to make an agent fall in love? Just as I am getting to the end of my list of agents, one of my very last possibilities responds to my query almost immediately and with a request for the full. She includes the hope-inspiring comment that my project intrigues her "long-dormant inner academic." Courtney works at what one of my writer friends enthusiastically dubs "a real agency," a full-scale New York City literary agency with a long history. When I double-check their website, my eyes widen (show, don't tell) on reading that they represented Sartre and Kafka. I send off the full, crossing my fingers. Within a month, this agent reads and responds to my work. Courtney doesn't offer to represent me but neither does she reject me outright. Instead, she proposes a detailed series of revisions to my manuscript, sending specific insider advice on exactly this point I've been trying to suss out about how to bring the story to the next level.

Over the course of the next seven months, she sends me notes, we talk on the phone, and we even have a brief chance to meet in person at the annual RWA conference. The meeting is in New York City this summer. One big motivation for aspiring writers such as me to attend is the chance to sign up for agent appointments. These pitch sessions are highly desired, and the agents' timeslots fill up fast. But the meetings are nerve-wracking as well. In the romance community, agent pitches induce a terror level worse even than that of the dreaded synopsis. My PRO status entitles me to book into the schedule in advance, and Courtney and I arrange to meet at one of these appointments that function on a speed-dating model. The agents sit in long rows of desks in a ballroom. I and the other hopefuls wait in sweaty, chattering clutches in an adjacent room until volunteers wrangle us into lineups based on our prearranged ten-minute timeslots. We nervously trade stories and practice our pitch lines as we edge slowly up to the front. Then a bell rings, someone shouts "Time!" and we're shoved into the pen like cows to slaughter. We sit in front of our designated agent and try to sell our story. When time is up and the bell rings again, you leave. It's considered a great breach of etiquette to try to squeeze in another pitch.

When the drill sergeant yells "Time!" for my pitch, I advance to meet Courtney, and the ten minutes fly by in a blur. She suggests that I switch the point-of-view character in a couple of the scenes in order to increase the impact of the story and to address show-don't-tell. "Raise the stakes," Courtney also advises me, for both Callista and Dominick. In other words, torture them more. Make her totter more dangerously on a genteel edge of poverty and loss of reputation at the opening; make him suffer more in his backstory. Set up the plot and get it rolling more quickly with problems and conflict immediately on the page. I feverishly take notes on Courtney's suggestions and agree to finish yet another draft before the end of the summer. There is no guarantee that she will represent me, but I like her ideas and agree that they will strengthen the manuscript no matter what happens next.

So I leave the cow pen and go home to rewrite again. I change the opening, have a pair of high-society ladies plot to destroy Callista's reputation. I get Callista evicted and her belongings thrown on the street. I give Dom a cold and jealous father and brew a murder plot with a "publish or perish" theme to amuse my own inner academic. My closing sex scene is a little risqué and nontraditional; Courtney had initially suggested that I tame it down. I admit here to a brief moment of self-righteousness: "Am I being policed?! Am I not allowed to stretch the conventions of the genre?!" But once we talked it through, I understand that Courtney was right. Callista's bold new self was unearned and too big a leap from her earlier stage of sexual innocence. Chastened, I realize it's not that the genre must stick to its tropes but that I need to write a better character arc. I edit to allow Callista a wilder side that awakens gradually throughout the story so as to give the final sex scene more resonance and credibility. I polish the prose throughout and resubmit the whole thing to Courtney when the school year starts up again in the fall. And then I wait.

And wait.

Finally, at year's end, when I've almost given up hope of hearing from her again, her email pings into my inbox one day.

> To: Roach, Catherine
> Subject: RE: QUERY: Master of Love
>
> Hi Catherine. It's taken far, far longer than I'd like, but I'm finally pleased to be able to say I've finished reading the revised MASTER OF LOVE. Long story short: I love it. I'd love to represent you. I have a few small "tweaks" I'd encourage you to make to the manuscript before sending it to publishers, but honestly (and I don't often say this) I'd be comfortable sending it out as-is.
> My Best,
> Courtney

WOW! Miracle of miracles—I actually have an agent!

Within a rather short time after that, Courtney finds an editor at Simon and Schuster who is willing to take on *Master of Love* and its follow-up, *Knight of Love*. But there's a catch, a rather big one. Simon and Schuster offers to publish my novels in its newly launched e-book only imprint, Pocket Star. E-readers are taking off, particularly for the romance and erotica titles that constitute a large share of digital fiction. The new business model for Simon and Schuster and other major publishers is to capture this emerging market with a strong focus on e-publishing. A different set of contract terms accompany this shift: higher royalty rates for e-books (reflecting the publisher's lower cost, as they don't have to produce physical copies and ship them around the country) but, in the case of a newbie author such as myself, a very small advance. It dawns on me the extent to which I am entering the world of fiction publishing at exactly the moment of huge sea change. For the first time since Gutenberg invented the printing press in the fifteenth century, a book no longer means a tangible product with pages that one turns over by hand. E-publishing makes it less expensive and less chancy for publishers to take on authors who lack an established fan base. One bestselling author warns me, however, that these realities may also lead publishers to commit less effort to developing the careers of debut authors.

Instead, these authors are expected to do much of their own publicity and marketing and generate their own sales. In this brave new world, computer literacy and social media savviness are the skill sets increasingly in demand. The *Romance Writers Report* and my listservs are full of tips about self-promotion. At the same time, the other new model beginning to emerge into the mainstream is self-publishing, formerly seen as a last-resort vanity option used by those unable to get a "real" press to take on their project. More and more, self-publishing is a viable and respected choice by which authors are circumventing the traditional publishers altogether and selling their work directly to readers via platforms such as Amazon Kindle. If Courtney hadn't taken me on and convinced Simon and Schuster to do the same, such independent publishing would probably have been my best option. But I'm a neo-Luddite who has neither an e-reader nor a Facebook page. I don't even own a cell phone. Figuring out the intricacies of publishing my own writing seems totally beyond me. I want to write books, not be an online marketing guru. I feel lucky to receive the contract offer from Simon and Schuster, although I am old-fashioned enough to be disappointed that my book won't exist in print copies on real bookstore shelves. To me, e-only doesn't quite feel like I'm publishing a real book. My mother, who is my biggest fan, won't be able to read my novels. But the editorial oversight and cover design are promised to be identical to the print books, my agent assures me. I will get to move up from PRO to PAN—the Published Authors Network of Romance Writers of America. And it is a start. Of course, I say yes.

The Simon and Schuster editor, naturally, has her own ideas for revision. She wants the whole story to be shorter and tighter. Clarify and heighten goal, motivation, and conflict. Start scenes as late in the action as you can and end them as early as you can. Keep the pace fast and the pages turning. I rewrite again, going through the whole manuscript one more time. Eventually, we move to the stage of the copyeditor, who does great work finding remaining infelicities of phrase and anachronisms. Did I know that *Diplodocus* fossils weren't discovered until the 1870s, and would I please change my reference to *Megalosaurus*? Did I realize that *Jane Eyre* didn't come out until October 1847 and that I have my heroine's little sister reading it in March? (A fact I did know but was hoping to ignore.) I catch myself feeling surprised that the publishing house edits romance novels so closely and carefully. What reader would be likely to know or care about *Jane Eyre*'s release month? But then I chide myself: Why shouldn't a romance editor have the highest standards? Am I selling the genre short, expecting less of it because it's "merely" popular fiction?

I rewrite. One. Last. Time.

At this point, one of the agents who had rejected me earlier sees my name listed in *Romance Writers Report* in the magazine's New Sales column, as having a two-book contract with Simon and Schuster/Pocket Star. She emails me to offer representation. It's a rather sweet moment, I must admit, when I can write back to thank her for reconsidering me but to let her know I've already found an agent.

And then finally—*finally*—the novel comes out. Not physically, of course, but it has its electronic debut on the virtual shelves of the Internet. (When the editor at Simon and Schuster first sends me the book's cover art, I hoot loudly enough in my office that my next door colleague calls out to see if I'm okay.) The date is December 3, 2012. Six years have passed since I settled on the goal of publishing a romance novel, with perhaps three years of truly buckling down to the task with a daily word count and revision schedule and a spreadsheet of constant queries to agents and editors. *Master of Love* goes live at a promotional discount that the publisher hopes will kick-start sales. (It doesn't. My sales stink.) Word spreads among some of my colleagues on campus, and within a week my email inbox receives this note from Jeremy, a friend and professor in another department:

> To: Roach, Catherine
> Subject: Master of Love!
>
> I can confirm that at least one Kindle edition of your book has sold! I trust you are applying your royalties to the boys' college fund.
> Regards,
> Jeremy

In my office, I reply:

> To: Butler, Jeremy
> Subject: Master of Love!
>
> Hell, no! I'm saving up to buy a bottle of champagne! Only another
> 99 copies at $1.99 each and I'll be there!
> Thanks for getting one—you're very sweet! I have to warn you,
> though—there are spicy bits!
> —Catherine

Later, reading my reply, I note the exclamation points after every sentence. Silly, giddy girl. I note as well my tongue-in-cheek warning about the "spicy bits." Despite my brave, sex-positive feminist words, am I anxious about going public with this writing? The book has a few sex scenes in it, as is standard for the genre. But its follow-up, *Knight of Love,* eventually earns a rating of only two out of five "Balls o' Fire" on the Simon and Schuster heat meter. *Master of Love,* which came out before my publisher invented this handy system, is ranked at the same lukewarm fieriness. (I admit to being rather disappointed that they rated my balls o' fire so low; I thought those books were pretty darn spicy.) It's not nerves, exactly, about letting such work out into the world, but I'm certainly aware that for some people even a single ball o' fire is one ball too much.

This theme of caution or wariness is a common one in interviews that I have with writers. One erotica author tells me she'd been at her grandfather's ninety-fourth birthday party the previous week. He'd asked her if she was also X, her erotic pseudonym. (Grandpa had Googled her.) She lied and said that no, that wasn't her. "It's not that I'm ashamed," she tells me, clearly conflicted, "but I don't really want my ten-year-old son and my parents and grandparents knowing about my erotica." I can relate. I've gotten good at hastily switching the computer screen when my kids wander into the room. Like sharks smelling blood, they try to read over my shoulder while I swat them away. "Are the scenes *explicit,* Mom?" asks my younger son, shaking his head. "Why do they have to be *explicit*?" One of my best friends in town, a working mom like me, loyally reads my novel but later admits that it's precisely these spicy bits that are hard for her.

She laughs as she mimes reading with a hand covering one eye, squinting sideways at her e-reader. She says that she tucked her son into bed and stayed in his room to read *Master of Love* but had to leave when the scene turns to lovemaking, as it felt wrong to be reading such things beside her sleeping child.

But all such is in the future. That day in my office, Jeremy's reply pings right back to my inbox:

> To: Roach, Catherine
> Subject: RE: QUERY: Master of Love
>
> Are you kidding me? I BOUGHT it for the spicy bits!

As we say in the South, bless his heart.

8

Happily Ever After

The Testament of Erotic Faith

In this last chapter, we arrive finally at a consideration of the romance novel's ending. Here is the moment we've been waiting for: that delicious and often tear-jerking emotional resolution where everything works out for the story's main characters. I often cry at the end of romance novels—indeed, I take it as a sign of a good book if the ending does make me cry. Do you know that opening scene of *Romancing the Stone*, where the romance novelist played by Kathleen Turner sits sobbing at her desk, typing out the final scene of her book? To the disgust of my boys, I confess to have done the same while working on my own novels.

In romance, this ending is crucial. One could argue that the romance story is defined by what insiders commonly refer to as the HEA. These initials stand for the Happily-Ever-After ending, which Romance Writers of America describes more fully on its website as the "emotionally satisfying and optimistic ending." In this ending, the protagonists resolve their various internal and external conflicts so as to work out their differences. They come to an understanding of their love for each other and commit their lives to that love. As the RWA website further explains, "The lovers who risk and struggle for each other and their relationship are rewarded with emotional justice and unconditional love." Stereotypically, this ending involves a hero and heroine declaring without reservation or irony

their mutual love, getting married, and conceiving or bearing a child. Increasingly in contemporary romances, the protagonists may not marry
and reproduce but will make some sort of deliberate decision to be together for the present. This "happy-for-now" ending—abbreviated as the
HFN, as opposed to the HEA—applies often in gay and lesbian romances
where only slowly is the option of marriage becoming a legal possibility,
and in some erotic romances where marriage or a similar promise of lifelong commitment seems too sudden for the plotline or too bourgeois for
the worldview of the novel. In all cases, the characters' commitment to
each other and to the central value of love brings to their lives a sense of
deep happiness, personal fulfillment, and the ongoing promise of hot sex,
even, as we've seen, if this sexual satisfaction is only implied.

Almost universally, authors with whom I talked view the ending as a
contract they have with their readers: No matter how wounded the characters are at a book's beginning and how further tortured these characters are by plot conflicts in a book's middle, all will be well by the end.
A historical romance author with a strong-selling series told me, "I was
devastated by the ending of *Gone with the Wind* when I read it at the
age of fourteen." In her writing, she takes seriously readers' desire for a
happy ending and celebrates this defining aspect of the genre: "I make
sure to give my readers the ending they want," she said. *New York Times*–
bestseller Lisa Kleypas gave a keynote talk at the 2007 Romance Writers
of America conference in which she spoke about the importance of the
romance story's ending as a description of what all women are entitled
to: a life where women are whole, safe, loved, sexually fulfilled, respected, in control of their choices, and *happy*. Many readers have told me that
they wouldn't read romance novels if they couldn't count on this happy
ending; they look for authors to whom they can "entrust their heart."
One aspiring author with whom I sat at an RWA luncheon told me it was
precisely the happy ending that initially got her hooked on the romance
genre. "Life is stressful and difficult and painful enough," she said. "I
don't want that in my books. I want to know that the relationship will
work out. I want to know that the book will be a good investment of my
time and money." For such readers, the HEA is a sacred guarantee. The
author will not let the readers down by failing to provide this emotional

resolution in the reading experience. Love *will* conquer all and love *does* heal all wounds, as the romance story resolves into the promise of happiness.

Two concepts help unpack the meaning of this ending and its significance for the romance story: *erotic faith* and *reparation fantasy.* These concepts allow us to see what is at stake in the ending of the romance. In short: (1) People have faith in love. The romance story functions similarly to a religious belief system that offers guidance on the end goal of how to live a good and worthy life. (2) The romance story is a reparation fantasy of the end of patriarchy. In this fantasy, the romance hero stands in for patriarchy itself in a vision wherein gender unfairness is repaired and all works out.

LOVE AS GOD, ROMANCE AS RELIGION

Here is my jumping off point: Robert M. Polhemus's powerful 1990 study of nineteenth-century British novels of love and romance, *Erotic Faith: Being in Love from Jane Austen to D. H. Lawrence.* In Polhemus's analysis of these novels, which stand as the high literary precursors to the popular romance fiction of the twentieth century, his key concept of erotic faith provides a reading of the emotional dynamic that the romance narrative then turns into story. Erotic faith, he writes, is "an emotional conviction, ultimately religious in nature, that meaning, value, hope, and even transcendence can be found through love—erotically focused love." Erotic faith is the belief "that people complete themselves and fulfill their destinies only with another . . . that in the quest for lasting love and the experience of being in love men and women find their real worth and character."[1]

Polhemus's point is that we have *faith* in love. We have a reverence for it. Starting in the late eighteenth century with the growth of secularism springing from the Enlightenment, in the art and in the marriages of Western Europe and North America, people increasingly fell in love with the idea of being in love. While others, such as the historian Jean H. Hagstrum in his *Esteem Enlivened by Desire: The Couple from Homer to Shakespeare,* have noted the earlier roots of this longstanding ideal of passionate marriage, what Polhemus identifies is a fuller flowering and more widespread acceptance of this ideal as erotic faith. In the context of rising secularism, Polhemus argues that faith in love becomes a new form of faith, to "augment or substitute for orthodox religious visions." Such similar psychological function links these two forms of faith that "religious feeling and eroticism run close together," and "love and theology may be surrogates for each other." The philosopher Simon May adds to this analysis in his *Love: A History,* the first chapter of which is even entitled "Love Plays God." While May refers more broadly to human love in its many forms, he too writes how "since the end of the eighteenth century, love has increasingly filled the vacuum left by the retreat of Christianity" to become in effect "the West's undeclared religion." We now worship love, May argues, as "our ultimate source of meaning and happiness, and of power over suffering and disappointment." Love becomes the Highest Good.[2]

The emotional intensity of the poetic tradition yields an illustration of this point. The iconic British Romantic poet John Keats writes of the eternal and unchangeable nature of true love in his 1820 sonnet "Bright Star," associated with his beloved Fanny Brawne. Keats wishes to be steadfast in love like the star:

> Pillow'd upon my fair love's ripening breast,
> To feel for ever its soft swell and fall,
> Awake for ever in a sweet unrest,
> Still, still to hear her tender-taken breath,
> And so live ever—or else swoon to death.[3]

In an 1819 letter to Fanny that he signs "Yours for ever," he tells her that "I have been astonished that Men could die Martyrs for religion—I have shudder'd at it. I shudder no more—I could be martyr'd for my Religion—Love is my religion—I could die for that. I could die for you. My Creed is Love and you are its only tenet."[4] Keats divinizes romantic love as a most worthy religion, indeed—one for which he'd willingly die. His dear Fanny is the "only tenet" of his creed, the central article of faith in which he believes. In this same tradition we may cite the twentieth-century American E. E. Cummings's beautiful, even mystical love poem "i carry your heart with me(i carry it in":

here is the deepest secret nobody knows
(here is the root of the root and the bud of the bud
and the sky of the sky of a tree called life;which grows
higher than soul can hope or mind can hide)
and this is the wonder that's keeping the stars apart

i carry your heart(i carry it in my heart)[5]

In Cummings's lush vision, romantic and passionate love is the secret of
the universe, the force behind life, a transcendent reality that animates all
being and knowing. The poem stands as testimony to erotic faith.

This erotic faith takes on story form in the romance narrative: spun
out in prose in the novel, be it the literary high fiction of *Pride and Prejudice* or the popular mass-market fiction of *The Sheik and the Vixen;* providing content for advertisements, Hollywood flicks, and pop lyrics; or used
as a mythic or archetypal template to make sense of one's own relationship practice. In all cases, the shared and underlying conviction is in the
power of love to make the world a better place. The realities of life and
the search for love are so often harsh and heartbreaking. In the romance
narrative, by contrast, love has a mythic or idealizing force strong enough
to mend tragedy. Romantic love offers—as does much traditionally defined religious faith—the promise of redemption. In novels, the love plot
is the story arc by which characters heal from past wounds and achieve a
new level of maturity. We can read the novel as teaching—or as preaching—that love is the means by which real-life people can mature as well.
For the novels' characters, love tempers pride, harsh judgment, and the
violent outbursts of a reflexive defensiveness. Love grants the inner peace
and self-confidence for the lover to become a stronger and wiser person.
It leads to compassion, mercy, understanding, and kindness. In all these
ways, erotic faith is the conviction, explored in the ups and downs of the
romance narrative—girl(s) and/or boy(s) meet, fall for each other, suffer
through internal and external conflicts, maybe break up, get back together, and ultimately live happily ever after—in the healing power of love.

In romance, love serves a traditionally religious function. As popular romance scholar Eric Selinger puts it, love or marriage can come to
function as that which we "believe in," as "a source of meaning and purpose and value . . . as a priority that determines other actions and beliefs."

Furthermore, the beloved can take the place of the godhead and come to function as the locus of "ultimate significance" in the life of the lover. Romantic love becomes a form of worship.[6] Here is one apt example, taken from the Regency romance *The Stanforth Secrets* by bestselling author Jo Beverley, member of the RWA Hall of Fame, in a tête-à-tête dialogue between hero and heroine:

> "Do you know how dreadful it is, my darling, to lie in my bed at night and know you are so close? A few steps to heaven. It is sacrilegious to ignore what we have here."
> [...] "That is a highly irreligious statement."
> He kissed the tip of her nose. "You are my religion, my goddess."
> Chloe used all her willpower. "Profanity too," she said, moving out of his arms.
> [...] "Not in my religion," he said lightly [...]. "There, the only sin is denial of love."[7]

The language of the passage is theological, through and through. For the couple to ignore or deny their love is sacrilegious and a sin, argues the hero. Although the heroine reproves him for profanity in such statements, the hero persists. He terms her his goddess, his religion, and his heaven.

One could dismiss such talk as no more than a pretty attempt at seduction. We see the heroine summon her willpower to resist, fearing exactly that. But the reader knows better. The romance genre *believes* in this religion of love. By the novels' endings, its characters are adherents to erotic faith—converts, if previous cynicism so requires. And along with these characters, I wager that many of the genre's authors and readers are believers in love as well. Note, as evidence, this comment by Beverley about the above quote from *The Stanforth Secrets*:

> I think there are a number of similar expressions in my early books and fewer later, which interests me. My early days of writing romance were an exciting exploration of the very matter of erotic love, whereas now I take the erotic faith in myself and the reader for granted. I wonder if that's a good thing. I hadn't thought of "erotic faith" but it's a powerful concept. I do believe in the reality and power of the human mating bond. It's obvious some don't, and that some of them see it as a fallacious or even wicked belief. That's why they get so agitated about romance novels.[8]

Beverley explains her belief in erotic faith—in the reality and power of the romantic mating bond—as an aspect of the human condition that is true and good. She views its exploration as central to the project of the romance narrative.

But we can go even further. The romance narrative is religious in its faith in the healing power of love, its focus on the beloved as "divine" or of ultimate significance, and its mythic quest for love. "Love is God" is the central dogma of such erotic faith. But we can also flip the equation and say that the core religious narrative of Western history is itself romantic. Christianity, that central religious story, is easily read as a love story: "God is Love," asserts a key New Testament passage (1 John 4:8, 16). In the context of Western culture, wherein the artistic, literary, philosophical, and scientific heritages are all strongly shaped by the Christian religious tradition, the narrative core of that tradition is essentially a romance story. The mythic narrative of Christianity follows the pattern of the romance narrative, with a guaranteed happy ending for the saved community of well-behaved believers or the recipients of grace. "Find your one true love and live happily ever after" is one way to describe the Christian story, in terms of the ideal relationship between the believer and the One True Love of Christ the Son or the Christian Father God, and then the believer's reward of life everlasting. "Are you the One?" the disciples of John the Baptist ask Jesus, as many a lover has pondered early in the game (Matthew 11:2–3; Luke 7:18–20).

One of the possible Latin etymologies for the term *religion* is *re-ligare*, "to re-bind" or "re-tie" (*ligament* has the same root). From this perspective, religion refers to a practice of reconnecting or of binding up a break, for example a break between humans and the divine or a breach within one's own self or soul. This etymology and way of understanding religion suggests a threefold aspect to the human condition and to the task of religion: an original unity, a break or loss or wound, and an attempt to repair and reconnect these sundered parts back into a unified whole. Plato's *Symposium* dialogue famously casts this threefold sense as the origin story of humanity in a tale of our foolish yet poignant quest for love. In the dialogue, the character of Aristophanes delivers a speech about how humans began as four-footed symmetrical beings (all male, all female, or androgynous half-male/half-female creatures), who were then cut in half by the gods and are now forever on a quest for their missing other part. Here is the original account of the beloved as our better half, our soulmate, our One True Love. Romantic love is a literal completion of self in this account. Plato writes of the mysterious—we may even say uncanny—pleasure felt by these reunited halves when and if they do find each other again: "The two of them are wondrously thrilled with affection and intimacy and love, and are hardly to be induced to leave each other's side for a single moment. These are they who continue together throughout life."[9] It is a happy-ever-after ending worthy of any modern romance novel.

This two-directional religious analysis allows us to see both the romance narrative within the Christian religious story—highlighting again how omnipresent and culturally powerful is this romance narrative—as well as the religious aspect of the romance story itself—highlighting the mythic work of healing and salvation that we assign to love. The point of this parallel is the deep-rootedness of this cultural belief in the resurrection power of love. The love of a good woman, or good man, or God, or Son of God, has the power to heal all wounds. Love has the power to forgive all sins stretching back to the stain of original sin, to resurrect a dead man, to save a lost soul, to integrate false persona and true self, to make a real man—or real woman—out of you. *This belief in the healing power of love is the central trope of erotic faith, of Western Christian culture, and of romance novels alike.* Whether the romance narrative borrows this belief from the Christian religious tradition or whether Christianity takes this perennial belief and incorporates it as central to its theology is a chicken-and-egg question that need not concern us here. Either way, love—in various forms of *agape, phile,* and *eros*—is the central emotional dynamic in the life-quest for meaning, happiness, and the crucial category of wholeness or healing.

Here is where the ending of the romance story becomes of central importance. The story resolves into a vision wherein the lovers love each other well. This love makes them whole and it makes them *into* a whole: not the eight-limbed roly-poly creatures of the *Symposium* but a blissfully bonded pair nonetheless. This fantasy is the idealized version of reality that the influential Canadian literary theorist Northrop Frye in his magisterial 1957 *Anatomy of Criticism* identifies as the central characteristic of the romance myth. In this idealized storyline is the seductive promise that pain will end. Whatever betrayal and disappointment and loneliness that haunt you will be banished by love. You will be cherished by a most worthy partner despite your flaws: devotedly, "for all eternity, and even beyond," promises award-winning romance author Mary Balogh's *The Secret Pearl*.[10]

From this perspective, the true significance of the HEA lies not in its presence at the end of every romance novel but its presence in the larger culture. The mythic narrative of the Christian tradition and that of the romance narrative each highlights the category of *eschatology*. Both are narratives concerned with the eschaton (from the Greek *eschatos*, "last" or "farthest"), the end of the world or the ultimate destiny of the characters involved. The HEA ending of the romance is inherent from the very beginning of the story, as part of its narrative structure. What I'm suggesting is that the romance story *is* narrative eschatology. A romance is a story about how to get to a particular type of end, an eschaton of love, healing, commitment, completion, happiness, generational continuity, maturity, and hope. What is most important about the romance story is this ending toward which it moves. At the end of our lives, suggests the poet Philip Larkin, "What will survive of us is love."[11] Larkin's phrase is one of the twentieth century's most memorable and ambiguous lines of poetry on the meaning of romantic love. In the end—the end of our lives, the end of our romance novels—what matters is love. We yearn, with an "almost-instinct almost true" says Larkin, for this ideal paradise where we are loved. Therein is the quest for wholeness granted, wounds made right, pleasure and security guaranteed. To be human, we may say, is to desire and to quest for this love. This is both what is wonderful and foolish—even dangerous—about the human condition. The romance narrative tells this story of love and humanity, in all of its shocking risk and glory.

As evidence of this power of erotic faith and its operation within the culture, let me bring in the example of gay romance fiction. These stories of two men romantically loving each other—and, again, having hot sex—constitute the increasingly popular subgenre of gay romances that are written and read primarily by women. *Force of Nature,* for example, is a 2007 *New York Times*–bestselling novel by romantic suspense author Suzanne Brockmann. To my knowledge, it is the first mainstream highly successful romance novel featuring a central gay couple. It tells the story of the complicated love between FBI agent extraordinaire Jules Cassidy and Robin Chadwick, Hollywood heartthrob, the "charismatic, closeted movie star for whom Jules feels a powerful attraction" (back cover). *Force of Nature* in fact features two parallel couples, also recounting the romance story of private investigator Ric Alvarado and his lovely assistant, Annie Dugan. All four characters work together to bring down a Florida crime lord. The intertwining of the heterosexual and homosexual love stories serves to make the point that romance transcends categories of same- and opposite-sex love. The follow-up novel, *All through the Night,* makes this point explicit. Here, Jules and Robin get married in Boston (with lots of romantic suspense complications including a killer stalker, intrusive reporters, ex-lovers, and home renovation disasters).

In an RWA conference talk that Brockmann gave and in her author's note at the end of *All through the Night,* she talks about her son Jason, who is gay; her longstanding support of gay rights organizations such as MassEquality, which works for equal marriage rights in Massachusetts (Brockmann lives outside of Boston); her donation of all earnings from the book to MassEquality; and her deliberate decision to write such a romance for purposes of celebrating and increasing mainstream acceptance of gay couples. They fall in love, have romantic trials, and seek to live happily ever after, just like all the heteros. Gay romance stories feature the exact same emotional dynamics as standard heterosexual romance: attraction, complicated by conflict, resolved to love. Brockmann, whose Twitter account proclaims her a proud and loving PFLAG (Parents, Families, and Friends of Lesbians and Gays) mom, writes, "I have this to say to the people who are rapidly becoming a minority themselves, people who don't think that gay Americans should have the same rights [i.e., the right to marry] as the rest of us—What part of *love* don't you understand?"[12]

From this exasperated perspective, erotic faith supports gay rights. In gay, lesbian, trans, and otherwise queer or non-heterosexual love stories,

the force of romance is powerful enough to trump the sexual orientation of those loving and being loved. Thus, it doesn't *matter,* there is little
import, to the fact that the two main protagonists happen, for example,
to both be men. Because these heroes truly love each other, they establish their legitimacy as practitioners of erotic faith—just like everyone
else—and their stories easily enter the mainstream. There is, as Brockmann suggests, something wonderfully revolutionary about these gay
romance novels. In them, erotic faith is powerful enough to triumph over
homophobia or hetero-normativity—the belief that all couplings should
be man-woman. The righteous power of romantic love is so strong that it
serves as a tool of social justice for the expansion of human rights and the
enfranchisement of sexual minorities. In this light, the gay romance subgenre is transgressive and radical as it queers traditional and restrictive
romance norms where it's always "boy meets girl," but never "boy meets
boy" or "girl meets girl."

Yet what I find really revolutionary about these gay romance stories
lies not in their affirmation of the traditional love story of erotic faith.
This story is, after all, restrictive in its own way: One still has to locate
that soulmate partner and bond deeply in order to find happiness. From
another perspective then, in the end—in the happily-ever-after ending or
the ending of happily for now—gay romance maintains the status quo.
While the stories do offer a new gender makeup for the protagonist pair,
the narratives otherwise reaffirm a traditional notion of romantic love
and repeat without question the central tenets of erotic faith: that love
conquers suffering (including that caused by homophobic society), that
sex isn't fully meaningful without love, that partner love ultimately provides more fulfillment than political activism. While erotic faith supports
the universality of romantic love—Cupid discriminates not when he lets
loose his arrow—it ironically can tame the import of non-heterosexual
stories. It tames them by subsuming lesbian, gay, bisexual, trans, asexual,
and queer identities under the category held to be more significant—and
less threatening—of the generic Lover.

So, instead, what really strikes me as transgressive in these novels is a
fantasy that aids in explaining the books' appeal to their largely female
readership. This fantasy is my second argument about what is at stake in

the ending of romance novels. As I see it, *these stories of love—gay and otherwise—offer a woman-centered fantasy of the end of patriarchy.*

GETTING A GOOD MAN TO LOVE: "COME BACK TO THE BED AG'IN, HONEY!"

True to eschatology, the Happily-Ever-After is not simply the ending of a comedic romance (as opposed to a Romeo-and-Juliet tragic romance). The end goal of erotic faith, like that of the Christian eschaton, is the end of all endings, an ending beyond endings. As erotic faith plays out in the popular romance genre, the goal is the end of patriarchy itself. By story's close, love levels the playing field for women and equalizes the gender balance of power. One author whom I interviewed—a midlevel historical romance author with a Ph.D. in English literature—put it this way: "The fantasy is only partly about romance. Even more, it's about women's empowerment. In the HEA, getting the love of your life is the icing on the cake. But getting the power of your destiny is the more seductive fantasy." For this author, the guarantee of women's power is what the HEA is really about. Within the imaginative space of the romance story, the fantasy is about patriarchy coming to an end.

This resolution and these fantasy dynamics are complex. It can be easy to miss or to dismiss the radical, reparative import of the traditional romance ending, since the storyline overlaps with the foundational premise of patriarchy. In a male-centered culture that enforces heterosexuality as the norm, it is axiomatic that a woman must be under the protection of a man, yoked to him and to at least some extent in his control. Traditional romance novels continue to end with the heroine married or on her way to marriage. As evidenced by the enormous female readership of these romance novels, this premise for happiness remains foundational to much of female fantasy life. Although the romance story doesn't disrupt this premise, the story does change its meaning. Yes, the woman is under the protection of a man, but that control is reciprocal: He, too, is yoked to her. She is not only protected but also pleasured by the love of a good man. Thus my argument that erotic faith within the romance story entails such strong belief in the transformative and redemptive power of love that this faith supports an imaginative world wherein patriarchy ends.

To unpack this argument, let me bring in another theorist, the mid-twentieth-century American literature critic Leslie A. Fiedler. For Fiedler, American fiction is driven by the dream of interethnic male bonding. He sees operating in this fiction what he calls the myth of the dark beloved, in which people of color forgive and love white folk despite the horrors of racism. "Come Back to the Raft Ag'in, Huck Honey!" is Fiedler's 1948 essay on *Huckleberry Finn* and *The Last of the Mohicans,* two iconic American stories authored by white males about a dark beloved, an African American or Native American male who shares an adventurous quest with a white male protagonist. Fielder's essay is essentially about the literature of white male America as a homosocial reparation fantasy for racism. In this fantasy, the predations of racism are repaired through an interracial buddy story, a narrative of a white male and a colored male who share friendship and brotherly love. The story is offered with remorse and affection on the part of whites and read with pleasure by them, partly because the friendship offered by the characters of color implies forgiveness and absolution for white people's acts and attitudes of racism.

Romance fiction engages in a reverse type of this reparation fantasy. Instead of springing from racism and white supremacy, the fantasy springs from sexism and patriarchy. It is offered not by those who perpetuated the discrimination (as in Fiedler's formulation where white male authors write from their fantasy position), but by those subjected to it: an overwhelmingly female industry of romance writers. Thus instead of Fiedler's myth of the dark beloved, we get a myth of the male beloved, the beloved hero of romance fiction. Women readers, authors, and fictional heroines, like Jim in *Huck Finn* and in Fiedler's provocative title, bear no grudge and invite the hero, "Come back to the raft"—or the bed—"ag'in, honey!" In this reading, romance fiction and—to stretch my thesis to its broadest applicability—the romance narrative in all of its various cultural manifestations is driven by the female dream of cross-gender romantic love and the myth of the male beloved. According to this myth, the hero—the alpha male, the patriarch—loves with tenderness, devotion, and sensitivity, even while maintaining his otherwise alpha ways. In this dream, the battle of the sexes is resolved. As Ann Barr Snitow writes, "The war between men and women who cannot communicate ends in truce."[13] Male and female bond in love. Gender disparity is healed. I adapt Fiedler's argument to the genre of romance fiction, then, in order to argue that the core appeal of romance fiction is this fantasy of the end of patriarchy in which the alpha male hero is revealed as the submissive.

Another scholar who helps to develop this point is the American queer literary theorist Eve Kosofsky Sedgwick. In an influential essay from 1997, Sedgwick draws a fruitful distinction between *reparative reading* and *paranoid reading,* two modes that represent different ways of knowing. Paranoid reading is a common academic form of analysis based on a hermeneutic of suspicion. When people engage in paranoid reading, they work to uncover the violence hidden in texts and culture, they are concerned about oppression and false consciousness, and they leverage the power of exposing injustice in order to bring about positive change. Sedgwick values this paranoid position and engages in it herself, but she worries about its dominance and even its contempt. She wants to articulate an alternative: a mode of reading and interpretation that is still sharply alive and critically engaged, but less oriented around suspicion and, perhaps, more loving.

One can easily outline a paranoid reading of romance fiction, aided by a fierce-eyed hermeneutic of suspicion. Romance novels brainwash women, goes this critique. The books give false pleasure with their impossible happy endings in order to keep women compliant under the heavy thumb of patriarchy, capitalism, and consumerism. But there is another way to read romance, the position, in fact, from which fans and authors of the genre generally view it: One may read romance reparatively. From this perspective, to love romance fiction is not to engage in a "self-hating complicity with an oppressive status quo," the notion Sedgwick likewise rejects in regard to the queer love of camp. Instead, the desire of the reparative impulse is to repair an object of relationship— say, the reader's relationship to the hero or heroine—that will then have resources to offer the self. To view romance fiction writing and reading as a communal exploration of reparative impulses, practices, and fantasies is, I think, to do better justice to the genre and to its creators and consumers. Sedgwick is moved, as I am, by "the many ways in which selves and communities succeed in extracting sustenance from the objects of a culture—even of a culture whose avowed desire has often been not to sustain them." Women readers "extract sustenance" from romance novels in the imaginative play of repairing the alpha male and of restoring gender relations.[14]

Reparative reading then, in Sedgwick's terms, involves a reparation fantasy, in the way that I am using Fiedler's theory. Since gay romance and its literary cousin slash fiction help to illustrate this argument, let me detour a little further through these narratives in order to develop my point. Gay romance enjoys increasing popularity within the community of female romance readers. In a paranoid reading the subgenre can appear conservative. Gay romance does help open up restrictive relationship norms that have narrowed people's options for love and consensual sex to the heterosexual, but it only opens these norms so far. Moreover, the lack of a lesbian romance subgenre of equal sales popularity to that of gay romance may be seen as evidence of a misogyny internalized by women romance aficionados, who have been conditioned by male-centered cultural norms (I could put myself in this category). Do heterosexual women need a man in their story in order to feel satisfied? Are two men better than one, as an explanation for the popularity of gay romance? Or—and here instead is the reparative reading in which direction I want to push this argument—it might simply be that women like to read about men, whether in gay male or heterosexual pairings, because it is men who are the problem, or, more specifically, because the problem is macho masculinity.

The subgenre of slash, a form of romance writing often erotic and related to gay romance, further illustrates this point. Slash derives from fanfiction, consisting of stories written by fans typically unpaid for their writing. These stories—frequently written and read by women—feature two male media characters represented typographically as m/m, thus the term "slash" (there is some f/f slash about women media characters, but much less than the m/m counterpart). As a form of fanfiction, the heart of slash is to imaginatively extend storylines already established, whether on page or screen, in an original or "canonical" fiction world. Slash fiction takes two compelling heterosexual male characters who function in the canonical story text as partners, co-workers, friends, or sometimes rivals and writes new storylines for these characters in which they admit their love for each other, are no longer able to deny their mutual sexual attraction, and come together romantically, despite the fact that they are heterosexual. Here are the alpha male pairs of fiction: Holmes and Watson, Batman and Superman, Edward (vampire) and Jacob (werewolf), Starsky and Hutch, Crockett and Tubbs—and, starting it all off, Kirk and Spock, among many others. All are the subjects of multiple online fanfiction slash stories.

Slash—even more so than gay romance—is the ultimate fictional expression of erotic faith. The romance heroes in these stories fall so in love with their male friend or partner, so embrace the religion of erotic faith, that they can't help committing themselves as lovers. These male heroes may not understand themselves as "really" gay and may be portrayed as heterosexual men whose beloved simply happens to be another man. But the love these men discover for each other is strong enough to defeat patriarchy's chief rule that a man must be straight. In a society that preaches the religion of erotic faith—where love provides meaning and fulfillment as the path to the promised land—the ultimate test of erotic faith is for a heterosexual alpha male to willingly and openly love in a romantic way another such male. To do so is much riskier than the expected path of loving a woman, for it is to breach the great taboo against same-sex male love that defines patriarchal masculinity. In this way, woman-oriented gay and slash romance pulls back the veil of patriarchy to dramatize the open-hearted man behind the mask, the full person behind the tough-guy guise that patriarchy imposes on men: risking love, fearing loss, committing heart and soul for the male beloved—despite the opprobrium of society at an alpha male who dares eschew the princess for another king. Such a man becomes the greatest practitioner of erotic faith. His story represents the end of patriarchy—the *fantasy* of the end of patriarchy—even while he stands as its central symbol.

I suspect that part of the appeal of gay and slash romance is that these m/m heroes are in this sense ironically *manlier* than the heroes in straight heterosexual romance. The m/m heroes are man enough to take on this risk of same-sex love. To return to chapter 6's category of the pussy-whipped man, it is true that these slash heroes are subservient to the desires of their female readers and writers: They serve a matriarchal author/authority and in this way cater to the pleasure of women. But within the world of the story, the fact that the hero's desire bends only to another man means that he isn't—he can't be—pussy-whipped. Heroes who love other men are, by definition, less enthralled to the female and thus less emasculated than are the straight heroes in traditional heterosexual romance. Same-sex male love stories keep the dynamics of the erotic wholly within the homosocial all-male world. In so doing, while these romances clearly violate the norm of compulsory heterosexuality, they are better able than heterosexual romances to keep intact patriarchy's other central standard, that men must never yield their dominance to women.

We arrive at the crux of the tension, the paradox at the heart and at the end of the romance narrative. Most baldly put, this paradox has women in a position of simultaneously desiring and fearing men. Romance novels can play an important reparative role in this regard for their women readers: exploring this paradox, negotiating its tension, healing its rift. If romance is one of the central narratives of popular culture—*the* central narrative of Anglosphere pop culture, as I argue in my boldest moods—with roots stretching down into the culture's foundational religious stories, then romance novels are indeed doing deep psychic work for their readers. The stories function as an antidote to patriarchy, as a way of pleasurably working through—in fantasy, in the safe and imaginative play world of fiction—this contradictory position of the heterosexual woman within rape culture. The complex work of the romance narrative involves acknowledging the limits and threats imposed on women by the culture, while also suggesting that women can refuse to accept such and empowering them to expect and demand better. (As an example, see the *In Death* futuristic suspense series by J. D. Robb—a pseudonym of top author Nora Roberts—where detective Eve Dallas deals with the ongoing traumatic memory of sexual and physical abuse by her dead father while supported by the healing love of her wildly rich and gorgeous, kick-ass husband.) In other words, as romance scholars before me such as Janice Radway and Tania Modleski have argued, a central purpose of the romance story's work is to assuage the rub and drag of living as a woman within a culture still marked by patriarchy. The genre creates a fantasy space of solace and possibility—and even revenge. In this space, women engage in reparative reading. They work out, within the realm of fiction, and make up, through the pleasures of the text, some of the inevitable cost to a woman's psyche of living in a culture that is in certain ways against her.

We can put it this way: If the name of the game is patriarchy, then a reparative reading of gender relations is one in which the domineering or uncaring patriarch becomes the good man. The most common narrative trope whereby this transformation occurs is in the romance narrative: Love blooms and tames his heart. Furthermore, if it is still a man's world out there, then for a woman to have a good man at her side is a good thing. A woman is safer from danger and has more resources to draw on, to the extent that she is in a committed relationship with, and thus protected and aided by, the good man. In this way, romance storytelling engages readers in a reparation fantasy that offers healing in male-female relations. Romance is fantasy in this sense of pleasurable escape from a harsher reality wherein true love does not always conquer all nor heal all gender wounds. Part of this reading pleasure is the fantasy conquest of patriarchy; herein the paranoid impulse of revenge meets the reparative impulse of love.

According to Northrop Frye's narrative theory of mythic structures and archetypal plots, one of the climactic images in the romance is that "of the monster tamed and controlled by the virgin." This taming is the central dynamic of the popular romance novel. Alongside or despite the realism imparted by plot and setting, these novels essentially represent a mythic fantasy world in which Woman—the Virgin, the Maiden, the Princess Warrior, Everywoman—tames and controls the monster, Man—the alpha hero, who has the power to harm her but who will not because he has learned how to love. Women authors control the alpha male through a strong female protagonist who is often his emotional superior. Through love, the dominant hero willingly takes up a stance of submission. He comes to realize, according to popular romance scholar Sarah S. G. Frantz's analysis of this dynamic in BDSM romance, that "the gendered expectation that he be dominant is a perversion of his identity, of BDSM, and of love itself." He submits in and to the romance; he gives up the power of patriarchy for the power of love.[15]

Romance storytelling in this way enacts the reparative impulse. It repairs Sedgwick's "relational object" of the male protagonist so that he may become fully actualized into what the genre unabashedly calls the hero. By the end of the novel's arc in the HEA, the hero ends up with the unlikely combined profile of high alpha traits that guarantee he can protect the heroine and that render him immune to the predations of patriarchy himself, paired with the high sensitivity of the most enlightened pro-feminist lover. The heroine and vicariously the female readers get that fantasy paradox of the alpha male who is strong yet lost without the heroine's love, dominant yet caring and sensitive, sexy yet with eyes for none but his beloved. This man who is made good is a fantasy as much as is the character of the alpha male warrior-king who strides across the beginning chapters of so many romance novels. He is the fantasy of the end of patriarchy.

This fantasy holds true even in stories without an overt alpha hero. For example, Mhairi McFarlane's British award-winning 2012 romantic comedy *You Had Me at Hello* tells the story of journalist Rachel and her former university classmate Ben, a classic beta hero. Ben is now a reasonably successful lawyer but more of a nice man and longstanding friend to Rachel than a Gorgeous and Dangerous Billionaire Tycoon. Such a hero represents neither power stacked against women at the story's opening nor monster tamed at her side by the story's end. The wider world of the novel, however, still operates within this space of man's world transformed and rebalanced for woman's pleasure. Rachel's initial boyfriend in the story consistently rides roughshod over her wishes (and provides only boring sex). Ben is the bad boyfriend's opposite: attuned to Rachel's needs, in sync with her sense of humor, supportive of her studies and career, interested in her friends. And he makes his alpha move in the end, riding to the rescue with a declaration of love just when Rachel has more or less contented herself with being alone forever. In that moment Rachel marvels that "Life transforms from black-and-white to colour." Thus even when the hero is not himself transformed by love as a symbol of the end of patriarchy, the reparative fantasy of such a beta-hero book still involves transformation to a life lived in color, with gender equality, and seasoned by sexual sizzle.[16]

This good man, the softened or end-state alpha hero, is the work of reparation, of the reparative fantasy. It—he—is an illusion, in the sense of a powerfully appealing figure based in wish fulfillment. As Freud noted in his analysis of religion as illusion, an illusion may have truth to it. For certain lucky young girls, their prince really does come (it worked for Grace Kelly). The romance story of the alpha hero has such truth to it—in that love does heal wounds, romance does offer sweetness to life, most people do seek and generally find such to at least some degree—but it is also a fantasy, or illusion, in the sense of a wish fulfillment that is unlikely to be literally and wholly true. Such truth-value is not, however, the point. The point of the story is the power of reparative reading and fantasy to offer a different type of truth and insight. The resonance of romance storytelling lies in this interconnected fantasy power of deep truth and wish-fulfilling illusion.

To read romance reparatively, then, as fan or scholar, is to take delight—voluptuous pleasure, even—in this more pliant image of masculinity (opened, softened, moldable, made putty in the hands), to play with its possibilities, to soak up its solace against the grimmer or simply more banal realities of daily life. Ultimately, a reparative reading of romance allows us to see and to know that patriarchy itself is a fantasy: a massive, neurotic, collective projection of fears and anxieties, worked out in cultural arrangements that are detrimental to so many of us, no matter what our gender. It allows us to see and to know that patriarchy could be different. Here's a thought: Patriarchy could end. If an angry god gives us the punishment of patriarchy, then a playful goddess could give us the pleasure of a Society of Love. Imagine social justice, civil rights, power-with instead of power-over, an end to violence, and body pleasure and consent-based play of all sorts. In romance novels, we get to keep imagining.

In support of this interpretation of the romance genre are three final examples of this reparation fantasy in the HEA's work of imagined healing. Two examples come from the romance subgenre of erotica and one from the paranormal—both areas of strong recent growth within the overall field—as both subgenres offer particularly effective literary means for women to use romance fiction as a way of working out their position within the culture. The messages to women readers in these novels are three: "You can't fight patriarchy" (The balance of power is stacked against women); "You must fight patriarchy" (A woman who wants a man should never settle for less than a good one who is fully supportive); and "Patriarchy will end" (You will teach this man how to truly love, so that he becomes the good man who will love you forever). All three of these messages are encapsulated in the complex HEA promise: *You will get a good man to love.*

Maya Banks's *Sweet Persuasion* is a 2009 BDSM romance featuring Serena, a successful businesswoman whose fantasy is to be a sex slave to Damon, the charismatic owner of a sex club. This and similar plotlines in erotic romance allow for exploration of a submission and surrender theme to the desire and possessiveness of a powerful man not widely seen since the bodice-ripper domination and rape plots of the 1980s. BDSM erotic romance allows for a more politically correct exploration of this dynamic, since the heroine surrenders willingly in a fantasy power game. In *Sweet Persuasion,* for example, Damon's complete authority over Serena—"I want the security of knowing I am . . . owned," she says—is ultimately benign. While Damon puts her in bondage and takes a crop to her, he also feeds, clothes, and bathes her; fully supports her professional ambitions; puts up charmingly with her meddling friends; buys her a wardrobe; and sends her to the spa. He demands total control over Serena, but the reader is also convinced that he is a good man who loves her well and devotedly. "I wanted to own her. I wanted her to own my heart," he says about another woman in a previous, failed relationship, when explaining his sexual and relationship desires to Serena. The lesson Serena learns in the end is that "it takes someone strong to give up ultimate power, to allow a man to take care of her, to make decisions for her."[17]

Patriarchy is literally the name of the game here: Serena wants to play sex-slave to a strong alpha master. Thus, the three messages: "You can't fight patriarchy," lest you be a bad slave and displease your master, but "you must fight patriarchy," in the sense of holding out for no less than this perfectly egalitarian master. For while the master here rules, no matter. By the time of the HEA, it is clear that he rules to serve, to cherish, and to love. And so, "patriarchy will end." Although the master, the alpha hero, is in charge, she *has* him. She fulfills his submissive desire to be owned by a woman, as she now owns his very heart. Through identification with both the heroine and hero, the female reader experiences her own vulnerable position within a still male-dominated culture as one that nevertheless promises safety and pleasure, precisely because Damon, this particular master, has capitulated to Serena, fully and completely.

In Joey W. Hill's BDSM romance novel *Natural Law* from 2004, the power dynamic is reversed between two undercover cops; here it's the mistress in charge. Violet is petite, a "pixie," yet formidable, a dominant mistress born. Patriarchy is already overturned here, in that the deep fantasy work of this story is that of resisting and rejecting male rule. Here instead is a matriarchy where man is the subordinate, required to obey the woman's every command and wanting nothing more than to fulfill her will and claim her satisfaction as his own. Yet although cop-hero Mac is a willing male submissive in this story, he is still the alpha through and through: physically much stronger than Violet, a seasoned detective, brave and protective (he takes a bullet for her by story's end). Like Serena and Damon, Violet and Mac finally find each other after a long and painful life-quest of loneliness and self-doubt. These couples complete each other and find healing and wholeness through surrender to their special form of love.

Violet, however, unlike Serena, upends the patriarchal dynamic; she is "someone strong" in a different sense than Serena, but not in any sense that emasculates Mac. He enjoys "serving a Mistress's pleasure," he says self-confidently, as much as he enjoys "being a cop, or watching a Buccaneers game, or spending a day out in the Gulf on my boat. Being a sub doesn't make me less of a man."[18] The female reader fantasy here is one of overt power, but although the heroine is nominally in charge (the message that "you must fight patriarchy"), the hero is the strong alpha male all the same (the message that "you can't fight patriarchy"), perhaps even more so—because if it takes a real man to eat quiche, wear pink, and drink chardonnay, surely it takes a man on the archetypal level of a romance novel warrior-king to accept bondage and open himself to the pleasures of dominance by his Mistress. What better way to symbolize and turn into storyline the fantasy message that "patriarchy will end" than to have the heroine quite literally anally penetrate the hero, as Violet does with Mac.

The warrior-king becomes real, and becomes vampire, in J. R. Ward's 2005 *Dark Lover* from the wildly popular *Black Dagger Brotherhood* series that I discussed in chapter 6 (one reader told me that for her, "the books were like crack"). In paranormal romance the hero can be more alpha: bigger, stronger, deadlier. He can grow fangs, possess supernatural strength, teleport, or heal miraculously fast. While Wrath is all that—indeed, his name says it all—there is one thing he cannot do, despite his superpowers. He, like all males emotionally stunted by patriarchy, cannot love. He can only disdain erotic faith as the religion of women and weak men. Yet he's immediately drawn to Beth, a beautiful woman thrust into his keeping, about to turn into a vampire herself. He gives in to lust but fights love. Nonetheless, by the end of the novel, as Wrath and Beth find peace and completion in their love bond and a new life mission to together rebuild vampire civilization, Wrath is a changed man. Still the ultra-violent patriarch toward any who would dare hurt his queen, he has literally had Beth's name carved into his back; kneeled at her feet; offered his body, heart, and soul as hers to command; and then asked her, with head bowed, "Will you take me as your own?"[19] The reader fantasy here is that patriarchy ends, yet patriarchy continues. In this end, you have the alpha-king for your own, since you have conquered him on the battlefield of love and taught him how to love.

In the romance novels above, as in that prototypical explanation in Plato's *Symposium,* love is a force that renders us whole, resolves life's quest, and grants deep peace. From this perspective, the romance story puts into narrative form the beliefs of erotic faith. It offers a fantasy of repaired gender relations. In the romance fantasy, a woman need not fear the dehumanizing violence and everyday injustices of a flawed world. She need not fear the alpha male in her bed—in her *body.* Instead, she invites that hero to "come back to the bed ag'in, honey." A woman can proffer this invitation because she has taken her stand against a male-ordered world and, although the system of gender inequality remains, so too has it ended. The romance fantasy is that the hero will come and come hard, in all his fierce and possessive warrior-king glory, but he will then forever stay: emotionally vulnerable, devoted unto death, serving his mistress with his sword and his heart. The fantasy is that patriarchy as an overall system remains in place—the hero remains a dominant alpha—but this system never threatens or diminishes the heroine, for the hero as its representative becomes submissive to her.

She gets a good man.

And she gets him to love.

Epilogue

*Lessons from Romancing
the Academic*

As conclusion, I offer a ruminative list of the Top Ten Lessons that I have learned from my auto-ethnographic project of writing romance novels as Catherine LaRoche.

10. *Writing romance fiction is hard.* A romance novel manuscript is not something one can toss off. At least I can't. A couple of times I got the "I should write one of those books, too!" response from people who seemed sure it would be easy. To manage even my very modest foray into publication, it took me a long time, much study of the craft, endless editing, and a huge dose of luck. Somewhat conversely, the quality of the writing is not what is ultimately most important in a romance novel. Bad or indifferent writing can nevertheless make for good or appealing romance fiction. What matters most, I believe, is something even harder to pull off: an emotionally gripping story. The reader's imaginative engagement in the world of the novel can happen whether or not the book meets traditional criteria of high literary style (e.g., care of word choice, elegance of sentence construction, original use of imagery and metaphor, layering of symbolism, depth and complexity of characterization, unexpectedness of plot turn). If

the writing is too literary, this structure or scaffolding may even call attention to itself and have the negative effect of pulling the reader out of the story to focus on the means by which the story is told. Fantasy escapism is one way the almost trance-inducing grip of ludic reading is described, but the term can be used derisively. I mean it instead as a compliment of high artistry. Creating this immersive reading experience through intense emotional storylines, repeatedly and on a tight publication schedule, is a very hard act to pull off.

9. *Writing romance fiction is fun.* This fun is different from the fun of strictly conceived academic writing. Scholarship tends toward the objective, the impersonal, the dry, and, on bad days, dare I say, the boring. As a professor of gender and culture studies, I find the same ideas and arguments playing out in my romance fiction as in my scholarly writing, albeit in very different forms. In this connection, I'm intrigued by the growing impact of the arts-based research movement, wherein a researcher writes up results in the form of a novel, play, or poetry, and by the possibilities offered through other experimental forms of hybrid academic discourse. Could academic writing gain wider impact— and be livelier and more enjoyable to read—if it adopted fiction elements of surprise, vulnerability, humor, suspense, emotion, and conflict? Can I incorporate fiction-writing techniques into my teaching in order to help students find their voice and make their arguments?

8. *The community is very important.* Fans of the romance genre— whether they are readers who dabble in writing or professional authors who make their living from their books—form a feisty group of friendly gals (and some very interesting guys). They come together, bonded by their common investment in the genre, in online forums and in-person writing events, in order to share their love of books. To be honest, most aspirational writers will not make a full-time living from romance publication. Many who start out won't even get published in traditional ways, although

e-books and self-publishing have opened up important new avenues for getting stories to the public. Regardless of such outcomes, the romance community functions as a highly supportive women's reading group, as a communal fan passion, as an online professional network, as a shared craft, as a love. I regularly tramped through miles of Yorkshire hills and woods in order to join my romance community for its meetings in a village pub. The group get-togethers were worth it every time, and I miss them now that I'm back home in Alabama.

7. *The solitude is very important.* The writing life is about the individual. It is about finding one's voice and putting words on the page. To quote Kafka again, the book exists to break open the frozen sea within us. This worthy work of solitude can forge a powerful self. The romance story may be particularly useful in developing a woman's voice, as it serves as a means for her to explore contradictions and quandaries of female desire. Although this work has a communal aspect, the writing is largely done alone. Through solitary imagination and the artisanship of word craft, this work can be therapeutic, transformative, reparative, empowering, and sometimes even remunerative.

6. *The genre needs defense.* Fans, writers, and many academics who study popular romance all make this point. In various corners of the culture, the novels are mocked as lowbrow smut, bad in all senses of the word, and the novelists are stigmatized and shamed. Defenders support the genre by developing arguments about the literary quality of the genre's best novels and novelists, about its significant role in the larger canon and the history of the novel, about the misogyny of the critique and its basis in anxiety around female sexuality, about the sexism of the critique and its absence in regards to parallel male-dominated popular genres such as suspense thrillers. All true.

5. *The genre needs no defense.* On the other hand, the sense that the genre is under special critique is overblown. This perception can be fueled by a defensiveness and internalized sense of inferiority

that women writers can acquire. In truth, lots of professions at-
tract slings and arrows. Politicians and Wall Street bankers are
regularly dissed. These generally male-dominated professions are
critiqued as the breeding ground of corrupt, power-hungry, and
greedy egomaniacs. The people in these professions laugh it off,
often all the way to the proverbial bank. Romance writers should
laugh it off too. Flipping the sense of stigma on its head, one
romance novelist did exactly that with me, joking, "Sometimes
I'm embarrassed to tell people I'm a lawyer!" The romance genre
needs no defense in the sense that it is what it is: entertainment,
light reading, escapist pleasure, with the deepest of issues at its
core. Let's own it and let no one shame us.

4. *A lot of it is about sex.* This might just be me, but I see questions
of sexuality as central to the genre. Sex itself is about a lot. As
humans, our sexuality is a nodal point of both possibility and
vulnerability. In territory well-trodden by psychoanalytic and
feminist theory, we know that sexuality represents a fascinating
crux of pleasure and danger, especially for women with their vulnerability to rape and their biological role as child-bearers. Our
sexuality connects us to others in some of life's most powerful
bonds, for better and for worse. Sexuality represents our physical-
ity as embodied selves, with all of the potential that entails for
ecstasy, intimacy, and reproduction as well as assault, disease,
and death. Sexual reproduction represents history and time: our
past through genetic links to parents and family, and our future
through generations to come. Sexual desire represents rationality
derailed and the thrill of living in our bodies in the now. Sex is a
pathway to knowledge of self and world, with dueling possibilities for insight and self-deception. Especially through the trope of
the virgin heroine, sexuality is a vector to a (not unproblematic)
sense of fuller womanhood. Romance fiction involves exploration
of all this and more in rich storytelling about the nature of desire.
Most broadly, it addresses the human longing for connection in
a world where love is fraught with complication and risk. Sex is
about a lot, indeed.

3. *The genre is conservative in its message of happily-ever-after pair bonding.* This is the part of the romance narrative with which I am most uncomfortable: the extent to which the narrative becomes imperative. It's not that the genre insists on heterosexual love, as romance storytelling is admirably open to sexual diversity. The problem is that the genre places so much insistence on pair-bonded romantic love as a necessity for maturity and happiness. Students—female and male, queer and straight—cry in my office about this pressure to find One True Love. We need more counter-narratives to romance, not to cancel out that storyline but to add alternatives to it. I'm heartened here by new cultural conversations around polyamory or consensual non-monogamy, asexuality, and the new singledom. The lesson? Don't cry, sweetie. Community and family come in all shapes and forms, as does love itself, well beyond the blinding glory of Princess or Prince Charming. Connect to people and things good and true, in order to find worthy love, to revel in consensually shared bodily delight, to develop your highest potential, and to be a force for goodness in the world. Be alone when you will, often, to know and love thyself. And here's an important lesson to get us all beyond the conservatism inherent in almost all cultural narratives about sex: It doesn't always have to be penetrative and phallic-centered. Remember the words of artist Sophia Wallace: *Democracy without Cliteracy? Phallusy.*

2. *The genre is radical in its liberating potential.* The romance publishing industry is woman-dominated and woman-oriented. Romance stories are our only cultural tales that always end with good women getting what they want. Not dead or damaged or left behind, but winning, every time, with all their needs met. And these stories model what a good man looks like: never abusive, always supportive, reliable in every way that counts, bringing his partner to orgasm every time. The genre clearly resonates with a huge number of readers and makes them happy. When women read these books, it's a way for them to claim personal time and space for themselves with stories that celebrate women and affirm their value. That *is* radical politics.

And the Number One lesson that I have learned about and from romance writing?

1. *Love matters.* Romance fiction raises critical questions for the reader about self and society. As is true of high literary fiction, genre romance has the ability to provoke reflection about the culture, to hold up a screen or mirror that allows us to see and judge ourselves. While the genre is escapist in its pleasures, make no mistake that it is mindless. Proof lies in the copious debate and commentary on the numerous online forums and in the fruitful scholarship of interdisciplinary popular romance studies. In and through storylines that deal with life, love, and family, romance readers and authors critically engage a host of pressing issues: women's and men's traditional roles, feminism, sexism, education, career choice, workplace stress, self-esteem, caregiver responsibilities, dating, sex, rape, domestic abuse, addiction, body image, pregnancy, miscarriage, childbearing, parenting, disability, divorce, friendship, sibling rivalry, and far more. Romance readers know that stories about love are some of the most important that we tell.

On that point, here's one final story. In 2013, while in England, I attended a wonderful book fair for readers and authors called the Festival of Romance. It was held in Bedford, a historic market town on the River Great Ouse. (In a coincidence that charmed me the entire time I was there, the Duke of Bedford is a minor character in my novel *Master of Love;* his land agent evicts my heroine Callista from her family home in London's Bloomsbury Square.) At the festival awards dinner, I sat next to a British romance blogger, a soft-spoken young woman with the translucent white skin of the English Rose described in so many of the historical romances I grew up reading. She told me a story about friends of hers, a couple who'd been married for twenty-three years. They owned a business where they worked together daily and a motorcycle that they drove all over Europe. The wife rode pillion on the back. The husband used to say that he knew his wife was falling asleep when he heard her helmet click against his. He adored her, the blogger told me, clearly admiring her friends' love. Just a few weeks ago, the wife died. My dinner companion had been at the funeral and said that the man looked literally deflated, like he'd sunk into himself. "She gave him his confidence," this young woman told me. "It's hard to talk about, but love makes us better. Love makes the world a better place." In a time when pundits question whether the book is dead, this woman looked me in the eye and said with quiet conviction, "Books are part of that goodness. Romantic novels make you feel better. They give you courage. I believe that books can change your life."

This project changed my life. It made me a better and more playful writer. It gave me insight into the romance novels that have overflowed my bookshelves for decades. It allowed me to meet a community of fun and creative people. And it underlined for me the importance of one of the central tasks of life: how to love well. This love can take on many forms. Popular romance fiction is the genre of literature that explores this task through a focus on amatory partnership. If you haven't read a romance recently, try picking one up. You'll find a whole world in it.

Happy reading.

Happy loving.

And happy endings to us all.

Notes

Prologue

1. The quotation comes from Christine Armario, "Hundreds Flock to Meet '50 Shades of Grey' Author," *Tuscaloosa News*, April 30, 2012, 2A.

2. *Romancelandia* is a term broadly used within the past decade or so by readers and writers of the popular romance genre. The term serves as metaphor for the literary landscape of popular romance fiction wherein heroes and heroines meet and play out their conflicts to happy resolutions; it refers equally to the physical community of authors, readers, and publishing professionals who engage with the genre and to their lively online discussions on reviewer websites, blogs, and Twitter. Romancelandia (I've seen it abbreviated as *Romland*) is thus at once literary landscape, human community, and online discussion world. It is a space simultaneously imaginary, physical, and virtual. I take the term as a fond and playful acknowledgment of the romance story's mythic nature. These stories are not fully realistic and of this world; they inhabit instead that happy other world of Romancelandia, where emotional justice reigns and all endings are satisfying. See, for example, extensive use of *Romancelandia* in Wendell and Tan, *Beyond Heaving Bosoms*; see also the new series *Romancelandia* by Anne Tenino, with the first book *Too Stupid to Live* (Hillsborough, NJ: Riptide, 2013).

1. Find Your One True Love

1. Coontz, *Marriage, A History*, 5. See also Polhemus, *Erotic Faith*, and May, *Love*.

2. Romance Writers of America (RWA) is the US-based professional writers' organization devoted to the publishing genre of popular romance fiction. It has a membership of approximately ten thousand published and aspiring authors. For all industry and reader statistics cited in this book, visit the RWA website at www.rwa.org/p/cm /ld/fid=580 and www.rwa.org/p/cm/ld/fid=582; see also RWA's *Romance Writers Report* 34.11 (November 2014): 9; "Mills & Boon," *Wikipedia*, http://en.wikipedia.org/wiki /Mills_%26_Boon; and "Romance Novel," *Wikipedia*, http://en.wikipedia.org/wiki /Romance_novel. See also Regis, *Natural History of the Romance Novel*.

3. These statistics come from Maria Connor, "Tough Economics: Publishing Industry Fallout and What It Means for Romance Writers," *Romance Writers Report* 29.4

(April 2009): 17; "2013 RomStat Report," *Romance Writers Report* 34.11 (November 2014): 9; and Liz Bury, "Self-Publishing Boom Sees 59% Increase in DIY Titles," *The Guardian,* October 11, 2013, http://www.theguardian.com/books/2013/oct/11/self-publishing -boom-increase-diy-titles.

　　4. Modleski, Loving *with a Vengeance,* xix. For some of these previous lines of academic inquiry, see Krentz, ed., *Dangerous Men and Adventurous Women;* Coddington, "Wavering between Worlds"; Regis, *Natural History of the Romance Novel;* Goade, ed., *Empowerment versus Oppression;* Vivanco, *For Love and Money;* and Frantz and Selinger, eds., *New Approaches to Popular Romance Fiction.*

　　5. *Anglosphere* refers broadly to the global community of native English-speaking peoples and nations with a British heritage. It is a fairly new term that proves useful for talking about the worldwide reach of popular romance fiction as a genre commonly written in Anglosphere countries and translated for global sales.

　　6. In this ethnographic research, I conducted interviews at four national conferences of the Romance Writers of America (Dallas, 2007; San Francisco, 2008; Washington, DC, 2009; New York City, 2011) and made extensive field notes as I participated in the conferences as a working member and aspiring author. About a dozen of my interviews were sit-down conversations lasting thirty to sixty minutes; I took notes instead of making audio recordings in order to maintain a more relaxed feel to these conversations. Most of the interviews, however, were more informal and consisted of many more conversations, both short and long, with fellow conference attendees and their guests in workshops and conference events, at meals and receptions, and in chance meetings such as at the elevator or on the shuttle bus. I aimed for these conversation partners to represent a broad cross-section. I ended up talking with women—and some men—ranging from the newly published to the *New York Times*–bestselling and who write across the gamut of romance subgenres; with industry insiders such as agents and RWA officers (chapter organizers, national board members, a past president); with hard-working aspirational authors trying to catch an agent's eye; and with women who have little serious ambition to publish but who love romance fiction and the camaraderie of the community. Using a semi-structured interview format, I asked open-ended questions about what these people think of the romance story: its appeal, the largely female aspect of its readership, its role and reception in pop culture, the changing nature of the romance genre and publishing industry, their own history of involvement as readers and writers, the limitations of the genre. Because I am not writing as a qualitative social scientist who performs formal analysis on interview data and instead as an interdisciplinary humanist who offers an interpretation of the romance narrative, the material from these interviews shows up in my text as illustrative quotations or examples but more often serves as background that informs my thinking. I seek to balance the limits of ethnography (e.g., its reliance on insiders' accounts for the meaning of their experiences) with analysis of the romance genre as a form of shared cultural fantasy space for working through deep ambivalences around sexuality and gender, especially for women (see, e.g., the model

of Modleski, *Loving with a Vengeance*). Thus, the ethnographic work of interviews and participation in the romance community shapes my interpretation of the romance story, along with my readings of primary texts (romance novels) and secondary texts (relevant academic literature), and my engagement in the academic discourse community of popular romance studies.

7. Johnson, *Gender Knot*, 5.

8. Snitow, "Mass Market Romance," 309. By focusing on a heterosexual woman reader, I do not intend for my analysis to erase the experience of readers of other gender expressions and sexual orientations. So what about the male reader, the lesbian reader, the queer reader, the asexual reader? What are the meanings, the pleasures, and the alienations of the romance reading experience for them? More generally, how does diversity in gender and sexuality change people's relationships to the wider romance story as it operates in the culture? How does this diversity queer the romance story? Although today's popular romance is not read exclusively by heterosexual women, such is the main target audience. As the genre continues to develop and change with the rise of more LGBTQ (lesbian, gay, bisexual, transgender, queer) books and publishing lines, it will be fascinating to think more about these larger questions and broader demographics.

2. Going Native

1. See Eisner, "Romantic Fandom."

2. Fiske, "The Cultural Economy of Fandom," 30, 37–39. For the romance review websites, see *Dear Author,* http://dearauthor.com/; *All about Romance,* http://likesbooks .com/; *Smart Bitches Trashy Books,* http://smartbitchestrashybooks.com; RT *Book Reviews,* www.rtbookreviews.com/; *The Romance Reviews,* www.theromancereviews.com/; *Romance in Color,* www.romanceincolor.com/; and *Romance Junkies,* www.romancejunk ies.com.

3. Jensen, "Fandom as Pathology."

4. Jenkins, *Confessions of an Aca-Fan.*

5. See, e.g., Swanson, *The Story of Viewers for Quality Television;* McCabe and Akass, eds., *Quality TV;* and Hills, *Fan Cultures.*

6. See oliviawaite.com, vacuousminx.wordpress.com, wonkomance.com, romance novelsforfeminists.blogspot.com, and *Something More* at myextensivereading.wordpress .com.

7. Phillips, "Embracing the 'Overly Confessional'"; Jenkins et al., "The Culture That Sticks to Your Skin," 3, 6.

8. Gunnels and Klink, "'We Are All Together.'"

9. Tedlock, "From Participant Observation to the Observation of Participation."

10. Lassiter, "Authoritative Texts, Collaborative Ethnography, and Native American Studies," 603. James Clifford and George E. Marcus's influential *Writing Culture: The Poetics and Politics of Ethnography* (1986) marked a watershed moment in the develop-

ment of this critique and its experimental alternatives. The broad set of these alternative practices inspired by postmodernism, postcolonialism, critical theory, and feminism includes narrative ethnography (Tedlock, "From Participant Observation to the Observation of Participation"), collaborative ethnography (Lassiter, "Authoritative Texts, Collaborative Ethnography, and Native American Studies"), autoethnography (Ellis, *The Ethnographic I*), life-world analytical ethnography (Pfadenhauer, "Ethnography of Scenes"), dialogic or hermeneutic ethnography (Tedlock and Mannheim, eds., *The Dialogic Emergence of Culture*), and public ethnography (Tedlock, "The Observation of Participation and the Emergence of Public Ethnography").

11. Pfadenhauer, "Ethnography of Scenes," par. 20; Jenkins et al., "The Culture That Sticks to Your Skin," 7. See also Moeran, "From Participant Observation to Observant Participation"; Whitehead, "Post-Human Anthropology"; and Lassiter, "Authoritative Texts, Collaborative Ethnography, and Native American Studies." Pfadenhauer's full enumeration of the characteristics of observant participation, as opposed to the more traditional method of participant observation, bears quoting:

> 1. with respect to the research objectives: ideally it [observant participation] is about the production of observation data *and* of experiential data; 2. with respect to the relevance assessment: participation—if a decision has to be made—takes priority over observation; 3. with respect to the researcher's perspective: he/she strives for an existential insider's perspective gained through subjective experience instead of for an (inevitably) aloof outsider's point of view; 4. finally, with respect to the consequences for the evaluation of the data gained: the interpretation of subjective experience data calls for a special, namely a *phenomenological* analysis. (par. 21)

12. Jenkins, *Fans, Bloggers and Gamers*, 4.

13. Ian Bogost, "Against Aca-Fandom: On Jason Mittell on Mad Men," *Ian Bogost Blog*, July 29, 2010, www.bogost.com/blog/against_aca-fandom.shtml#.

14. Gergen and Gergen, "Performative Social Science and Psychology." See also Pfadenhauer, "Ethnography of Scenes," par. 21. Performative ethnography partakes in a growing area, variously called alternative academic discourse, hybrid academic writing, or lyric scholarship, that seeks to open up orthodoxies of scholarly communication which emphasize impersonal voice and analytical prose. These alternatives incorporate instead personal narrative, fiction and poetry, nonlinear writing, and a host of other experiments with written word to explore a given research topic. See, e.g., Schroeder et al., eds., ALT DIS: *Alternative Discourses and the Academy*; Kouritzin et al., eds., *Qualitative Research*; and Anita Lahey, "Academic Papers Get Poetic," *University Affairs*, January 2012, 24–28. See also the example of the "Social Fictions Series" emerging from the arts-based research movement and published by Sense Publishers, a collection of books informed by traditional social research but written in fictional format (www.sense publishers.com/catalogs/bookseries/social-fictions-series/).

15. Whitehead, "Post-Human Anthropology," esp. 5; Wacquant, *Body and Soul;* Mc-Tavish, *Feminist Figure Girl.* See also Lianne McTavish, "Scholarly Gym Rat," *Chronicle Review,* November 25, 2011, B20.

16. See Deirdre Donahue, "Scholarly Writers Empower the Romance Genre," *USA Today,* July 6, 2009, updated July 10, 2009, www.usatoday.com/life/books/news/2009-07-06-romance-novels_N.htm, and Lee Tobin McClain, "Sweet, Savage Academe: True Confessions of a Pulp Professor," *Chronicle of Higher Education,* August 15, 2003, B19.

17. Whitehead, "Post-Human Anthropology," 5, 7; Jenkins et al., "The Culture That Sticks to Your Skin," 4; Tedlock, "The Observation of Participation and the Emergence of Public Ethnography," 160.

18. Wacquant, *Body and Soul,* vii, 4, 4n3. Wacquant further explains how "breaking with the moralizing discourse—that indifferently feeds both celebration and denigration—produced by the 'gaze from afar' of an outside observer standing at a distance from or above the specific universe, this book seeks to suggest how boxing 'makes sense' as soon as one takes pains to get close enough to it to grasp it *with one's body,* in a quasi-experimental situation" (7).

19. Coker and Benefiel, "We Have Met the Fans." "Look Hot While You Fight the Patriarchy" functions as the tagline to Lianne McTavish's blog at feministfiguregirl.com and as the subtitle to her book *Feminist Figure Girl.*

4. Sex: Good Girls Do

1. Perrin, *Getting Some,* 133.

2. The chapter subtitle "Good Girls Do" was partly inspired by the title of a newspaper article about women taking pole-dancing and stripper aerobics classes at local gyms, in the context of a claimed new freedom that women are enjoying to explore their sexuality. Marilisa Racco, "Good Girls Do," *Globe and Mail,* April 8, 2006, http://search.proquest.com/docview/383563676?accountid=14472. "Good Girls Do" was equally the title of a romance fiction program hosted at the Bowling Green Public Library in Kentucky that featured authors and readers celebrating the genre. Clinton Lewis, "The Business of Romance," *Bowling Green Daily News,* June 30, 2004, www.bgdailynews.com/romance-authors-sherrilyn-kenyon-from-left-annie-soloman-cheryl-zach/article_b4904b80-8040-58f6-9279-6701a5e8aa3e.html?mode=jqm.

3. American Dialect Society, www.americandialect.org/woty/all-of-the-words-of-the-year-1990-to-present. See also the online magazine *Cliterati,* a blog group featuring writing about women's sexual fantasies, www.cliterati.co.uk/about/.

4. Illouz, *Hard-Core Romance,* 34. For analyses of sex-positive culture, see, e.g., Nagle, ed., *Whores and Other Feminists;* McNair, *Striptease Culture;* Johnson, ed., *Jane Sexes It Up;* Roach, *Stripping, Sex, and Popular Culture;* Nikunen et al., eds., *Pornification;* and Taormino et al., eds., *Feminist Porn Book.*

5. Jeff Bercovici, "The World's Top-Earning Authors," *Forbes*, August 12, 2013, www
.forbes.com/sites/jeffbercovici/2013/08/12/the-worlds-top-earning-authors-with
-50-shades-e-l-james-debuts-at-no-1/; "Fifty Shades of Grey," *Wikipedia*, http://en.wiki
pedia.org/wiki/Fifty_Shades_of_Grey; Illouz, *Hard-Core Romance*, 7.

6. Annie Sprinkle, *Hardcore from the Heart: The Pleasures, Profits and Politics of Sex
in Performance* (New York: Continuum, 2001); Taormino et al., eds., *Feminist Porn Book*;
Carol Queen, *Real Live Nude Girl: Chronicles of Sex-Positive Culture*, 2nd ed. (San Francisco: Cleis Press, 2002); Vance, ed. *Pleasure and Danger.*

7. I build my argument partly on Snitow's earlier important essay "Mass Market Romance."

8. "Porno-, comb. form," *Oxford English Dictionary Online* (Oxford: Oxford University Press, 2014), www.oed.com/view/Entry/148007; Douglas Harper, "Pornographic,"
Dictionary.com: Online Etymology Dictionary, http://dictionary.reference.com/browse
/pornographic.

9. See, e.g., Russell Moore, "Can Romance Novels Hurt Your Heart?" *Crosswalk.
com*, May 18, 2011, www.crosswalk.com/blogs/russellmoore/can-romance-novels-hurt
-your-heart.html; Kimberly Giles, "Romance Novels Can Become Addictive," *KSL
.com*, May 30, 2011, www.ksl.com/?nid=1010&sid=15609384; Caryn Rivadeneira, "Why
Romance Novels Aren't Emotional Porn," *Christianity Today*, June 2011, www.chris
tianitytoday.com/women/2011/june/why-romance-novels-arent-emotional-por
.html?paging=off; Joe Carter, "How Romance Novels Are Like Pornography," *First
Things*, July 11, 2011, www.firstthings.com/blogs/firstthoughts/2011/07/how-romance
-novels-are-like-pornography-part-ii; and Slattery, *Finding the Hero in Your Husband.*

10. Steinem, "Erotica vs. Pornography," 241; Snitow, "Mass Market Romance." See
also Whissell, "Linguistic, Emotional and Content Analysis."

11. Snitow, "Mass Market Romance," 320.

12. Greer, *The Female Eunuch*, 180.

13. Snitow, "Mass Market Romance," 316, 320. Although sometimes credited to Gloria Steinem, this slogan, much reprinted on T-shirts and bumper stickers, was coined by
Australian writer, activist, and senator Irina Dunn in 1970. See "Irina Dunn," *Wikipedia*,
http://en.wikipedia.org/wiki/Irina_Dunn.

14. See, e.g., Wendell and Tan, *Beyond Heaving Bosoms*, and the fan-scholar blog sites
that I mention in chapter 2 such as oliviawaite.com, *Vacuous Minx, Wonk-o-Mance*, and
Romance Novels for Feminists.

15. See, e.g., Maria Mora, "Is Gay Male Erotica the Next Big Thing?" *All Parenting*,
April 2, 2014, www.allparenting.com/my-life/articles/970447/is-gay-male-erotica-the
-next-big-thing.

16. See Good For Her and the Feminist Porn Awards, goodforher.com and feminist
pornawards.com.

17. With the growth of a contemporary asexuality movement, we can ask questions
about asexual romance in this connection as well; see, e.g., www.asexuality.org for the

Asexual Visibility and Education Network; Cerankowski and Milks, "New Orientations"; and De Luzio Chasin, "Theoretical Issues in the Study of Asexuality." There can certainly be companionate marriage—for example, Christian couples who took vows of married chastity in the history of Christianity or long-term couples who no longer have sex—but I mean something different. What about a relationship that blooms and unites two people in a lasting romantic love bond that involves no sexual desire or consummation? Perhaps my insistence on eros constitutes a form of discrimination or bias on my part.

18. Penley et al., "Introduction," 14.

19. See details of the installation at www.sophiawallace.com/, http://sophiawallace .tumblr.com/post/33308221940/cliteracy, and http://sophiawallace.tumblr.com/post /44862453647/cliteracy-day33.

20. Nagoski, *Come as You Are.* For the text of her presentation at the 2013 Feminist Porn Awards academic conference, see Nagoski, "Vaginas of Science, Vaginas of Justice." See also Lloyd, *The Case of the Female Orgasm.*

21. "Is Sleep the New Sex?" *The Week,* http://theweek.com/article/index/97049 /is-sleep-the-new-sex; Ruby Warrington, "Why Sleep Is the New Sex," *Huffington Post,* www.huffingtonpost.com/2010/03/02/why-sleep-is-the-new-sex_n_482796.html.

22. The phrase "a feminist is a woman who writes" comes from Spender, *The Writing or the Sex?* 47. Cixous, "Laugh of the Medusa," 876, 877, 880, 881.

23. George Orwell, "Inside the Whale" (1940), in *A Collection of Essays* (New York: Houghton Mifflin Harcourt, 1981), 242.

24. Franz Kafka to Oskar Pollak, January 27, 1904, Franz Kafka, *Letters to Friends, Family and Editors,* transl. Richard Winston and Clara Winston (New York: Schocken Books, 1990), 14.

25. Fletcher, *Historical Romance Fiction.*

26. McFarlane, *Here's Looking at You,* 282–83, emphasis added.

6. Love

1. hooks, "Love as the Practice of Freedom," in *Outlaw Culture,* 243–50.

2. Jenkins, *Indigo,* 1.

3. hooks, "Love as the Practice of Freedom," in *Outlaw Culture,* 250.

4. "Free, *v.*" and "free, *adj., n.,* and *adv.*," *Oxford English Dictionary Online* (Oxford: Oxford University Press, 2015), www.oed.com/viewdictionaryentry/Entry/74376, www .oed.com/viewdictionaryentry/Entry/74375.

5. James Mellon, ed., *Bullwhip Days: The Slaves Remember, An Oral History* (New York: Grove Press, 1988), 455, quoted in Jenkins, *Indigo,* 357.

6. Jenkins, *Indigo,* 30, 81–82.

7. Pat Benatar, "Love Is a Battlefield," by Mike Chapman and Holly Knight, on *Live from Earth* (Chrysalis Records, 1983). See video at www.youtube.com/watch ?v=BcOixjbPC4I.

8. James Sterling's prefatory poem "To Mrs. Eliza Haywood on Her Writings" appeared in the third and subsequent editions of Haywood's collection *Secret Histories, Novels, and Poems* (London, 1732); Sterling's epithet from his poem stuck in many subsequent references to Haywood and her prolific body of work. For a well-contextualized discussion of Sterling's epithet, see George Frisbie Whicher's *The Life and Romances of Mrs. Eliza Haywood* (New York: Columbia University Press, 1915), 15–20. See also David Brewer, "'Eliza Haywood,' Secret History, and the Politics of Attribution," in *The Passionate Fictions of Eliza Haywood: Essays on her Life and Work,* ed. Kirsten T. Saxton and Rebecca P. Bocchicchio (Lexington: University Press of Kentucky, 2000), 217–39.

9. Haywood, *Fantomina,* 239

10. Ibid., 234, 238. For further commentary on Haywood, see Backscheider and Richetti's introduction in *Popular Fiction by Women,* ix–xxiii; see also Margaret Case Croskery, "Masquing Desire: The Politics of Passion in Eliza Haywood's *Fantomina,*" in *The Passionate Fictions of Eliza Haywood,* 69–94.

11. Spenser, Sonnet 37, *Amoretti.*

12. The J. Geils Band, "Love Stinks," by Peter Wolf and Seth Justman, on *Love Stinks* (EMI Records, 1980); Taylor Swift, "Blank Space," by Taylor Swift, Max Martin, and Johan Shellback, on *1989* (Big Machine Records, 2014). I thank Christopher Fox for bringing this song to my attention.

13. hooks, *All about Love,* 13, 4, 14.

14. Thaddaeus Quince, "This Heart," on *The One You Love* (Wreckloose Records, 2007).

15. Jenkins, *Indigo,* 1.

16. See Illouz, *Hard-Core Romance.*

17. National Leather Association–International, *Abuse versus Healthy* BDSM*: Know the Difference,* brochure, part of the NLA-I Domestic Violence Project, 2007, distributed at the panels of the Romance section, Popular Culture Association national conference, St. Louis, MO, April 2010.

18. Buchanan, *Hard Fall,* 199, 215. For other interesting examples of these dynamics within the BDSM romance genre, see Hill, *Natural Law* and *Rough Canvas.*

19. On the archetypes of manhood in the mythopoetic men's movement, see, e.g., Robert Moore and Douglas Gillette, *King, Warrior, Magician, Lover: Rediscovering the Archetypes of the Mature Masculine* (New York: HarperCollins, 1990).

20. hooks, "Love as the Practice of Freedom," in *Outlaw Culture,* 246.

21. Ward, *Dark Lover,* 3, 186–87.

22. Rotham, *Big Temptation,* 285.

23. Chantal Gabel, "Pinnacle Vodka: Flavor of Choice," *Steppin' Out Magazine,* August 17, 2011, 71; *Steppin' Out* bills itself as New York and New Jersey's no. 1 weekly entertainment and nightlife magazine. Christina Jelski, "Pinnacle Whipped on Fire in 2011," *Impact: Global News and Research for the Drinks Executive,* July 15, 2011, 6. For the ads as presented on Pinnacle Vodka's website, see www.pinnaclevodka.com/advertising. For

blog comments on the ad campaign, see http://goddessblue.wordpress.com/tag/stereo type and http://salucking.wordpress.com/tag/get-him-whipped/.

24. Vincent, *Self-Made Man*, 277.

25. Jenkins, *Indigo*, 356.

7. Notes from the Writing

1. See *Aphra Behn: Oroonoko, The Rover, and Other Works*, ed. Janet Todd (London: Penguin, 2003).

2. For 2013 figures, see Jeff Bercovici, "The World's Top-Earning Authors," *Forbes*, August 12, 2013, www.forbes.com/sites/jeffbercovici/2013/08/12/the-worlds-top-earning -authors-with-50-shades-e-l-james-debuts-at-no-1/. For 2014 figures, see Natalie Robehmed, "The World's Top-Earning Authors," *Forbes*, September 8, 2014, www.forbes.com /sites/natalierobehmed/2014/09/08/the-worlds-top-earning-authors-veronica-roth -john-green-and-gillian-flynn-join-ranking/.

8. Happily Ever After

1. Polhemus, *Erotic Faith*, 1, 27.

2. Ibid., 4, 10, 19; May, *Love*, 1.

3. Keats, "Bright Star!" in Keats, *John Keats: The Complete Poems*, 452.

4. Keats, *Complete Works*, Letter CXLII.

5. E. E. Cummings, *Complete Poems: 1904–1962*, ed. George J. Firmage (New York: Liveright Publishing, 1991), 766.

6. Eric Selinger, "Love and Religion (John Lennon Edition)," *Teach Me Tonight*, July 17, 2012, http://teachmetonight.blogspot.co.uk/2012/07/love-and-religion-john -lennon-edition.html. See his further quote in the same blog post: "Sometimes the intersection of love and religion involves seeing the beloved as a divine (or quasi-divine) figure—love as worship, or love as idolatry, I suppose—and sometimes it involves seeing something 'of God' in the person you love." See also the blog post "What's It All About, Arnold?" by Eric Selinger at *The Popular Romance Project*, July 5, 2012, in which Selinger quotes Karen Lystra from her book *Searching the Heart: Women, Men, and Romantic Love in Nineteenth-Century America* (New York: Oxford University Press, 1992): "By the 1830s, the personhood of the loved one . . . had become a powerful rival to God as the individual's central symbol of ultimate significance" (http://popularromanceproject.org /talking-about-romance/2304/#more-2304).

7. Jo Beverley, *The Stanforth Secrets* (1989; reprint, New York: New American Library, 2010), 255–56. I thank Laura Vivanco for finding this example in relation to my use of Polhemus's concept of erotic faith and for posting it in a blog post, "Quick Quotes: Faith, Hope and Love," *Teach Me Tonight*, March 12, 2012, http://teachmetonight.blog spot.co.uk/2012/03/quick-quotes-faith-hope-and-love.html.

8. Jo Beverley, comment on Vivanco's post "Quick Quotes: Faith, Hope and Love," *Teach Me Tonight,* March 12, 2012, http://teachmetonight.blogspot.co.uk/2012/03/quick -quotes-faith-hope-and-love.html?showComment=1331549442231#c83324823247476 07527.

9. Plato, *Symposium,* 192c.

10. Although what Frye means by *romance novel* differs from the popular genre fiction under consideration here, there is significant continuity between these forms of prose fiction as well. Frye, *Anatomy of Criticism.* This issue of the historical lineage of contemporary romance novels in terms of the long-established literary forms of both *novel* and *romance* bears further study. Balogh, *Secret Pearl,* 386.

11. The line is from Larkin's poem "An Arundel Tomb" in the final stanza: "Time has transfigured them into / Untruth. The stone fidelity / They hardly meant has come to be / Their final blazon, and to prove / Our almost-instinct almost true: / What will survive of us is love." For commentary on various meanings of the poem and its cultural contexts, see, e.g., James L. Orwin, "'An Arundel Tomb'—An Interpretation," *About Larkin* 17 (April 2004), and Jeremy Axelrod, "Philip Larkin: 'An Arundel Tomb': Does a Notoriously Grumpy Poet Believe in Everlasting Love?" www.poetryfoundation.org /learning/guide/237912.

12. Brockmann, *All through the Night,* 340.

13. Snitow, "Mass Market Romance," 314.

14. Sedgwick, "Paranoid Reading and Reparative Reading," 27, 35. Sedgwick's work on the reparative and paranoid reading positions is quite suggestive for an analysis of popular romance studies. She draws on a psychoanalytic tradition through Freud, Paul Ricoeur, and the British object relations theorist Melanie Klein. Klein's theory of the infant's relational positions of the paranoid/schizoid and the depressive/reparative allows Sedgwick to develop her own theory about reading strategies and ways of knowing. Sedgwick's suggestion that queer, feminist, literary, and critical theory need not be suspicious (paranoid, accusatory) in order to be effective is a fruitful one for popular romance studies as well: "No less acute than a paranoid position, no less realistic, no less attached to a project of survival, and neither less nor more delusional or fantasmatic, the reparative reading position undertakes a different range of affects, ambitions, and risks" (35).

15. Frye, *Anatomy of Criticism,* 201; Frantz, "'How We Love *Is* Our Soul'," 58. See also Frantz, "'Expressing' Herself."

16. McFarlane, *You Had Me at Hello,* 433.

17. Banks, *Sweet Persuasion,* 70, 253, 284.

18. Hill, *Natural Law,* 277.

19. Ward, *Dark Lover,* 333.

Bibliography

Backscheider, Paula R., and John J. Richetti. *Popular Fiction by Women, 1660–1730: An Anthology.* Oxford: Clarendon Press, 1996.

Balogh, Mary. *The Secret Pearl.* 1991. Reprint, New York: Bantam Dell, 2005.

Banks, Maya. *Sweet Persuasion.* New York: Berkley Heat, 2009.

Bersani, Leo. "Is the Rectum a Grave?" *October* 43 (1987): 197–222.

Brockmann, Suzanne. *All through the Night.* New York: Ballantine Books, 2007.

———. *Force of Nature.* New York: Ballantine Books, 2007.

Buchanan, James. *Hard Fall.* Albion, NY: ManLoveRomance Press, 2009.

Cerankowski, Karli June, and Megan Milks. "New Orientations: Asexuality and Its Implications for Theory and Practice." *Feminist Studies* 36.3 (2010): 650–54.

Cixous, Hélène. "The Laugh of the Medusa." Translated by Keith Cohen and Paula Cohen. *Signs* 1.4 (1976): 875–93.

Clifford, James, and George E. Marcus, eds. *Writing Culture: The Poetics and Politics of Ethnography.* Berkeley: University of California Press, 1986.

Coddington, Lynn. "Wavering between Worlds: Feminist Influences in the Romance Genre." *Paradoxa* 3.1–2 (1997): 58–77.

Coker, Catherine, and Candace Benefiel. "We Have Met the Fans, and They Are Us: In Defense of Aca-Fans and Scholars." *Flow* special issue, "Revisiting Aca-Fandom," 13.05 (2010). http://flowtv.org/2010/12/we-have-met-the-fans/.

Coontz, Stephanie. *Marriage, A History: How Love Conquered Marriage.* New York: Penguin, 2005.

De Luzio Chasin, C. J. "Theoretical Issues in the Study of Asexuality." *Archives of Sexual Behavior* 40.4 (2011): 713–23.

DePaulo, Bella. *Singled Out: How Singles Are Stereotyped, Stigmatized, and Ignored, and Still Live Happily Ever After.* New York: St. Martin's Griffin, 2007.

Douglas, Ann. "Soft-Porn Culture." *The New Republic,* August 30, 1980, 25–29.

Eisner, Eric. "Romantic Fandom: Introduction." *Romantic Circles Praxis Series,* April 2011. http://romantic.arhu.umd.edu/praxis/fandom.

Ellis, Carolyn. *The Ethnographic I: A Methodological Novel about Autoethnography.* Walnut Creek, CA: AltaMira Press, 2004.

Fiedler, Leslie A. "Come Back to the Raft Ag'in, Huck Honey!" *Partisan Review* 15.6 (1948): 664–71.

Fiske, John. "The Cultural Economy of Fandom." In *Adoring Audience: Fan Culture and Popular Media,* edited by Lisa A. Lewis, 30–49. London: Routledge, 1992.

Fletcher, Lisa. *Historical Romance Fiction: Heterosexuality and Performativity.* Aldershot, UK: Ashgate, 2008.

Frantz, Sarah S. G. "'Expressing' Herself: The Romance Novel and the Feminine Will to Power." In *Scorned Literature: Essays on the History and Criticism of Popular Mass-Produced Fiction in America,* edited by Lydia Cushman Schurman and Deidre Johnson, 17–36. Westport, CT: Greenwood Press, 2002.

———. "'How We Love *Is* Our Soul': Joey W. Hill's BDSM Romance *Holding the Cards.*" In *New Approaches to Popular Romance Fiction: Critical Essays,* edited by Sarah S. G. Frantz and Eric Murphy Selinger, 47–59. Jefferson, NC: McFarland, 2012.

Frantz, Sarah S. G., and Eric Murphy Selinger, eds. *New Approaches to Popular Romance Fiction: Critical Essays.* Jefferson, NC: McFarland, 2012.

Freud, Sigmund. *The Future of an Illusion.* Translated and edited by James Strachey. 1927. Reprint, New York: Norton, 1989.

Frye, Northrop. *Anatomy of Criticism: Four Essays.* 1957. Reprint, Princeton, NJ: Princeton University Press, 1990.

Gergen, Mary M., and Kenneth J. Gergen. "Performative Social Science and Psychology." *Forum: Qualitative Social Research* 12.1 (2011): art. 11. www.qualitative-research.net /index.php/fqs/article/viewArticle/1595/3105.

Goade, Sally, ed. *Empowerment versus Oppression: Twenty First Century Views of Popular Romance Novels.* Newcastle upon Tyne, UK: Cambridge Scholars Publishing, 2007.

Greer, Germaine. *The Female Eunuch.* London: Paladin, 1970.

Gunnels, Jen, and M. Flourish Klink. "'We Are All Together': Fan Studies and Performance." *Flow* special issue, "Revisiting Aca-Fandom," 13.05 (2010). http://flowtv.org /2010/12/we-are-all-together/.

Hagstrum, Jean H. *Esteem Enlivened by Desire: The Couple from Homer to Shakespeare.* Chicago: University of Chicago Press, 1992.

Haywood, Eliza. *Fantomina; or, Love in a Maze* (1725). In *Popular Fiction by Women, 1660–1730: An Anthology,* edited by Paula R. Backscheider and John J. Richetti, 227–250. Oxford: Clarendon Press, 1996.

Hill, Joey W. *Natural Law.* In the *Nature of Desire* series. Akron, OH: Ellora's Cave Publishing, 2004.

———. *Rough Canvas.* In the *Nature of Desire* series. Akron, OH: Ellora's Cave Publishing, 2007.

Hills, Matt. *Fan Cultures.* London: Routledge, 2002.

hooks, bell. *All about Love: New Visions.* New York: HarperCollins, 2000.

———. *Communion: The Female Search for Love.* New York: HarperCollins, 2002.

———. *Outlaw Culture: Resisting Representations.* New York: Routledge, 1994.

———. *Salvation: Black People and Love.* New York: HarperCollins, 2001.

Illouz, Eva. *Hard-Core Romance: Fifty Shades of Grey, Best-Sellers, and Society.* Chicago: University of Chicago Press, 2014.

———. *Why Love Hurts: A Sociological Explanation.* Cambridge: Polity Press, 2012.

James, E. L. *Fifty Shades Trilogy.* New York: Random House, 2011.

Jenkins, Beverly. *Indigo.* 1996. Reprint, Lincoln, NE: iUniverse, 2000.

Jenkins, Henry. *Confessions of an Aca-Fan: The Official Weblog of Henry Jenkins.* www .henryjenkins.org.

———. *Fans, Bloggers and Gamers: Exploring Participatory Culture.* New York: New York University Press, 2006.

———. *Textual Poachers: Television Fans and Participatory Culture.* New York: Routledge, 1992.

Jenkins, Henry, Tara McPherson, and Jane Shattuc. "The Culture That Sticks to Your Skin: A Manifesto for a New Cultural Studies." In *Hop on Pop: The Politics and Pleasures of Popular Culture,* edited by Henry Jenkins, Tara McPherson, and Jane Shattuc, 3–25. Durham, NC: Duke University Press, 2002.

Jensen, Joli. "Fandom as Pathology: The Consequences of Characterization." In *Adoring Audience: Fan Culture and Popular Media,* edited by Lisa A. Lewis, 9–29. London: Routledge, 1992.

Johnson, Allan G. *The Gender Knot: Unraveling our Patriarchal Legacy.* Revised and updated edition. Philadelphia: Temple University Press, 2005.

Johnson, Merri Lisa, ed. *Jane Sexes It Up: True Confessions of Feminist Desire.* New York: Four Walls Eight Windows, 2002.

Kamble, Jayashree. *Making Meaning in Popular Romance Fiction: An Epistemology.* New York: Palgrave Macmillan, 2014.

Keats, John. *The Complete Works of John Keats,* vol. 5, *Letters 1819 and 1820.* Edited by H. Buxton Forman. New York: Thomas Y. Crowell, 1900.

———. *John Keats: The Complete Poems.* 3rd edition. Edited by John Barnard. London: Penguin Books, 1988.

Kouritzin, Sandra G., Nathalie A. C. Piquemal, and Renee Norman, eds. *Qualitative Research: Challenging the Orthodoxies in Standard Academic Discourse(s).* New York: Routledge, 2008.

Krentz, Jayne Ann, ed. *Dangerous Men and Adventurous Women: Romance Writers on the Appeal of the Romance.* Philadelphia: University of Pennsylvania Press, 1992.

LaRoche, Catherine [Catherine Roach]. *Knight of Love.* New York: Pocket Star–Simon and Schuster, 2014. Book 2 in the *Society of Love* series.

———. *Master of Love.* New York: Pocket Star–Simon and Schuster, 2012. Book 1 in the *Society of Love* series.

Lassiter, Luke Eric. "Authoritative Texts, Collaborative Ethnography, and Native American Studies." *American Indian Quarterly* 24.4 (2000): 601–14.

Levy, Ariel. *Female Chauvinist Pigs: Women and the Rise of Raunch Culture.* New York: Free Press, 2005.

Lloyd, Elisabeth A. *The Case of the Female Orgasm: Bias in the Science of Evolution.* Cambridge, MA: Harvard University Press, 2006.

May, Simon. *Love: A History.* New Haven, CT: Yale University Press, 2011.

McCabe, Janet, and Kim Akass, eds. *Quality TV: Contemporary American Television and Beyond.* London: I. B. Tauris, 2007.

McFarlane, Mhairi. *Here's Looking at You.* London: Avon/HarperCollins, 2013.

———. *You Had Me at Hello.* London: Avon/HarperCollins, 2012.

McNair, Brian. *Striptease Culture: Sex, Media, and the Democratisation of Desire.* London: Routledge, 2002.

McTavish, Lianne. *Feminist Figure Girl: Look Hot While You Fight the Patriarchy.* Albany, NY: SUNY Press, 2015.

Modleski, Tania. *Loving with a Vengeance: Mass-Produced Fantasies for Women.* 2nd edition. New York: Routledge, 2008.

Moeran, Brian. "From Participant Observation to Observant Participation: Anthropology, Fieldwork and Organizational Ethnography." In *Creative Encounters,* Working Papers no. 2, Copenhagen Business School, July 2007. Revised version published in *Organizational Ethnography: Studying the Complexities of Everyday Life,* edited by S. Ybema et al., 139–155. London: Sage, 2009.

Nagle, Jill, ed. *Whores and Other Feminists.* New York: Routledge, 1997.

Nagoski, Emily. *Come as You Are: The Surprising New Science that Will Transform Your Sex Life.* New York: Simon and Schuster, 2015.

———. "Vaginas of Science, Vaginas of Justice: Representations of Healthy Female Sexual Functioning in Feminist Porn." *The Dirty Normal,* April 6, 2013. www.thedirty normal.com/2013/04/06/vaginas-of-science-vaginas-of-justice-representations-of -healthy-female-sexual-functioning-in-feminist-porn/.

Nell, Victor. *Lost in a Book: The Psychology of Reading for Pleasure.* New Haven, CT: Yale University Press, 1990.

Nikunen, Kaarina, Susanna Paasonen, and Laura Saarenmaa, eds. *Pornification: Sex and Sexuality in Media Culture.* London: Bloomsbury, 2007.

Penley, Constance, et al. "Introduction: The Politics of Producing Pleasure." In *The Feminist Porn Book: The Politics of Producing Pleasure,* edited by Tristan Taormino et al., 9–20. New York: Feminist Press, 2013.

Perrin, Kayla. *Getting Some.* Don Mills, ON: Spice, 2007.

Pfadenhauer, Michaela. "Ethnography of Scenes. Towards a Sociological Life-World Analysis of (Post-Traditional) Community-Building." *Forum: Qualitative Social Research* 6.3 (2005): art. 43. www.qualitative-research.net/index.php/fqs/article/view Article/23/49.

Phillips, Tom. "Embracing the 'Overly Confessional': Scholar-Fandom and Approaches to Personal Research." *Flow* special issue, "Revisiting Aca-Fandom," 13.05 (2010). http://flowtv.org/2010/12/embracing-the-overly-confessional/.

Plato. *Symposium: Plato in Twelve Volumes.* Vol. 9. Translated by Harold N. Fowler. Cambridge, MA: Harvard University Press, 1925.

Polhemus, Robert M. *Erotic Faith: Being in Love from Jane Austen to D. H. Lawrence.* Chicago: University of Chicago Press, 1990.

Radway, Janice A. *Reading the Romance: Women, Patriarchy, and Popular Literature.* 1984. Reprint, Chapel Hill: University of North Carolina Press, 1991.

Regis, Pamela. *A Natural History of the Romance Novel.* Philadelphia: University of Pennsylvania Press, 2003.

Roach, Catherine M. *Stripping, Sex, and Popular Culture.* Oxford: Berg, 2007.

Romance Writers of America (RWA). "Romance E-Book Market Share Rose." RWA *eNotes,* January 21, 2015.

———. "Romance Literature Statistics." www.rwanational.org/cs/the_romance_genre /romance_literature_statistics.

Rotham, Robin L. *Big Temptation.* Akron, OH: Ellora's Cave Publishing, 2008.

Schroeder, Christopher, Helen Fox, and Patricia Bizzell, eds. ALT DIS: *Alternative Discourses and the Academy.* Portsmouth, NH: Boynton/Cook, 2002.

Sedgwick, Eve Kosofsky. "Paranoid Reading and Reparative Reading; or, You're So Paranoid, You Probably Think This Introduction Is about You." In *Novel Gazing: Queer Readings in Fiction,* edited by Eve Kosofsky Sedgwick, 1–37. Durham, NC: Duke University Press, 1997.

Slattery, Julianna. *Finding the Hero in Your Husband: Surrendering the Way God Intended.* Deerfield Beach, FL: Health Communications, 2004.

Snitow, Ann Barr. "Mass Market Romance: Pornography for Women Is Different." In *Women and Romance: A Reader,* edited by Susan Ostrov Weisser, 307–22. 1979. Reprint, New York: New York University Press, 2001.

Spender, Dale. *The Writing or the Sex? or, Why You Don't Have to Read Women's Writing to Know It's No Good.* New York: Pergamon Press, 1989.

Spenser, Edmund. Sonnet 37, *Amoretti* (1595). In *Edmund Spenser's Amoretti and Epithalamion: A Critical Edition,* edited by Kenneth J. Larsen. Tempe: Arizona State University, 1997.

Steinem, Gloria. "Erotica vs. Pornography." In *Outrageous Acts and Everyday Rebellions.* 2nd edition. New York: Henry Holt, 1995, 238–251.

Stepp, Laura Sessions. *Unhooked: How Young Women Pursue Sex, Delay Love, and Lose at Both.* New York: Riverhead Books, 2007.

Swanson, Dorothy Collins. *The Story of Viewers for Quality Television: From Grassroots to Prime Time.* Syracuse, NY: Syracuse University Press, 2000.

Taormino, Tristan, et al., eds. *The Feminist Porn Book: The Politics of Producing Pleasure.* New York: Feminist Press, 2013.

Tedlock, Barbara. "From Participant Observation to the Observation of Participation: The Emergence of Narrative Ethnography." *Journal of Anthropological Research* 47.1 (1991): 69–94.

———. "The Observation of Participation and the Emergence of Public Ethnography." In *Strategies of Qualitative Inquiry,* 3rd edition, edited by Norman K. Denzin and Yvonna S. Lincoln, 151–172. Thousand Oaks, CA: Sage, 2008.

Tedlock, Dennis, and Bruce Mannheim, eds. *The Dialogic Emergence of Culture*. Urbana: University of Illinois Press, 1995.

Vance, Carole S., ed. *Pleasure and Danger: Exploring Female Sexuality*. Boston: Routledge and Kegan Paul, 1984.

Vincent, Norah. *Self-Made Man: One Woman's Year Disguised as a Man*. New York: Penguin Books, 2007.

Vivanco, Laura. *For Love and Money: The Literary Art of the Harlequin Mills and Boon Romance*. Tirril, Penrith, UK: Humanities EBooks, 2011.

Wacquant, Loïc. *Body and Soul: Notebooks of an Apprentice-Boxer*. New York: Oxford University Press, 2004. Excerpted as "Participant Observation/Observant Participation," in *Sociology: Introductory Readings*, 3rd edition, edited by Anthony Giddens and Philip W. Sutton, 69–73. Cambridge: Polity Press, 2010.

Wallace, Sophia. *Cliteracy: 100 Natural Laws*. www.sophiawallace.com/cliteracy-100-natural-laws.

Ward, J. R. *Dark Lover: A Novel of the Black Dagger Brotherhood*. New York: Signet Eclipse, 2005.

Weisser, Susan Ostrov. *The Glass Slipper: Women and Love Stories*. New Brunswick, NJ: Rutgers University Press, 2013.

Wendell, Sarah. "'You Call Me a Bitch Like That's a Bad Thing': Romance Criticism and Redefining the Word 'Bitch.'" In *New Approaches to Popular Romance Fiction: Critical Essays*, edited by Sarah S. G. Frantz and Eric Murphy Selinger, 178–94. Jefferson, NC: McFarland, 2012.

Wendell, Sarah, and Candy Tan. *Beyond Heaving Bosoms: The Smart Bitches' Guide to Romance Novels*. New York: Fireside, 2009.

Whissell, Cynthia. "Linguistic, Emotional and Content Analysis of Sexually Explicit Scenes in Popular Fiction." *Canadian Journal of Human Sexuality* 7.2 (1998): 147–59.

Whitehead, Neil L. "Post-Human Anthropology." *Identities: Global Studies in Culture and Power* 16.1 (2009): 1–32.

Index

CATHERINE M. ROACH is Professor of Gender and Culture Studies in New College at the University of Alabama. A recipient of grants from the Fulbright program and the Romance Writers of America, her most recent academic book was *Stripping, Sex, and Popular Culture* (2007). She publishes romance fiction as Catherine LaRoche.

31901059266132